Cozy Little Landscapes in Watercolor

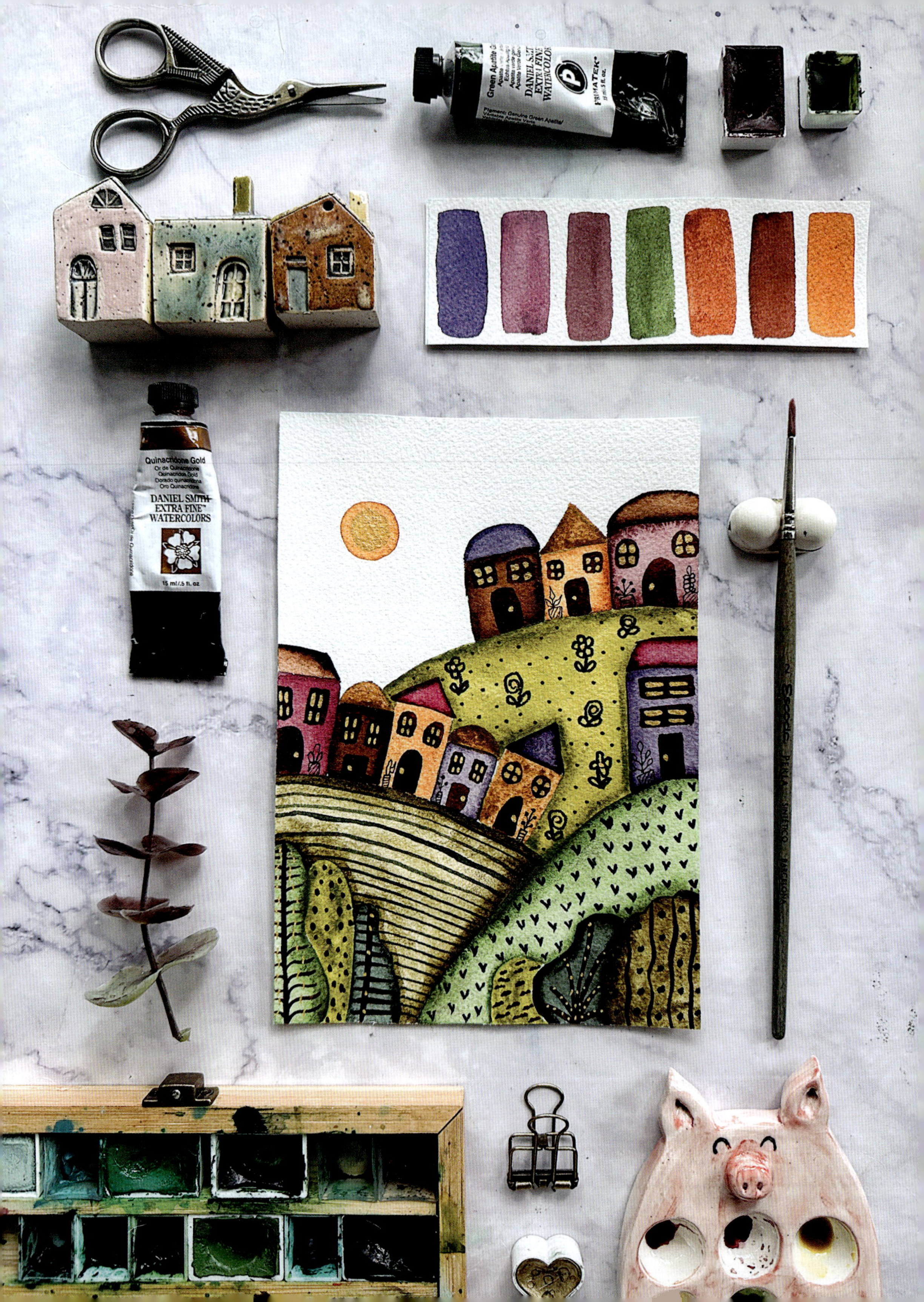

Cozy Little Landscapes in Watercolor

Super-Easy, Mini Painting Projects for Whimsical Forests, Charming Villages, and More

Mayo Moreno
Creator of Safari of Ideas

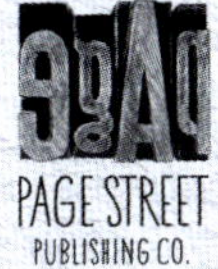

PAGE STREET
PUBLISHING CO.

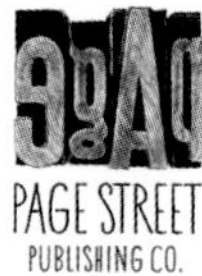

PAGE STREET
PUBLISHING CO.

First published in 2026 by

Page Street Publishing Co.

27 Congress Street, Suite 1511

Salem, MA 01970

www.pagestreetpublishing.com

Distributed by Macmillan, sales in Canada by The Canadian Manda Group.

30   29   28   27   26   1   2   3   4   5

ISBN-13: 979-8-89003-429-8

Library of Congress Control Number: 2025940564

Edited by Sadie Hofmeester
Cover and book design by Molly Kate Young for Page Street Publishing Co.
Photography and artwork by Mayo Moreno

Printed and bound in the United States of America

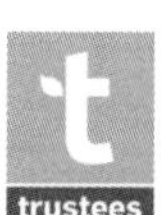

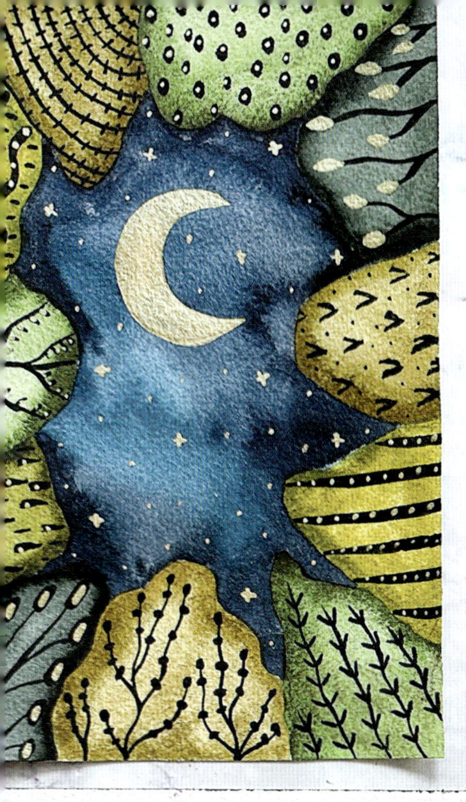

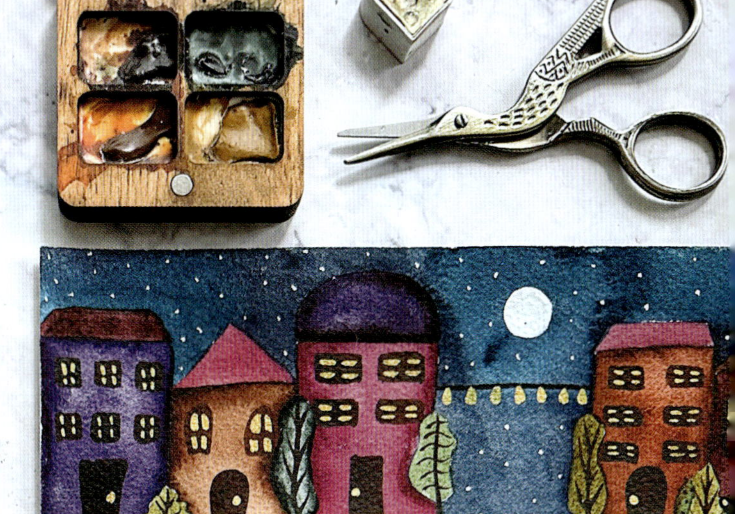

Dedication

To my beautiful Sandy, who always inspired me to dream big and reminded me that the world becomes even more magical when we fill it with music, colors, and fairy tales.

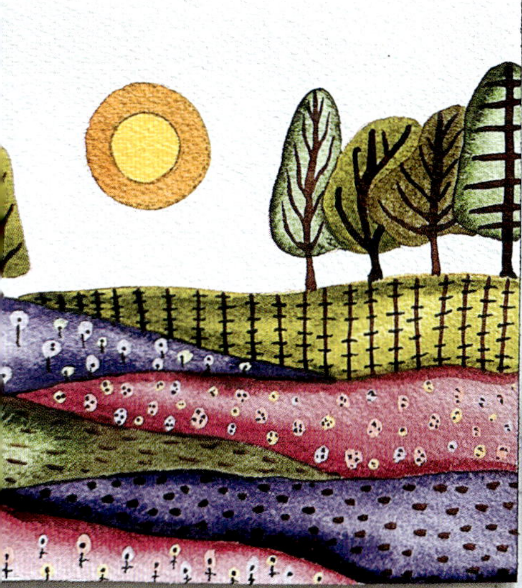

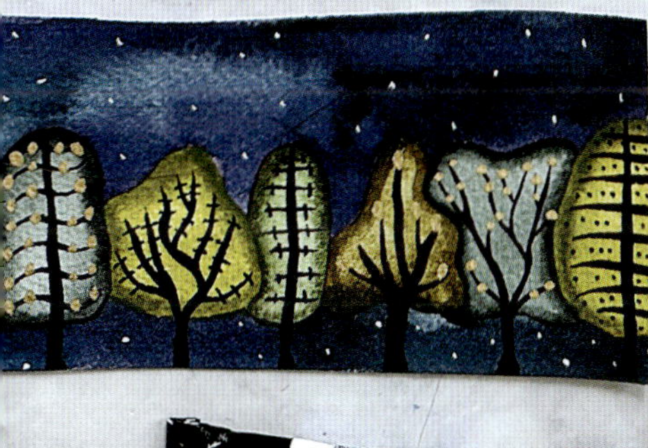

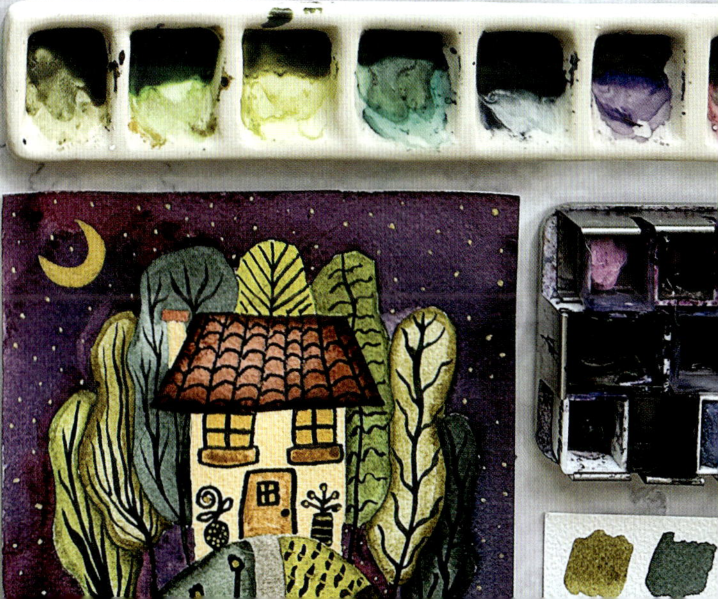

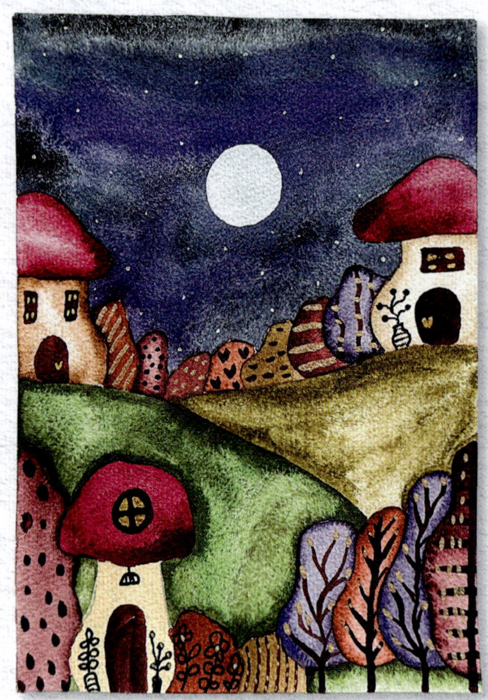

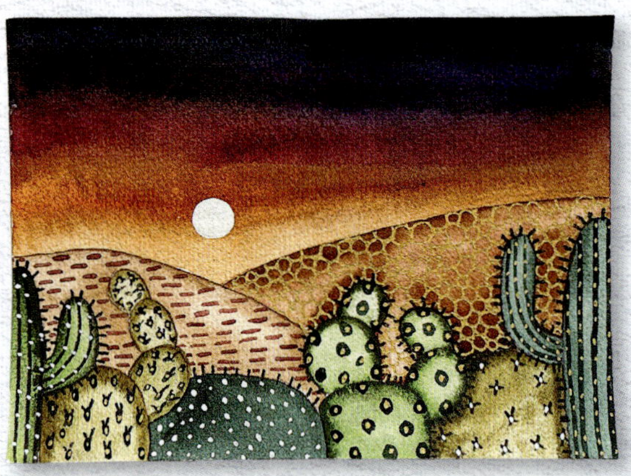

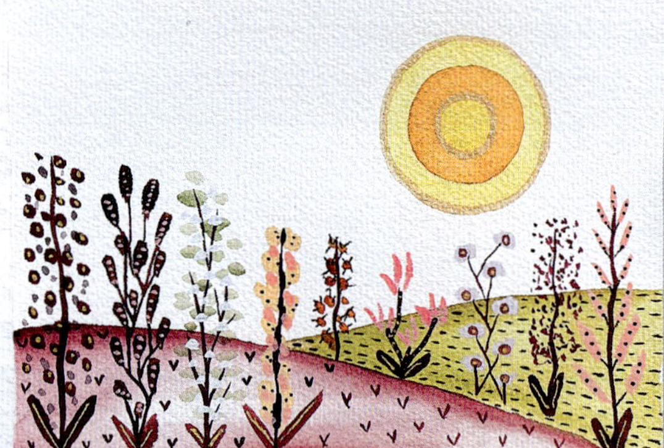

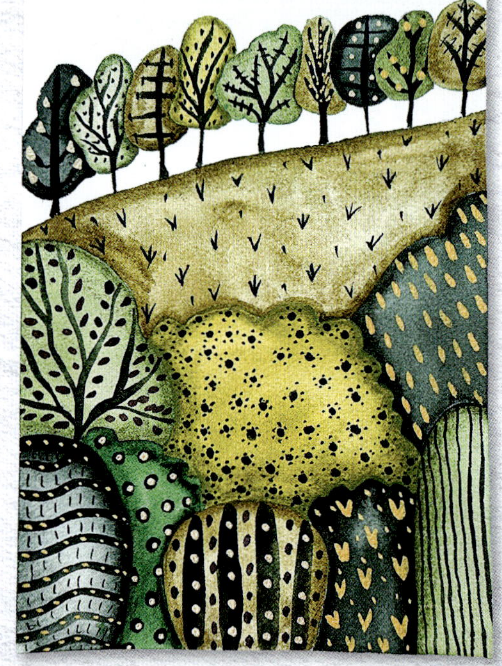

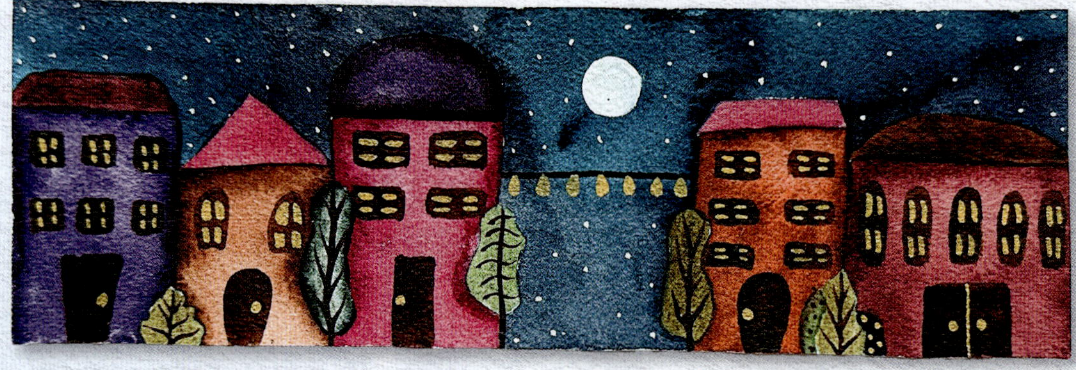

Contents

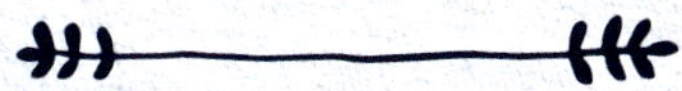

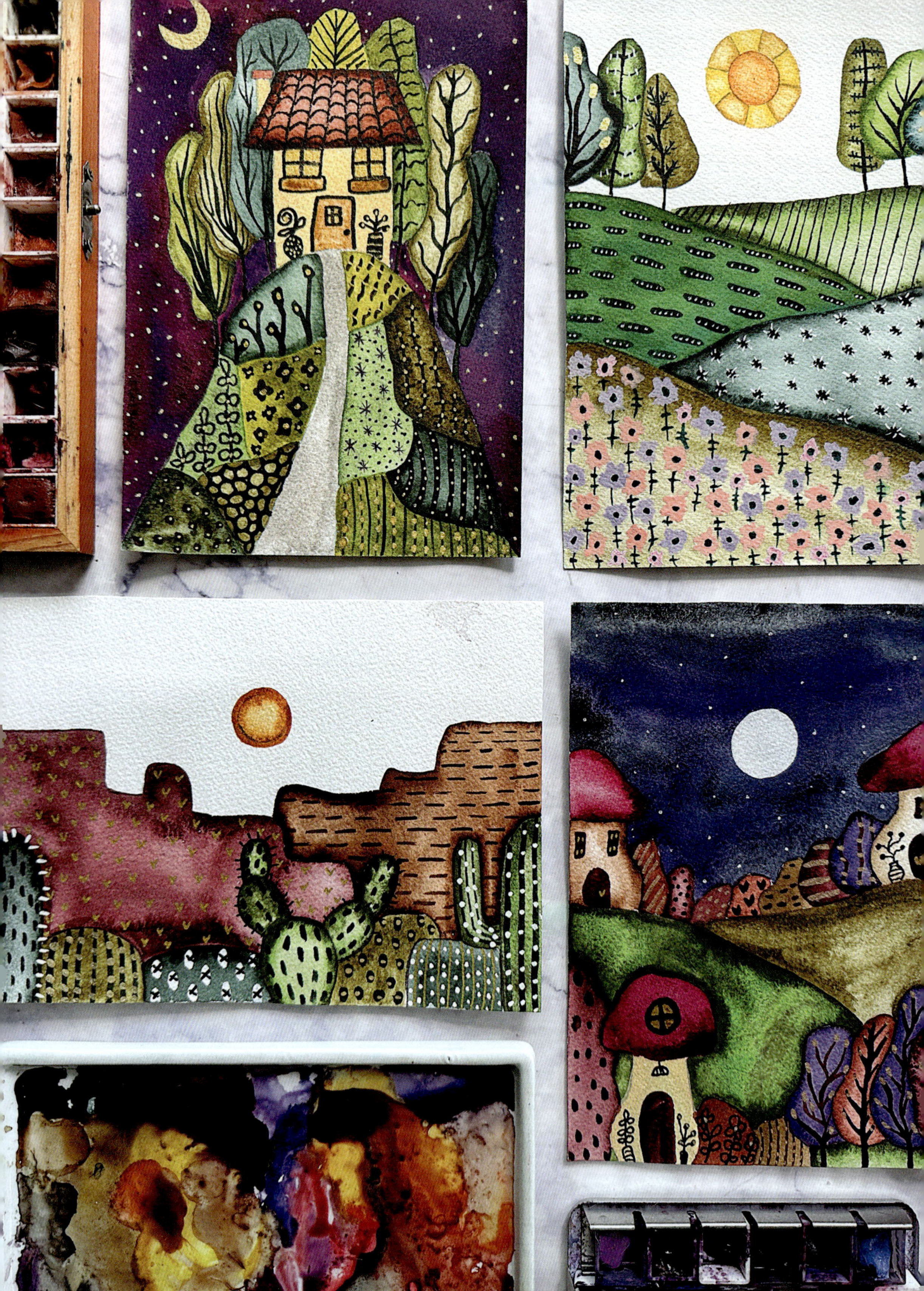

Introduction

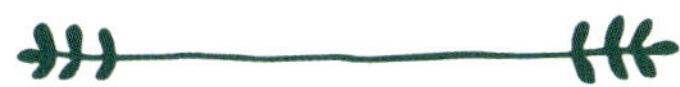

Landscapes have always been an inexhaustible source of joy for me. Since I was a child, I have spent hours exploring nature, marveling at the beauty of mountains, forests, and rivers. Observing how light filters through the leaves and how colors change with the seasons has always inspired me deeply. Each landscape has its own story to tell, and every nook is a little world full of life.

When I think of those perfect moments, I imagine myself surrounded by cozy colors, with a warm cup of tea in hand and a soft blanket wrapped around me. Those are the moments when the stress of everyday life fades away, and the magic of nature becomes the center of my attention. In those instances, I feel connected to the world around me, and painting becomes an extension of that connection.

In this book, I want to share with you an easy and fun way to enjoy landscapes, where each brushstroke transports you to a place of calm and joy. Through the pages, you will find step-by-step guides to create small forests, gentle hills, and cozy scenes that will warm your soul. It's not just about learning to paint; it's about immersing yourself in a creative process that allows you to relax and find peace in every stroke.

With watercolor, we can let our emotions flow; it is a practical and beautiful medium to work with. Each color and each drop of water become a reflection of our inner state, allowing us to explore not only the outer world, but also the landscape of our being. Watercolor is like an intimate conversation between the paper and the brush, where imperfections transform into beauty, and mistakes become opportunities to create something unexpectedly wonderful.

I invite you to join me on this artistic adventure, where watercolor will take us to a magical world full of bright colors and soft textures. Imagine, for a moment, being surrounded by gentle breezes and birdsongs while your hands dance on the paper, creating little works of art that capture the essence of the landscapes we love. Each chapter of this book will be like a path we walk together, discovering new techniques, sharing anecdotes, and letting our imagination soar freely.

So get your brushes ready, choose your colors, and allow the beauty of nature to inspire you. Together, we will explore what it means to create and enjoy the magic that the world offers us, one landscape at a time. This journey will not only lead us to create art but also to find a refuge in the calm that only painting can provide. Let's bring those dreamed-of landscapes to life!

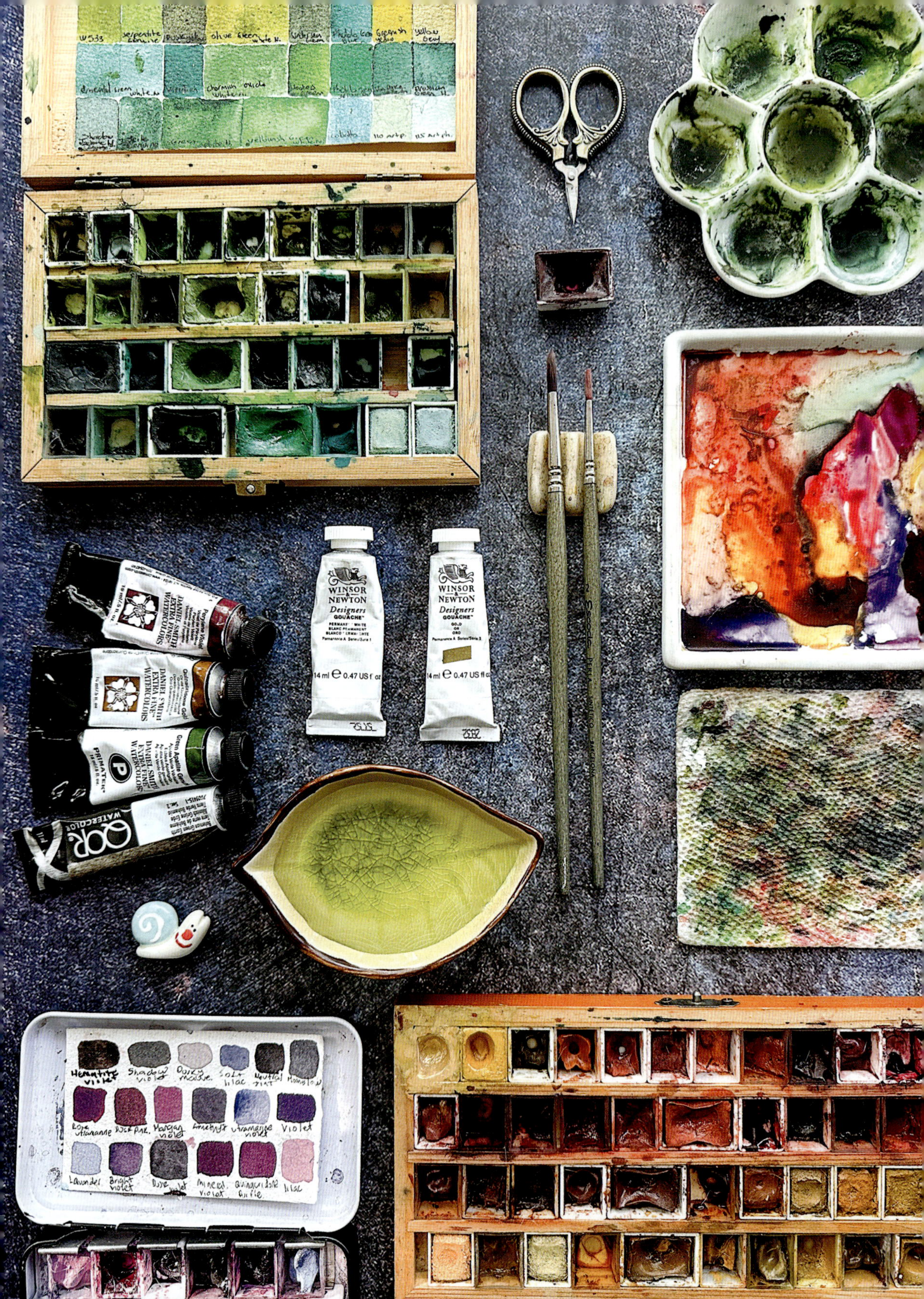

Getting Ready for Our Watercolor Adventure

In this chapter, we'll explore the tools and gentle techniques that open the door to watercolor magic. These essentials will help you feel grounded, inspired, and ready to create.

Materials

Before we dive into painting, let's talk briefly about supplies. The right tools make a big difference in watercolor, and while you don't need a huge collection to begin, choosing carefully will help you get the best results. If you are on a budget, I recommend prioritizing good paper. Watercolor paper absorbs and shows color in a way that regular paper simply cannot. Next, invest in a few quality brushes and paints rather than buying a large, inexpensive set. It's much better to slowly build your kit than to feel overwhelmed with too many low-quality materials.

In addition to your art supplies, you'll also want to keep a few simple household items nearby: one or two cups of clean water, a paper towel or reusable cloth for dabbing, and a pencil for sketching. You may notice in some of my examples that my sketch lines are a soft blue or red. This is because I use colored leads in a mechanical pencil. They dissolve easily with water, so the marks don't remain harsh or visible underneath the watercolor layers.

Remember, the goal is not to have every supply possible, but to enjoy the process with the essentials that let the paint and water flow beautifully.

Watercolors

Watercolors are water-based paints. They often come in pans or tubes. Pans have dried cakes of paint that need to be rehydrated or activated with water before use. Tubes contain ready-to-use liquid paint; however, if you squeeze tube paint onto a palette and let it dry, it will also need to be activated with water before painting. Personally, my favorite paints are pans because they last a long time and are much easier to store.

Buying watercolors is a very exciting exercise because of the wide variety of colors available. As a watercolor collector with over 400 paints, I wanted to create a specific color palette to achieve a cozy effect in our landscapes. For this reason, I selected just 15 colors for us to use in our exercises. If you do not have these exact shades, feel free to use similar colors from your own palette.

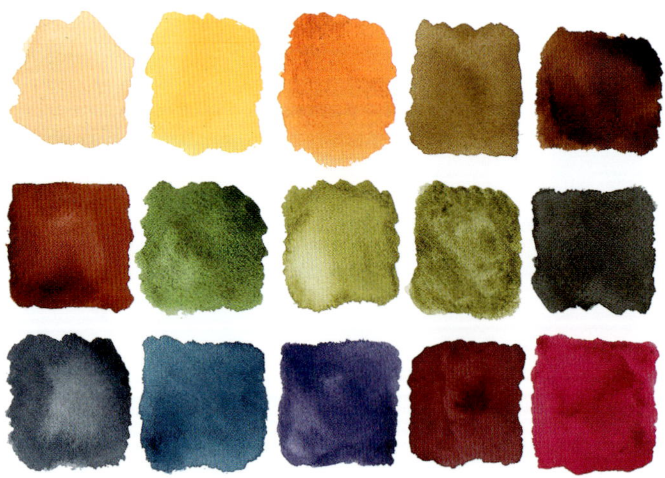

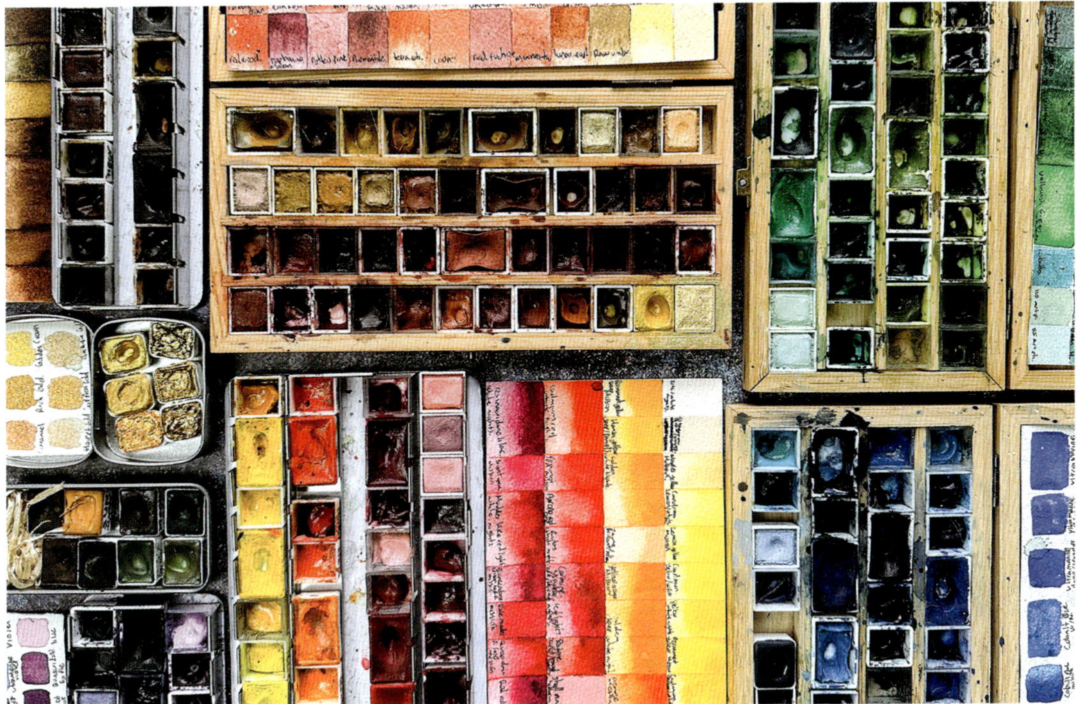

These are the colors we will be using:

- Naples Yellow (Schmincke)
- Nickel Azo Yellow (Daniel Smith™)
- Quinacridone Gold (Daniel Smith)
- Raw Umber (Daniel Smith)
- Burnt Umber (White Nights®)
- Permanent Brown (Daniel Smith)
- Green Apatite Genuine (Daniel Smith)
- Olive Green (Daniel Smith)
- Bohemian Green (QoR®)
- Shadow Green (Holbein)
- Indigo (Holbein)
- Turquoise (White Nights)
- Violet (White Nights)
- Perylene Violet (Daniel Smith)
- Quinacridone Lilac (White Nights)

All these colors can vary depending on the brand. In fact, I often buy the same color from different brands to have various shades of the same hue.

Here are my recommended brands for beginners, which are both affordable and of good quality:

- Art Philosophy®
- White Nights

However, if you're really falling in love with watercolors and can invest a little more, please try specific colors from these brands:

- Daniel Smith
- Holbein
- Schmincke
- QoR

If you wish to support a handmade watercolor brand, that would also be great since you can find different textures and granulation.

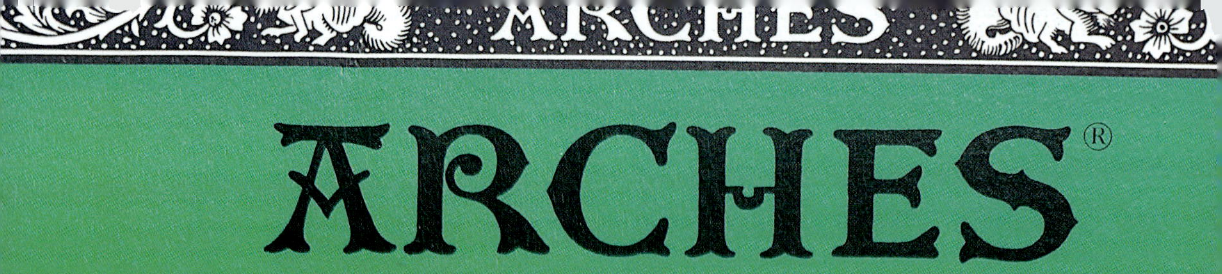
ARCHES®
AQUARELLE - WATERCOLOUR - AC
GRAIN FIN
COLD PRESSED
GRANO FINO
300 g/m² - 140 lb
m x 41 cm
acquareLLo
watercoLour
ENHANCED
IMPROVED COLOUR LIFTING
INCREASED SURFACE RESISTANCE
VEGAN FRIENDLY
QUALITY
Made in Italy

Paper

When it comes to watercolor, paper is one of the most important elements you can choose. The variety available is astounding, from cellulose to cotton and beyond. Each type offers unique characteristics that can transform your painting experience. The texture, finish, and weight of the paper play a crucial role in the outcome of your artwork.

For our landscape exercises, I always recommend a paper that can withstand a good amount of water. This not only allows the watercolors to blend beautifully but also gives us the opportunity to create fascinating textures in the skies, enhancing the depth and luminosity of our landscapes. The paper's ability to absorb water is key: The right paper can make every brushstroke an adventure, allowing us to explore the magic of watercolor without limitations.

Hot-pressed and cold-pressed papers absorb water differently. Cold-pressed paper, with its slightly textured surface, tends to hold more water and allows for richer blending and soft washes that are perfect for natural landscapes. Hot-pressed paper, with its smooth surface, absorbs water more quickly and works best for fine details or when combining watercolor with ink. So, for the landscapes in this book, I use cold-pressed paper throughout.

Paper weight is another important factor: Heavier papers (140 lb [300 gsm] and above) can hold more water without buckling, while lighter papers may warp unless stretched.

Finally, material matters. Cotton papers absorb and release water evenly, giving you time to work with the paint, while cellulose papers dry faster and are less forgiving, but are often more affordable.

When it comes to size, I usually buy large watercolor blocks and cut them down to the size I need. This gives me flexibility and often better value. However, sometimes you can find discounts on smaller blocks, and those are also a great option if you're just starting out or want something convenient to carry.

One of my favorite papers is fine-grain Arches® cold-pressed cotton. Its exceptional quality provides the perfect surface to work on, ensuring that your colors flow and blend seamlessly. I use this paper for almost all my paintings because it gives me the balance I need between durability, texture, and luminosity.

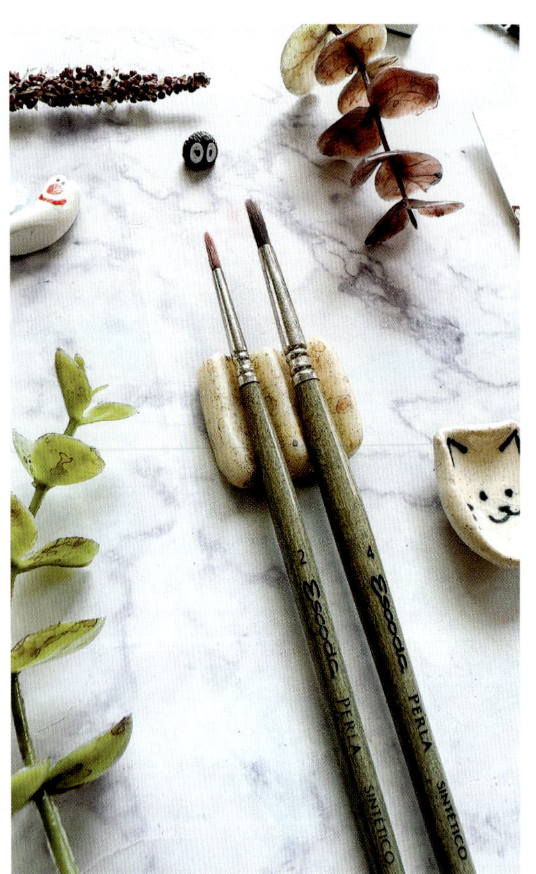

Brushes

My favorite brushes are round. I like to alternate between synthetic and natural brushes depending on what I am painting. My preferred synthetic brushes are white Toray hair brushes, which are made from high-quality Japanese nylon fibers that mimic natural hair while offering durability and springiness. They give me greater control over the pigment and allow me to achieve precise details in my work. These brushes are perfect for a more controlled application of pigment. On the other hand, I also enjoy using natural-hair brushes, especially for painting backgrounds and skies. These brushes are ideal for holding a large amount of water, which helps blend colors smoothly, and are more agile when filling in larger spaces. The versatility of these tools enables me to experiment with different techniques and create unique effects in my paintings.

For the paintings in this book, I elected to use only my white Toray synthetic round brushes. Here are the sizes we will be using:

- Size 2 round
- Size 4 round

Extra Materials: Textures and Details in Watercolor

To bring our landscapes to life, having some additional materials is essential. Here are some things to have on hand that can transform your artwork:

Permanent White Gouache

Permanent white gouache is perfect for highlighting and accentuating details in your watercolors. Its opacity allows for vibrant contrasts and adds depth to your landscapes.

Gold Gouache

Gold gouache adds a touch of magic and luminosity. This metallic medium can highlight key elements, such as reflections or architectural details. Its ability to be applied over dry colors lets you experiment without limits.

Size 5 and Size 12 Fineliner Pens

Fineliners are excellent for adding fine details to your watercolors. A size 5 is ideal for delicate outlines and intricate patterns, while a size 12 allows for bolder strokes. They are best used once the watercolor is completely dry, allowing you to add textures, outlines, and extra character without smudging. The combination of ink and watercolor creates a captivating visual contrast.

Mixing Palette

A palette is essential for blending your colors before applying them to the paper. I recommend porcelain palettes because they keep colors clean and don't stain easily, but plastic or other types of palettes can also work. Personally, I'm obsessed with porcelain palettes, and I buy and collect as many as I can.

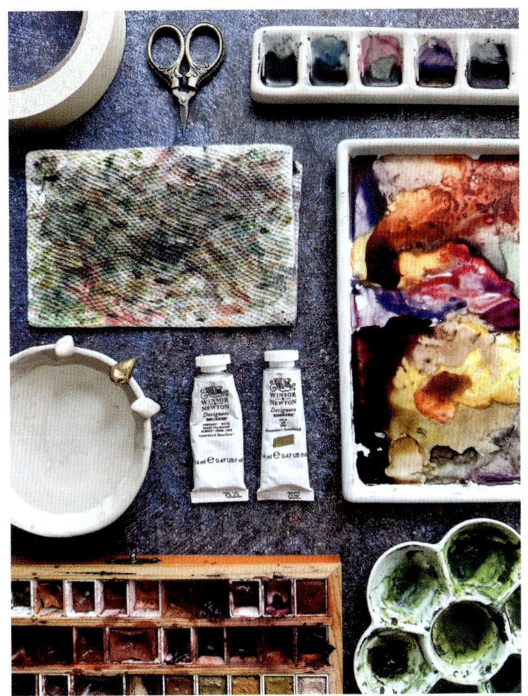

Kitchen Towel or Cloth

Having a clean kitchen towel or cloth on hand is essential for watercolor painting. It allows you to gently dab your brush to remove excess water or pigment, control moisture, and keep your strokes crisp. Unlike tissues, which can break apart, a towel or cloth is durable and reusable throughout your painting sessions.

Water Containers

A jar or cup of water is one of the most important tools in watercolor. You'll use it constantly to rinse your brushes, dilute pigments, and control transparency. It's always best to keep two containers nearby—one with clean water for mixing colors and another for rinsing your brushes. This ensures your colors stay fresh and vibrant.

Watercolor Techniques

Controlling water is the fundamental technique for creating our landscapes in watercolor. Below, I introduce the techniques we will be using throughout the book, including wet-on-wet, wet-on-dry, layering, and other simple methods that will help you achieve beautiful textures and effects.

Wet-on-Wet

We will use the wet-on-wet technique to create our skies. This involves loading a brush with plenty of water and applying it to the area you intend to paint. Without letting it dry, you then pick up the paint with your brush and apply touches of color in specific areas. We can use different pigments to allow the watercolors to blend naturally, creating unexpected blooms.

One of the fascinating aspects of this technique is that it offers limited control over the pigment, resulting in incredible and beautiful effects that we can achieve.

Wet-on-Dry

The wet-on-dry technique is the one we will use most often, as it gives us greater control over both water and pigment. This technique involves applying watercolor to dry paper. One way I particularly enjoy using this technique to create luminosity in shapes is by applying a generous amount of pigment along the edges of the forms and then spreading it with water (see the gradual wash technique explanation on page 21). This method makes the edges darker than the center of the shape, adding depth and dimension to our paintings.

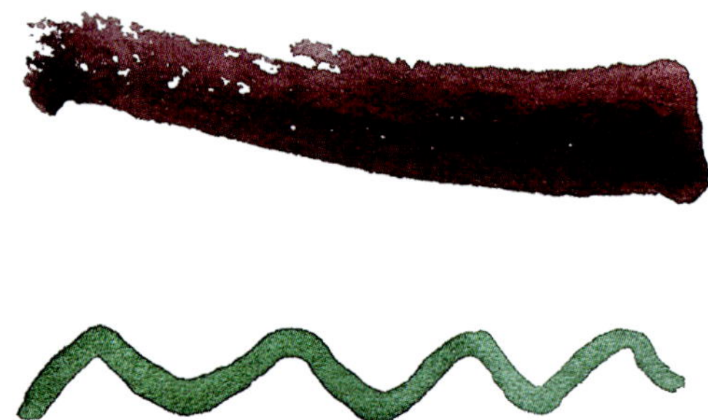

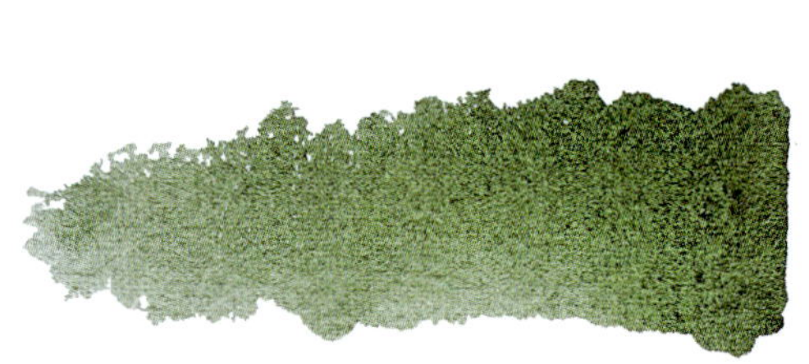

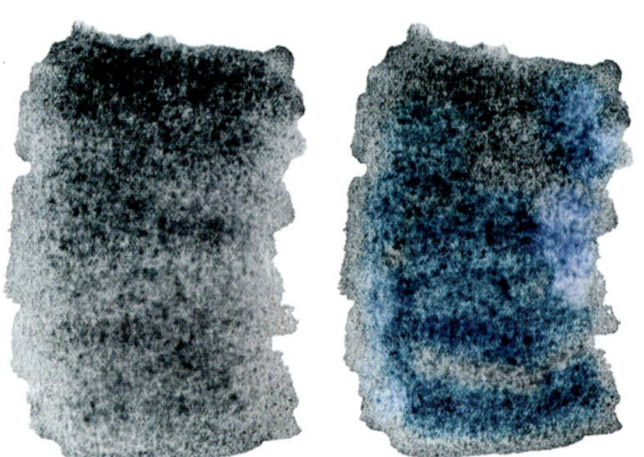

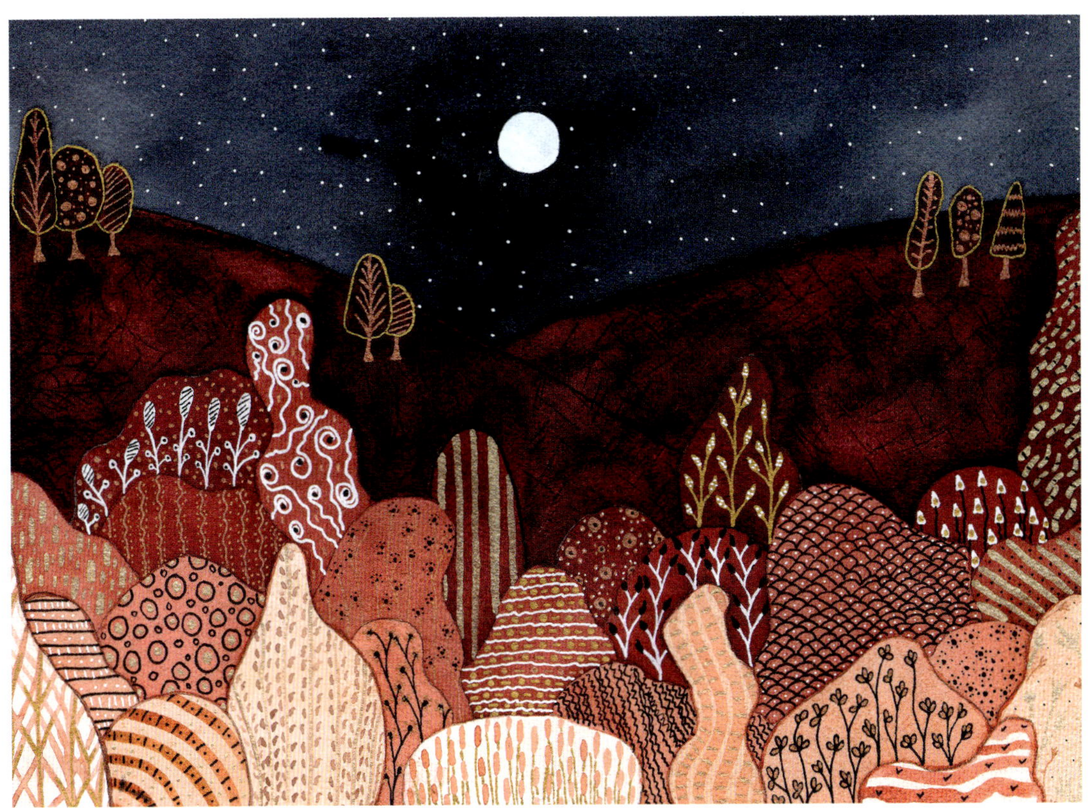

Layers

The use of layers is an essential technique in watercolor that adds depth and complexity to your works. By applying multiple layers of color, you can transform a simple wash into a vibrant and detailed painting.

The layering technique involves applying colors sequentially, allowing each layer to dry before adding the next. This lets you mix and overlap colors, adjusting intensity and creating visual dimensions.

Applying the Base Layer

Start with a gradual wash (page 21) or a flat wash (page 21) that covers most of the area. These washes set the initial tone and provide a background for the subsequent layers. I often use a gradual wash for my first layer because it creates smooth color transitions that add depth and variation, while a flat wash gives a clean, even background that works beautifully for skies or larger shapes. Later layers can also be applied using different approaches—for example, wet-on-wet for soft blends or wet-on-dry for sharper edges. But beginning with a gradual or flat wash provides a strong and versatile foundation for building up the painting.

Building Dimensions

Once your base layer is dry, add intermediate layers with more intense colors or shadows to build depth. Leave some areas of the base color visible to create an effect of light and three-dimensionality.

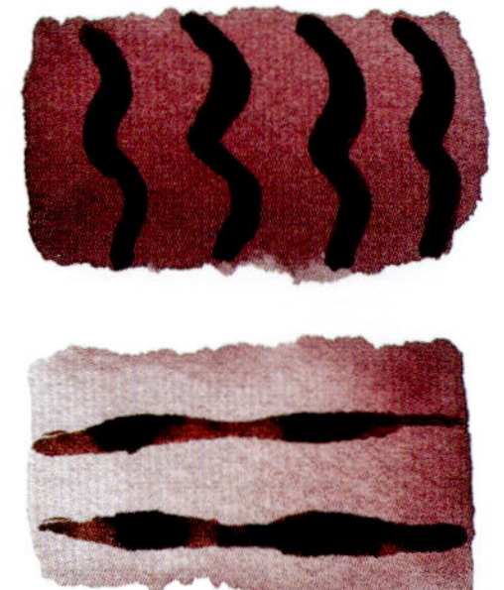

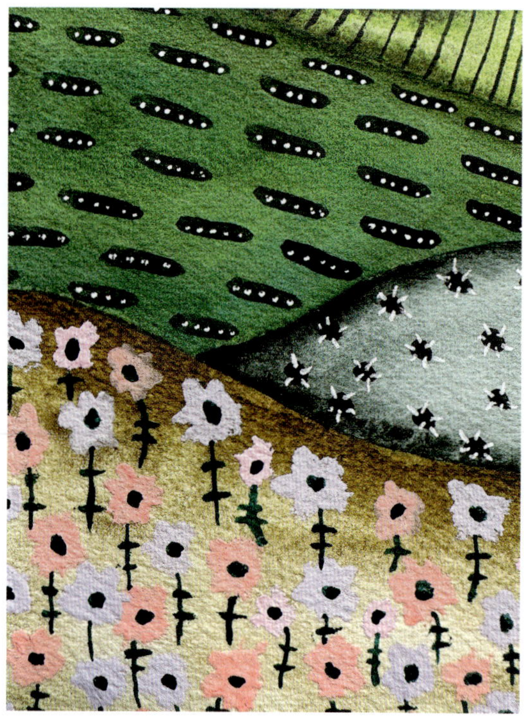

Textures and Details

In the art of watercolor, texture and pattern are fundamental elements that can transform even the simplest shapes into vibrant and dynamic works. Through various techniques, we can add depth and character to our paintings, achieving a unique style that highlights the theme of our artwork. In this section, we will explore different methods to create textures and patterns that complement your watercolor forms.

The Importance of Texture

Texture in a painting not only adds visual interest but also evokes a tactile sensation that invites the viewer to engage with the work. Textures can convey feelings of softness, roughness, light, and shadow, and they are essential for bringing life to your landscapes, flowers, or any other form you are painting.

Techniques for Creating Textures

Flat wash: A flat wash is one of the most fundamental watercolor techniques. It consists of loading your brush with diluted pigment and applying it evenly across the paper in long, continuous strokes, usually working from top to bottom. The goal is to create a smooth, uniform layer of color without streaks or visible edges. Flat washes are ideal for painting skies, large shapes, or backgrounds where you want an even tone.

Watercolor paints have different levels of granulation. When applied as a flat wash, granulating watercolor paints will show some organic texture where the large pigment particles clump together on your paper. The Dusk Pink below is granulating, while the Quinacridone Purple above is non-granulating.

Gradual wash technique: By implementing a color wash that decreases in intensity, you can create smooth gradations that add subtle texture to a shape. This approach is excellent for giving the illusion of both depth and dimension. It is also my preferred technique for painting trees: I load the edges of the tree shape with more concentrated pigment, then use a clean brush filled with water to gently pull the color toward the center. This creates a soft gradient, with darker edges that suggest texture and volume, while the lighter center conveys depth and natural variation. Readers can return to this technique throughout the book whenever they want to create trees with richness and dimension.

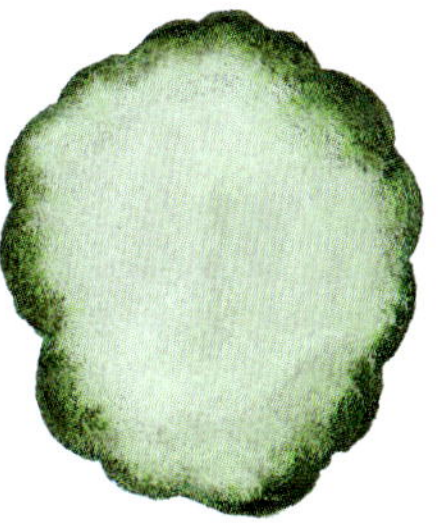

Splattering and dripping: By applying splashes of watercolor or gouache, you can create organic and dynamic effects. Load the bristles of an old brush or toothbrush with your paint, and tap the handle gently to create splattering and dripping textures on top of your watercolor layers. This method adds spontaneous, natural details that bring energy and movement to your painting.

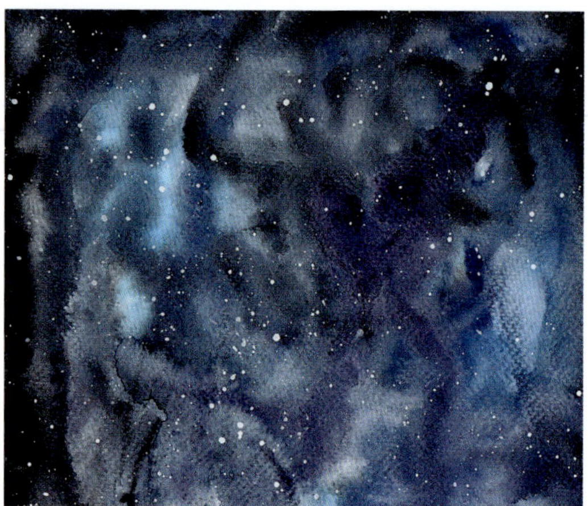

Patterns that complement your forms: Creating patterns is another effective way to add interest to your watercolors. Patterns can be geometric, organic, or abstract, and they can help guide the viewer's eye through the composition. Some ideas include:

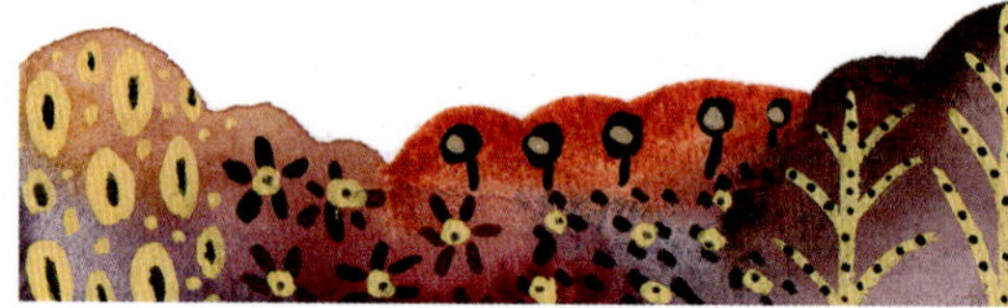

- **Repetitions:** Use repetitive shapes such as circles or lines to create a pattern that complements the main subject of your painting.
- **Color zones:** Apply different colors to specific areas to form a pattern that highlights the shapes. This can make your composition more vibrant.

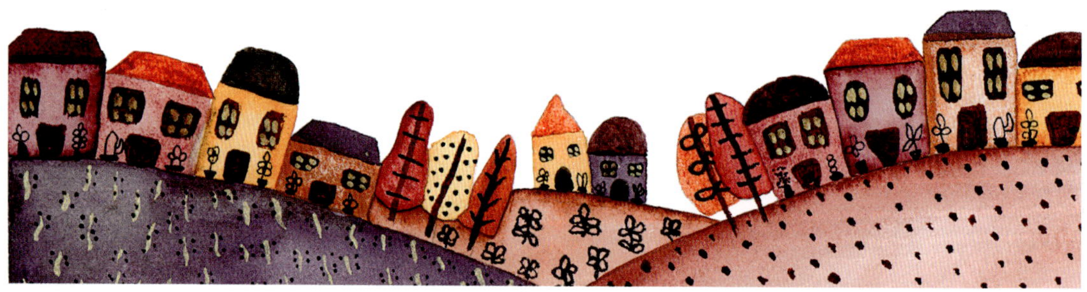

Paint Landscape Shapes

When painting landscapes in watercolor, the simplest shapes often carry the most meaning. Trees, houses, the sun and moon, and even the wide expanse of the sky can be reduced to basic forms that allow us to capture their essence without worrying about perfection. In this section, we'll explore easy ways to paint these shapes with fluid brushstrokes and soft washes, letting the watercolor do the work of creating texture and light. Each element becomes not just a shape on the page, but a piece of the story of your landscape.

Trees

1. Sketch the shapes: Lightly sketch simple, uniform shapes for the tree canopies. These can be rounded ovals or elongated forms, depending on the type of tree you want to create.

2. First wash: Choose different colors for the canopy. Sometimes I like to blend two colors within the same shape or use the gradual wash technique (page 21) to create smooth transitions and variation. Let this first layer dry completely.

3. Paint the trunk and branches: With a thin brush, like a size 2, and highly pigmented watercolor, paint the trunk starting from the bottom and moving upward. As you pull the brush upward, the lines naturally branch out, forming delicate limbs.

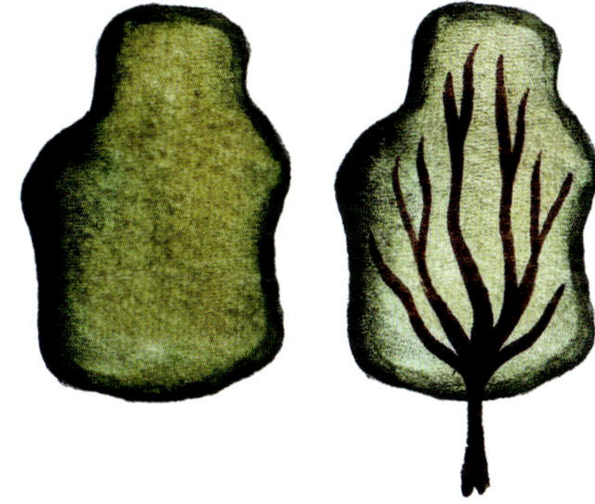

4. Add leaves and fruits: Once the trunk and branches are dry, add small textures to suggest foliage or fruits. These can be simple circles, lines, or dots painted with different watercolors. For extra detail and contrast, you can also use gold gouache or a fineliner to highlight the leaves and add intricate touches. For additional inspiration, you can reference Melody Among the Trees (page 31) and Forest in the Galaxy (page 123).

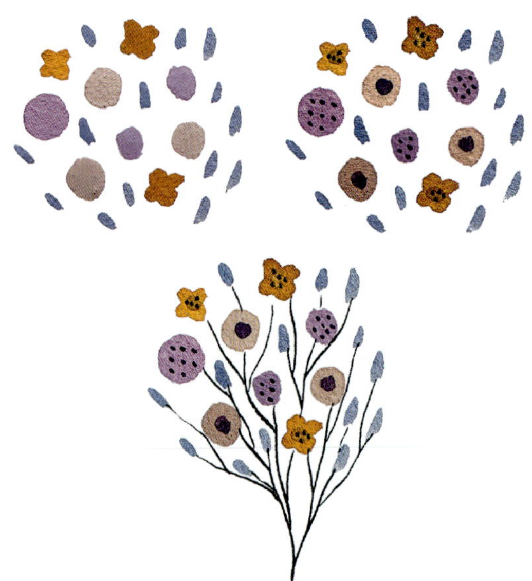

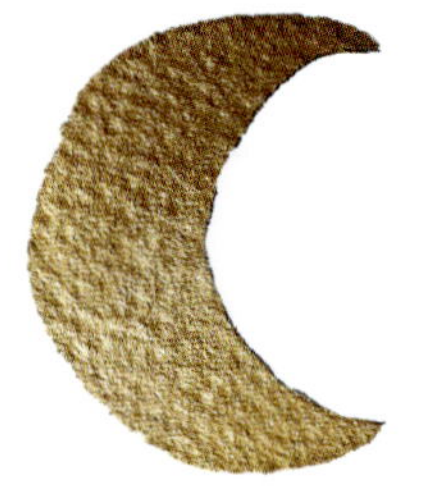

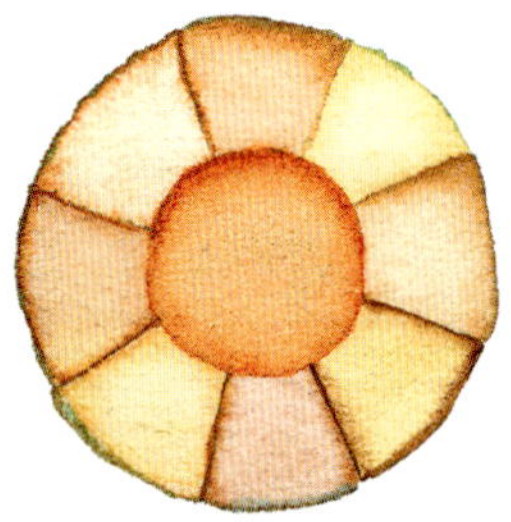

Flowers and Plants

1. First layer: Use watercolor (or you can use white gouache mixed with a little watercolor to create soft pastel tones) with a size 2 brush to create simple circles, lines, and dots for basic flower shapes. Let this first layer dry completely. (See Whimsical Wildflowers [page 149].)

2. Paint the centers: Once the base shapes are dry, add the centers of the flowers. I like to use gold gouache, highly pigmented watercolor, or sometimes a fineliner for more precise detail. (See Melody Among the Trees [page 31].)

3. Add stems and leaves: With a darker color than the flower petals, paint the stem starting from the bottom and pulling upward. This helps the stems feel connected and natural. From the stems, add simple leaves with upward strokes to complete the plant forms.

Sun and Moon

1. Sketch the geometric shapes: Sketch simple geometric forms to define the sun or moon. For example, use overlapping circles or triangles for the sun's rays or a crescent or full circle for the moon. (See Dreaming in the Forest [page 35] and Blooming Peaks [page 141].)

2. Paint the sun: Use different tones of yellow watercolor to fill the sections of the sun. To highlight brightness, add gold gouache to certain areas, layering the tones to give each zone a radiant and dimensional look.

3. Paint the moon: Use gold or white gouache as your main medium. Apply it evenly within the shape, layering it to create a luminous, glowing effect that contrasts beautifully against the sky.

4. Layer for depth: Add additional washes or overlapping shapes to create depth. The combination of watercolor washes and gouache gives both the sun and moon a magical, textured quality.

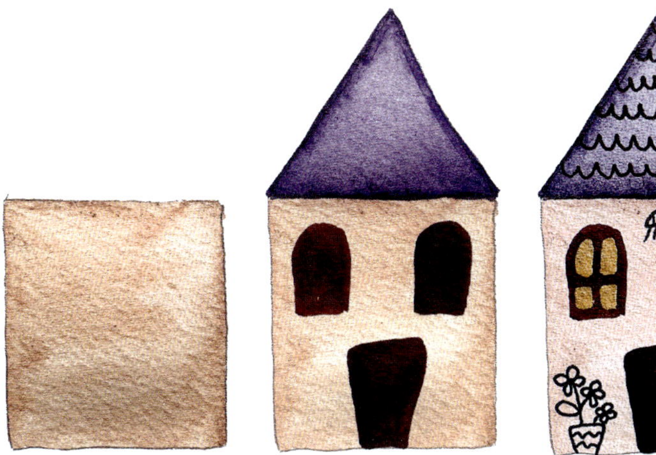

Houses

1. Sketch the base: Draw the basic structure of the house. I usually start with a rectangle or square for the walls and add a triangle or an arch on top to form the roof. Then, I sketch geometric shapes for windows and rectangular doors.

2. Paint the facade: Apply a light wash of watercolor in pastel or soft tones to paint the facade. I prefer using diluted pigment so the color feels gentle and serves as the foundation for the rest of the design. Let this layer dry completely.

3. Paint the roof, windows, and doors: Paint the roof with a stronger color to give contrast. Use another color to paint the windows and the door, adding variety and charm to the house.

4. Add details: After all the base colors are dry, add the fun details. With gold gouache, paint tiny glowing lights inside the windows. Use a fineliner to draw details such as roof tiles, chimneys, or little accents. At the base of the house, you can doodle extra elements like potted plants or lamps to bring the scene to life.

Paint the Sky

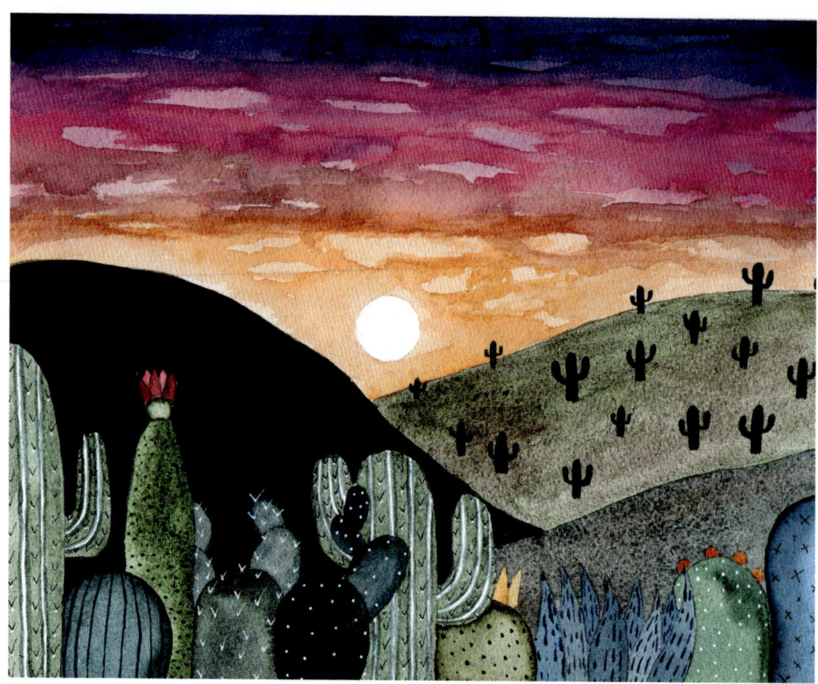

Almost every landscape has a sky, and throughout this book, we'll explore the captivating art of painting different skies, focusing on the ephemeral beauty of sunsets and the enchanting allure of starry nights.

Sunset

1. Prepare your colors: Select the tones for your gradient sky—starting with dark blue, followed by violet, lilac, and finishing with yellow. Make sure to have them ready and well-diluted with enough water, since speed is essential for this technique.

2. Start on dry paper: Work directly on dry paper rather than pre-wetting it. This gives you more control over the edges of your gradient.

3. Apply the gradient: With a medium brush, such as a size 4, begin painting horizontally from the darkest color (blue) at the top, moving down through violet, pink, and finally yellow.

4. Blend quickly: Apply each color while the previous one is still wet. The key is to move fast so the pigments merge naturally, creating smooth transitions between each band of color.

5. Final check: Look at the sky effect once the wash is complete. Adjust slightly if needed while the surface is still damp, but avoid overworking so the transitions stay soft and luminous. (See Shadows of the Sunset [page 83].)

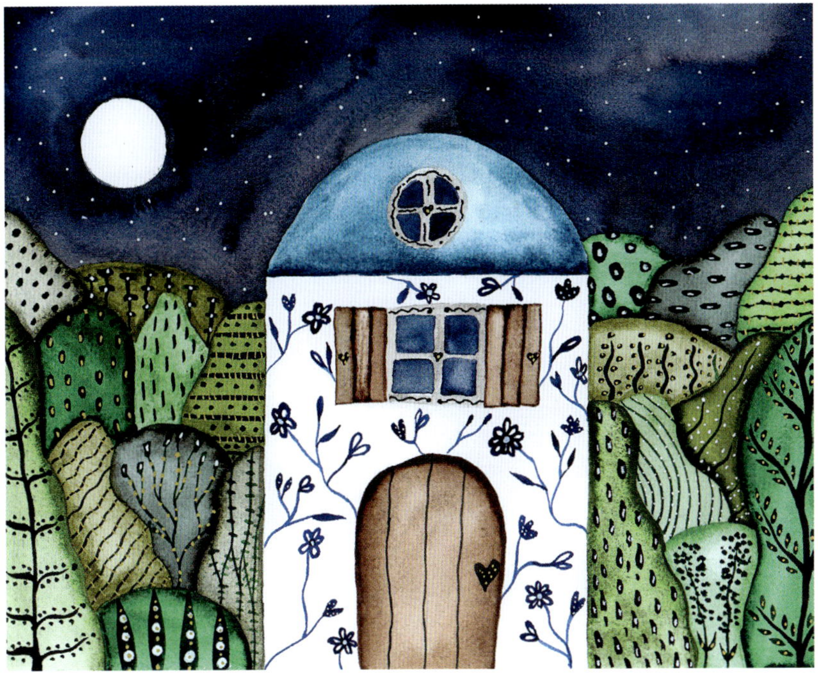

Starry Night

1. Dark background: Apply a wash of different blues and violets to represent the night sky. This base will create a dramatic backdrop for the stars to shine against. Allow it to dry before moving forward.

2. Paint the stars: To create stars, use a small brush, such as a size 2, with white gouache to paint dots for small stars or starbursts (little asterisk-like shapes) for larger ones.

3. Add a moon: A crescent or full moon can enhance your night sky. Paint the moon using white or gold gouache, ensuring it stands out against the darker background.

Note: I often keep the white of the paper as the background because watercolor shines beautifully when it has room to breathe. Leaving areas untouched allows the light of the paper to become part of the painting, creating a natural glow and soft contrast without adding extra layers. This is also how I create the moon in many of my starry night scenes, letting the untouched white paper suggest a bright, luminous moon against the darker sky. This simplicity helps the colors feel fresh, airy, and full of life.

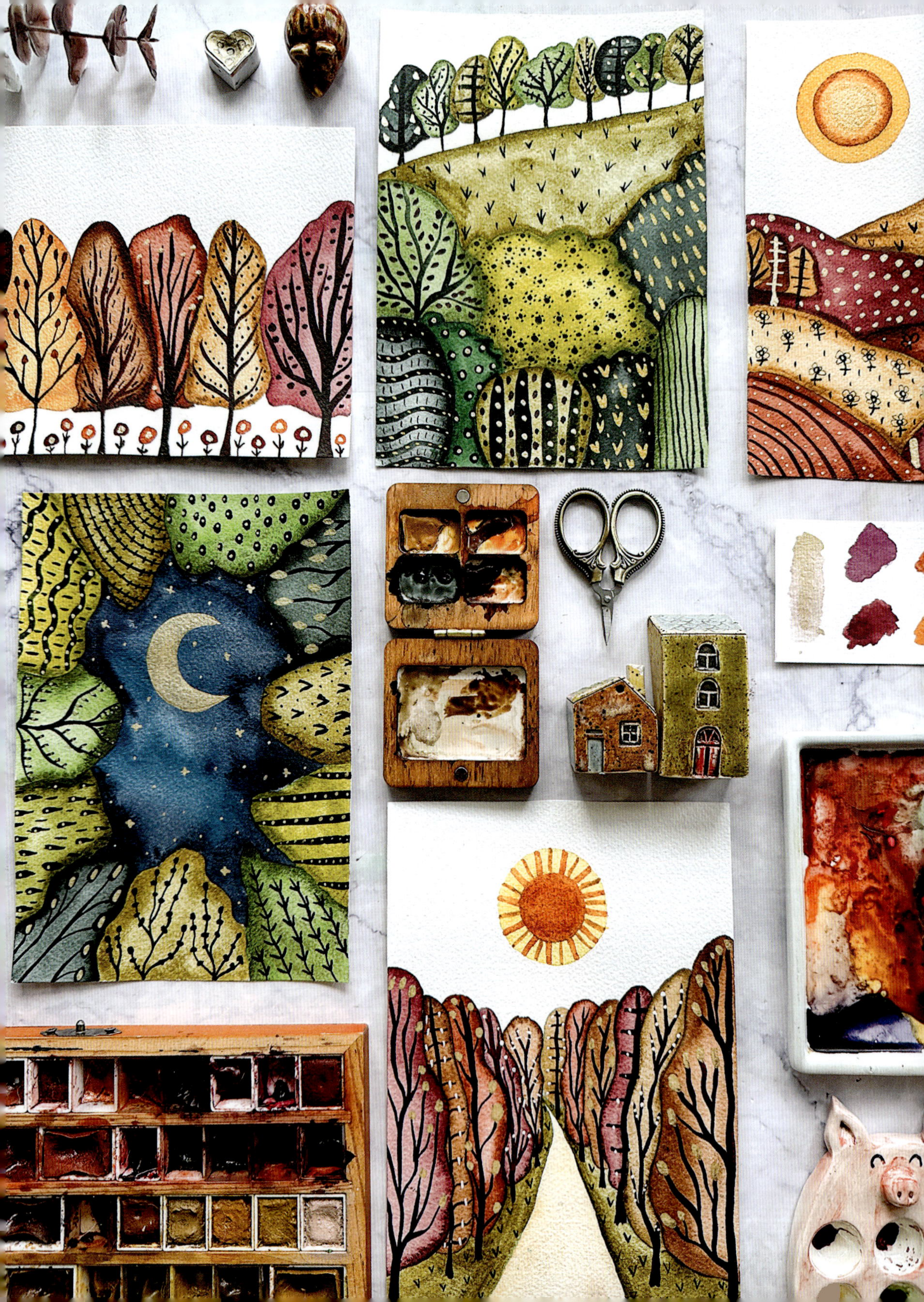

In the Enchanted Forest

Entering an enchanted forest is like stepping into a universe where trees hum quiet melodies, golden leaves whisper beneath your feet, and sunlight weaves threads of magic through the canopy above.

In this chapter, I invite you to wander watercolor paths where nature becomes both sanctuary and mystery, where every corner hides a secret and every brushstroke tells a story. You'll discover hidden cabins nestled among trees, dreamlike mountain silhouettes, dancing lights flickering through foliage, and autumn afternoons beaming with gentle nostalgia.

Here, you won't just paint landscapes: You'll listen to the wind rustling through the pines, feel the warmth of golden leaves, and drift with the heartbeat of a forest that sings and embraces.

Brush in hand, heart wide open . . .

Let the journey begin.

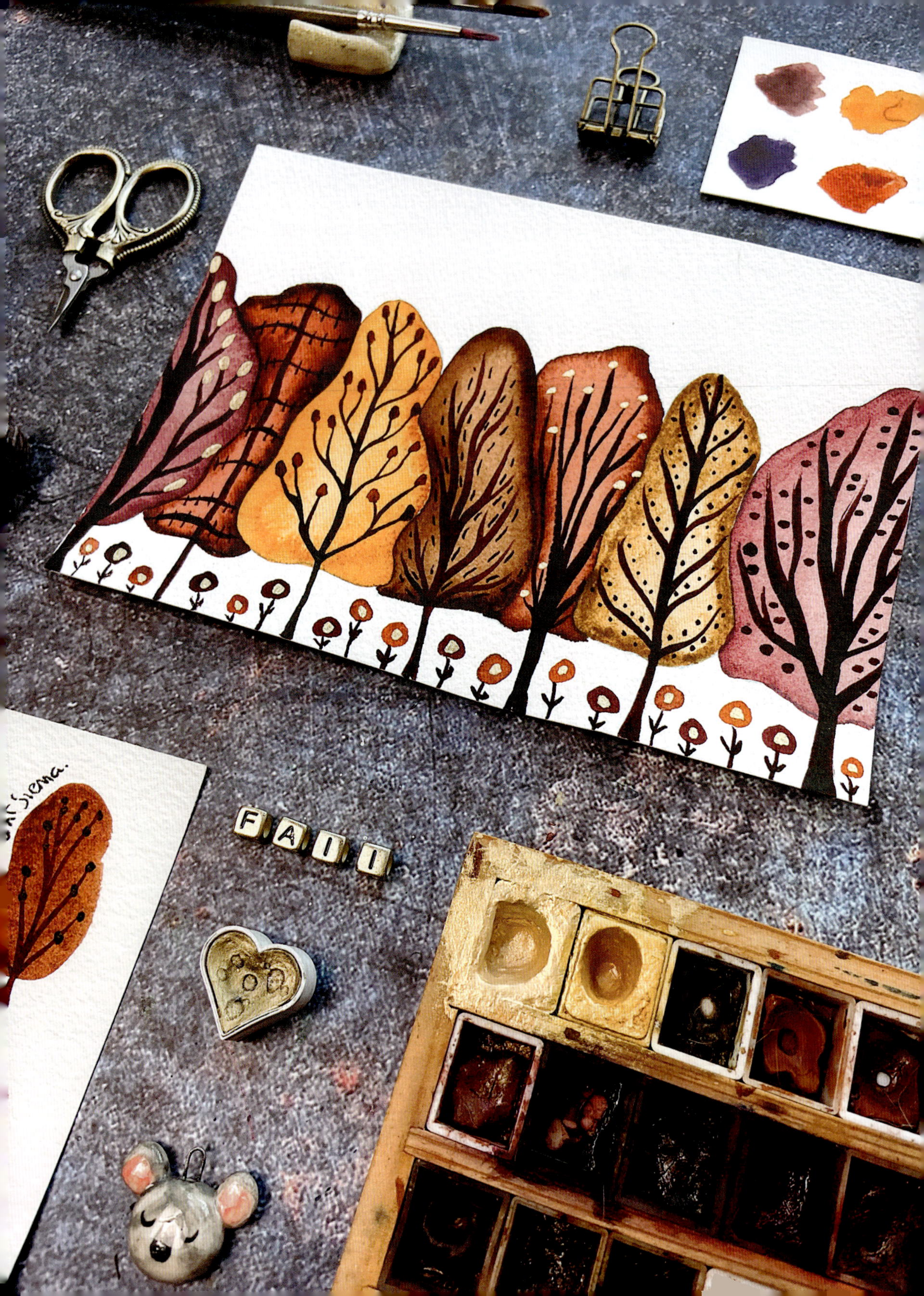

FALL

Melody Among the Trees

Autumn is a season of quiet beauty, where every tree seems to glow in its own shade of gold, red, or amber. In this exercise, we'll paint a horizontal row of trees, each with different colors, branches, and details that reflect the richness of fall. With golden leaves and little flowers by their trunks, we'll create a gentle, colorful melody among the trees.

Materials

Paper size
5 x 7" (13 x 18 cm)

Brushes
Size 4 and size 2

Watercolors
Perylene Violet
Nickel Azo Yellow
Permanent Brown
Burnt Umber
Raw Umber
Quinacridone Gold

For details
Gold gouache

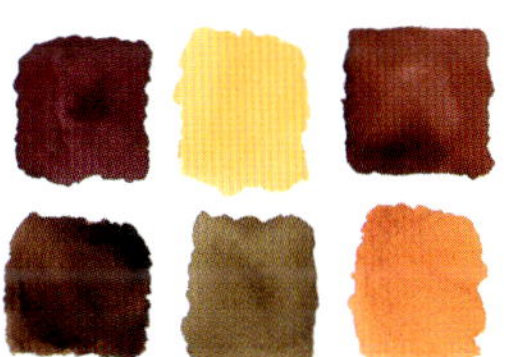

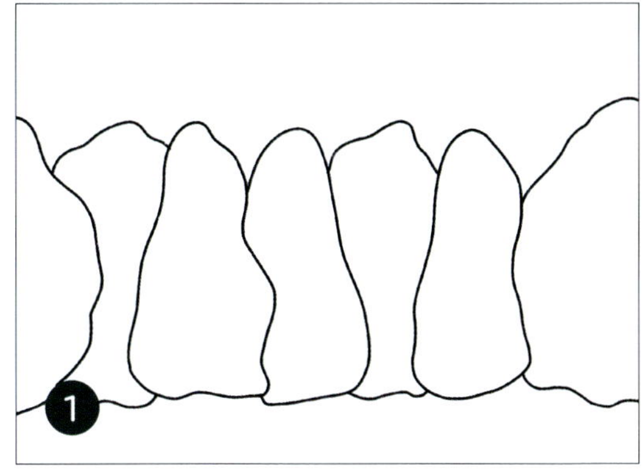

Step 1

Place your paper horizontally. Lightly sketch the shapes of seven trees in a horizontal row. They don't need to follow a specific form—each tree can be different in size and shape, with a natural, uneven look. Let them slightly overlap to create a sense of closeness and flow, as if they're part of the same quiet forest melody.

Step 2

Activate your paints with a bit of water. Then, paint every other tree from left to right using the gradual wash technique (page 21). With the size 4 brush, pick up a generous amount of concentrated Perylene Violet and paint the edges of the first tree. Rinse your brush, and with clean water, gently pull the pigment from the edges toward the center of the tree to create a soft gradient. Repeat this process for the other trees: Use Nickel Azo Yellow for the third tree, Permanent Brown for the fifth, and Perylene Violet again for the seventh. The gradual wash allows the colors to fade beautifully toward the center, giving each tree subtle depth and dimension.

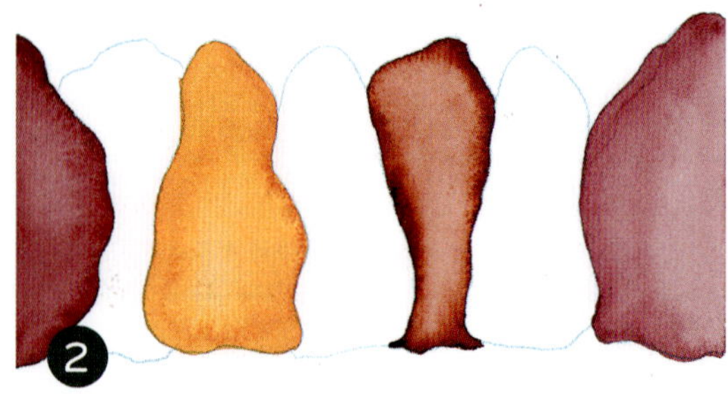

Step 3

Before moving on, make sure the first layer of watercolor is completely dry. This prevents the colors from blending unintentionally and will make the next details crisp. Paint the remaining trees using the same process as in Step 2. From left to right, paint the second tree Permanent Brown, the fourth Burnt Umber, and the sixth Raw Umber. Allow these trees to dry fully before moving to paint the trunks in the following step.

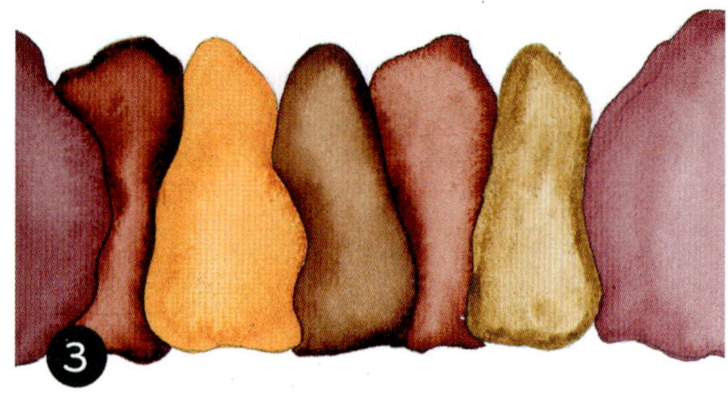

Step 4

Using the tip of your size 2 brush and a generous amount of Burnt Umber or Perylene Violet, begin painting each tree trunk. Start from the base of one and follow an upward line toward the top of the tree. This will be your main trunk. From this central line, gently extend smaller branches outward, varying their direction and pattern slightly for each tree to create a more natural, organic look.

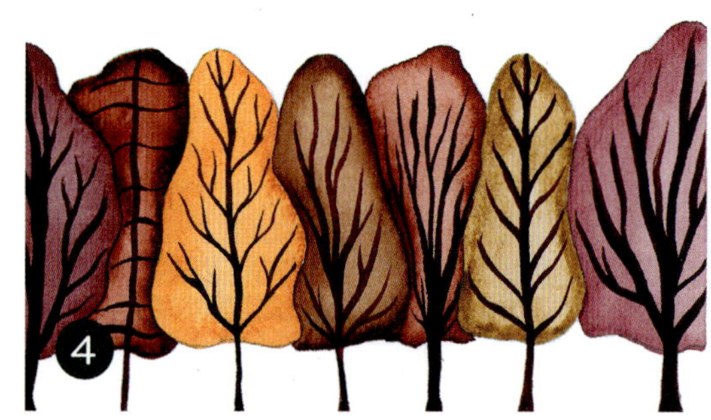

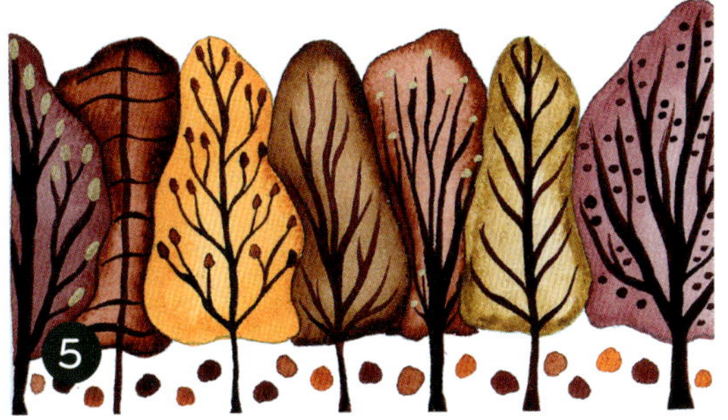

Step 5

Using your size 2 brush, paint small ovals between the tree trunks and branches with either Permanent Brown, Quinacridone Gold, or Perylene Violet, varying the color with each oval. These will become the base for your flowers. Then, with the same brush and using gold gouache and Perylene Violet, add leaves and small circles along different parts of the branches to bring texture and depth to the trees.

Step 6

Using Permanent Brown, add more texture to the branches with small lines and tiny tree shapes to bring them to life. To complete this magical autumn forest, paint the flowers nestled between the tree trunks. With the tip of your size 2 brush and plenty of Perylene Violet, paint the flower stems and a couple of small leaves. Then, use gold gouache to add a tiny circle inside each oval to form the centers of the flowers. With these final touches, your painting is complete.

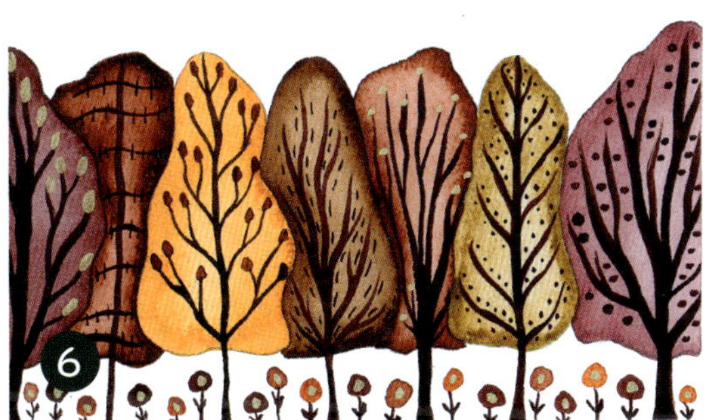

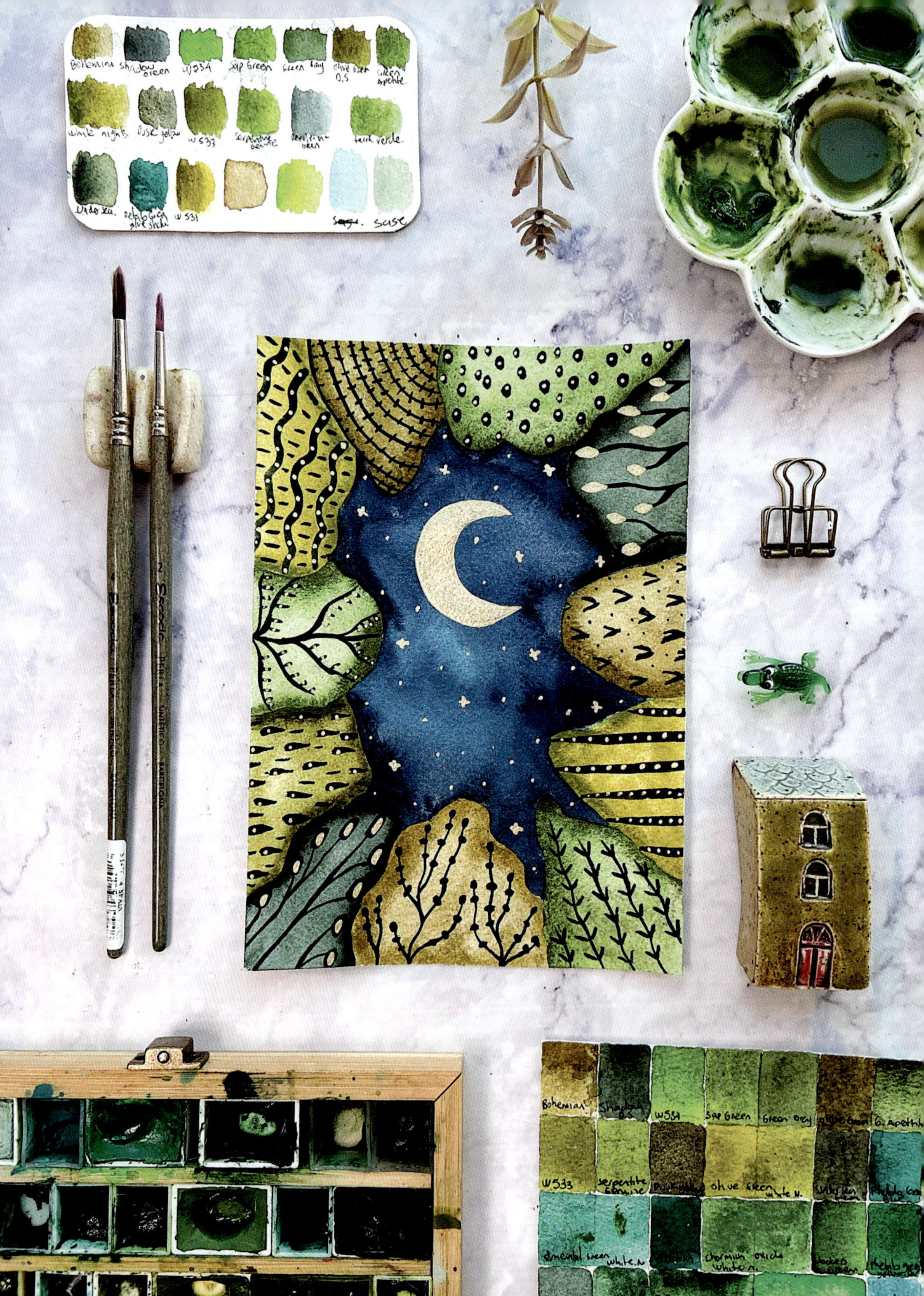

Dreaming in the Forest

This is a journey where watercolor transports us to a magical forest under the cloak of night. In this exercise, we will immerse ourselves in the beauty of trees reaching toward a starry sky, where a golden moon lights our path. Through each brushstroke, we will capture the serenity of darkness and the sparkle of stars, inviting our dreams to blossom in this surreal landscape.

Materials

Paper size
5 x 7" (13 x 18 cm)

Brushes
Size 4 and size 2

Watercolors
Bohemian Green
Green Apatite
Shadow Green
Olive Green
Indigo
Turquoise

For details
Gold gouache

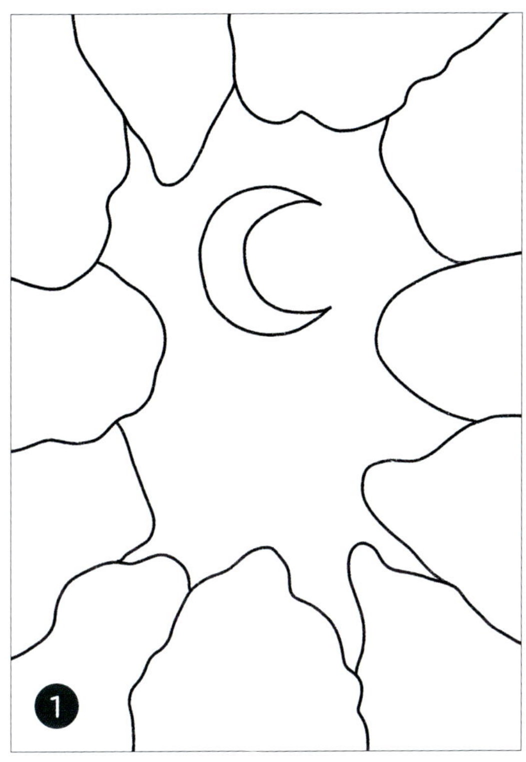

Step 1

Place your paper vertically. Lightly sketch a frame of uniform trees, leaving space in the center to sketch a crescent moon. Imagine this scene as if you were lying in the middle of the forest, gazing up at the starry sky.

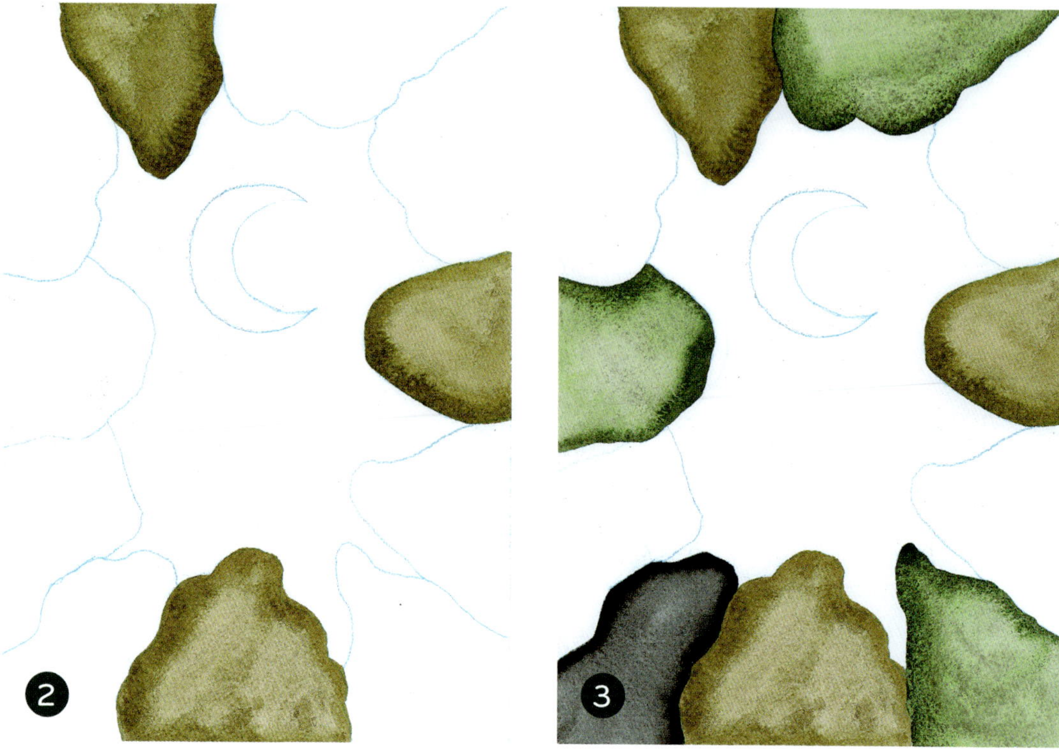

Step 2

Activate your paints with a bit of water. With the size 4 brush, take Bohemian Green and paint a tree on each side of your painting using the gradual wash technique (page 21): Load your brush with plenty of pigment to paint the edges. Then, with a clean brush loaded only with water, gently spread the pigment toward the center of each shape to create light and a soft gradient. Allow the trees to dry completely before moving to the next step. This will prevent the colors from bleeding when we add new layers.

Step 3

Using Green Apatite, paint the trees next to those from the previous step. Continue using the gradual wash technique, keeping the edges of each tree darker and pulling the color toward the center with clean water for a softer, lighter interior. This creates subtle depth and variation in the foliage. Then, paint the tree in the bottom left-hand corner with Shadow Green. Make sure the Bohemian Green from Step 2 is completely dry before applying the Shadow Green so the colors stay clear and defined.

Note: I continued to use the gradual wash technique here, but feel free to experiment. You might give one tree a smooth, flat wash, another a gradual gradient, and one more blooms to add texture and surprise.

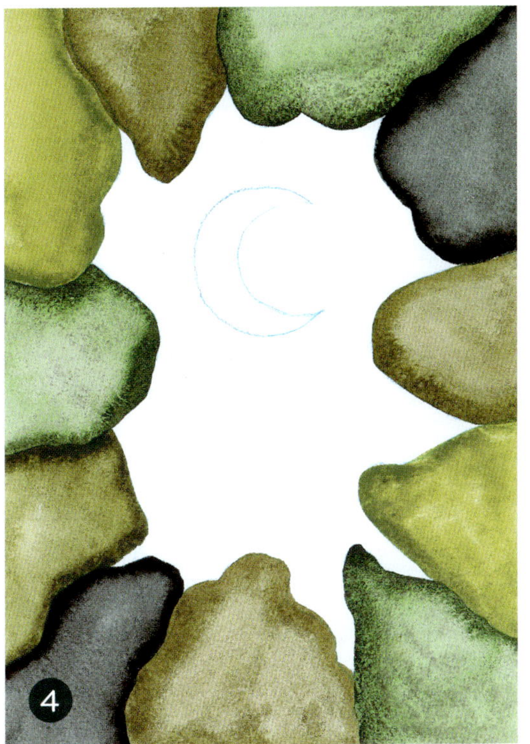

Step 4

Now, let's finish the first layer of the trees that are still unpainted using Shadow Green and Olive Green. It's important that no two adjacent trees are painted with the same color. Try to create a distribution where the tones blend naturally and harmoniously. Once you've completed this layer, allow the paint to dry completely before moving to the next step.

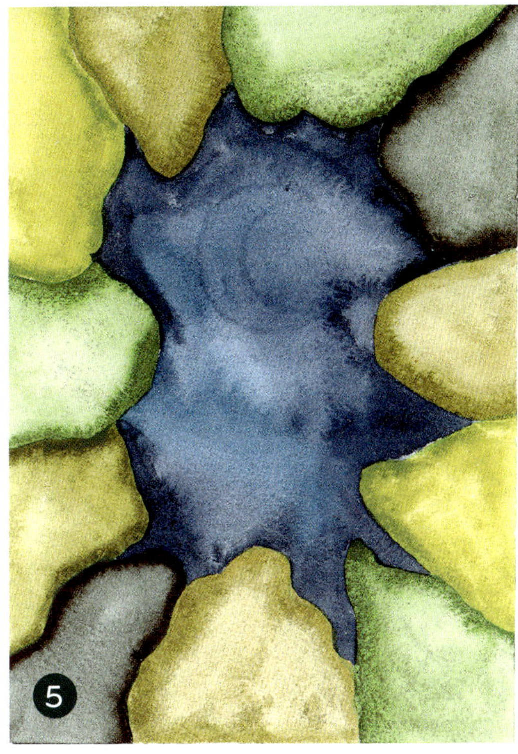

Step 5

For this step, we will paint the sky using Indigo and Turquoise, but we won't mix them initially. Start by loading your brush with Indigo and applying it along the edges of the sky. Once the edges are painted, clean your brush thoroughly, and then load it with Turquoise. Gently add a few touches to the sky, creating some accents. Next, clean your brush again and load it with just water. Use the wet brush to spread and diffuse the existing pigment, helping the colors blend naturally. The goal is for the pigments to merge on their own in the sky, creating a beautiful, textured effect.

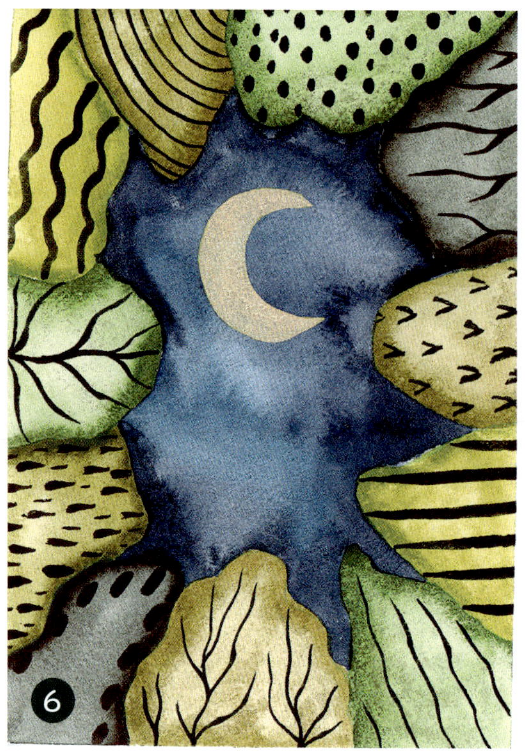

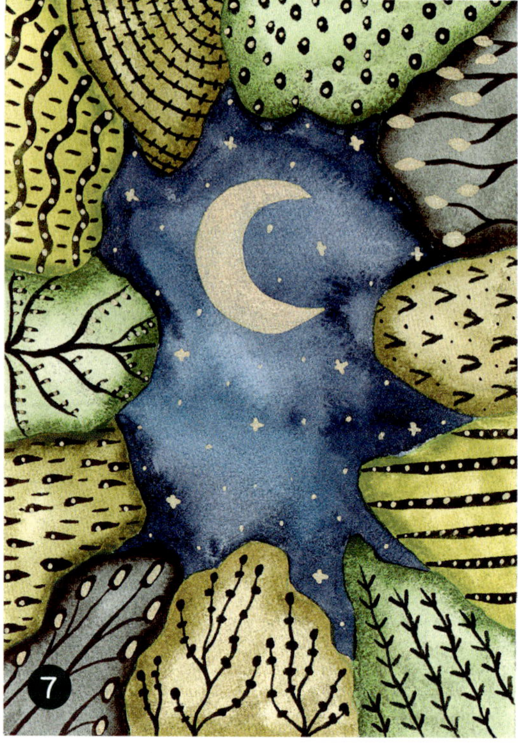

Step 6

Now comes the fun part: creating textures. With the size 2 brush loaded with plenty of Shadow Green, start painting over the trees. You can add waves, branches, dots, stripes, hearts, or leaf shapes. The idea is to play with the brush and let the textures appear naturally. Add a crescent moon in the middle of the sky using gold gouache. Start by outlining the shape of the moon with the fine tip of the size 2 brush, and then fill it in with the same golden pigment.

Step 7

For the final step, use gold gouache to enhance your painting. With the tip of your size 2 brush, apply the gouache over the textures you previously painted with Shadow Green. Follow the reference image and add overlapping details such as dots or small leaves. To finish, paint a few asterisks and dots in the sky. These golden touches will give your starry night a magical sparkle.

In the Golden Woods

In this exercise, we'll paint a sunlit path surrounded by golden autumn trees. Using warm and gentle tones, we'll capture the calm and beauty of a walk beneath glowing branches and soft autumn light . . . a warm scene to get lost in the peacefulness of nature.

Materials

Paper size
5 x 7" (13 x 18 cm)

Brushes
Size 4 and size 2

Watercolors
Burnt Umber
Naples Yellow
Nickel Azo Yellow
Perylene Violet
Quinacridone Gold
Permanent Brown
Raw Umber
Bohemian Green
Shadow Green

For details
Gold gouache
White gouache

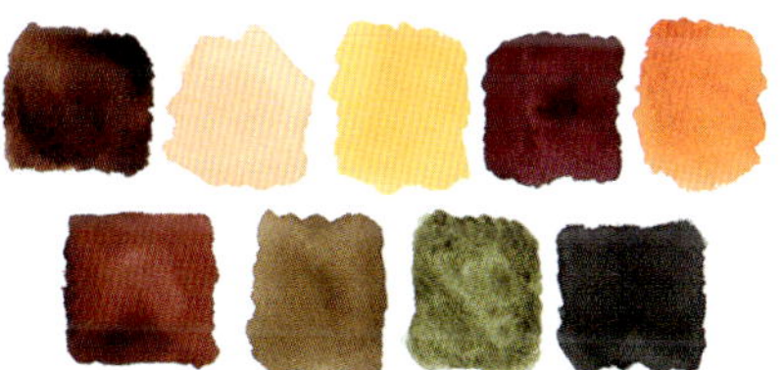

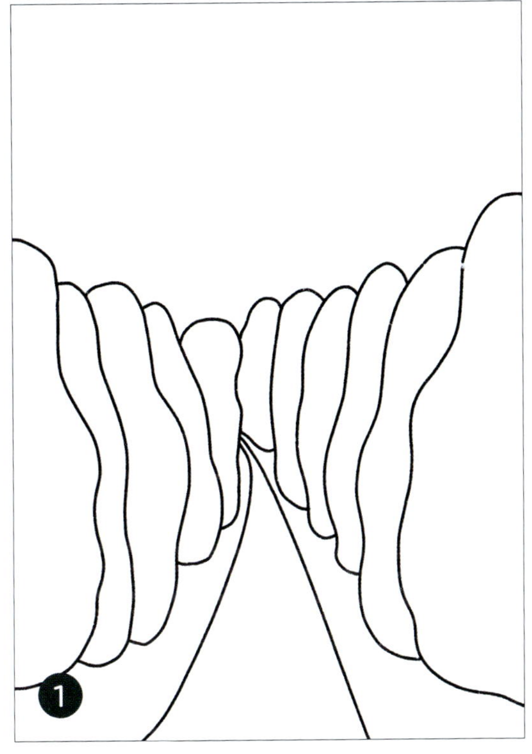

Step 1

Place your paper vertically. Lightly sketch the outlines of trees along both the left and right edges of the page. On each side, begin with a large tree, then draw a smaller one next to it, followed by an even smaller one, creating rows that gradually decrease in size as they move toward the center. Continue both sides until the trees almost meet in the middle. Finally, at the bottom of the page, draw a path that runs through the center, leading into the golden woods.

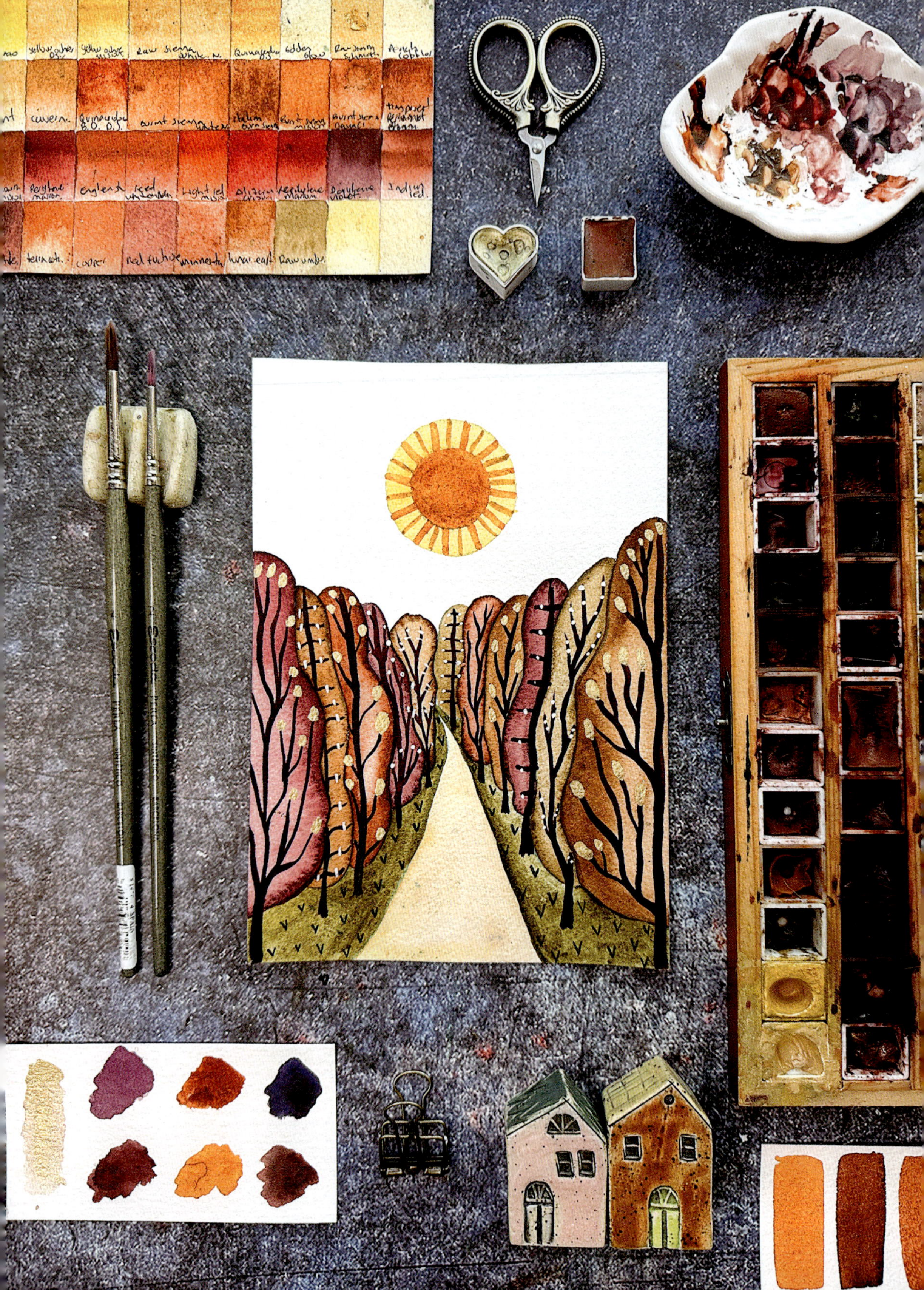

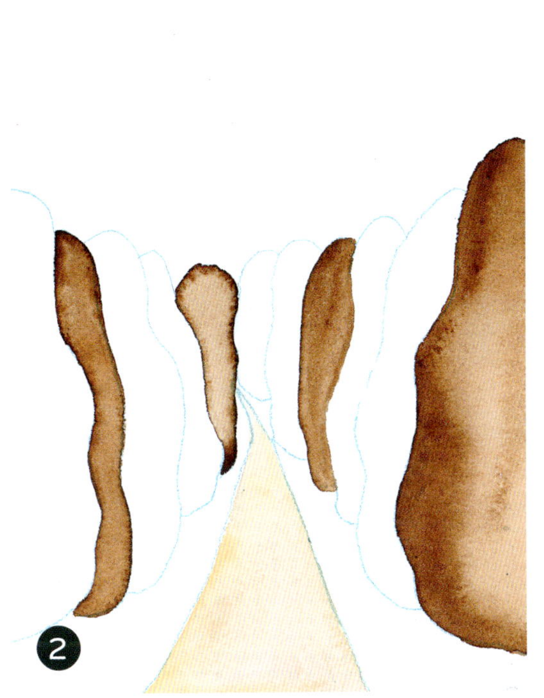

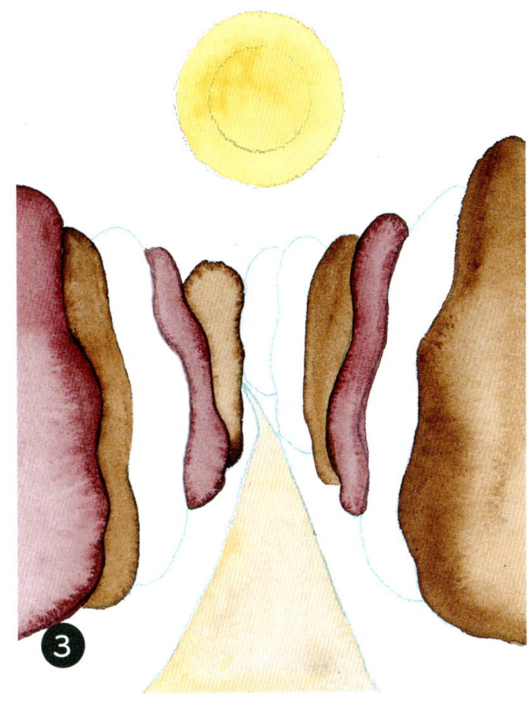

Step 2

Activate your paints with a bit of water. Use Burnt Umber and the size 4 brush to paint the first tree on the right, the fourth tree from the right, the second from the left, and the fifth from the left. Begin by outlining each tree with plenty of pigment. Then, rinse your brush, and using only clean water, gently pull the color from the edges toward the center. This gradual wash technique (page 21) will give the trees a natural look, and it's the method you'll continue using for all the trees in this painting. Next, take Naples Yellow and paint the path in the center of the scene.

Step 3

Once the watercolor is completely dry, sketch a circle in the center of the sky—this will be your sun. Inside that circle, sketch a smaller one to create a glowing effect. Paint the sun Nickel Azo Yellow. Next, using Perylene Violet, paint the first tree on the left, the fourth tree from the left, and the third tree from the right, following the same technique as Step 2. Allow everything to dry completely before moving to the next step.

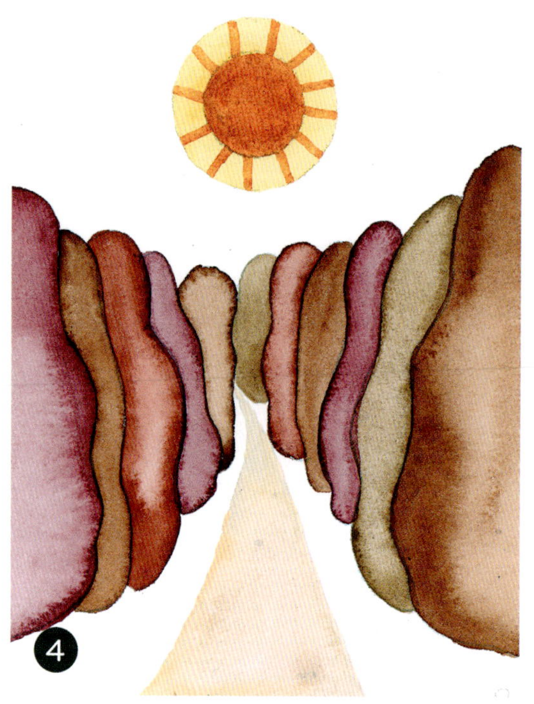

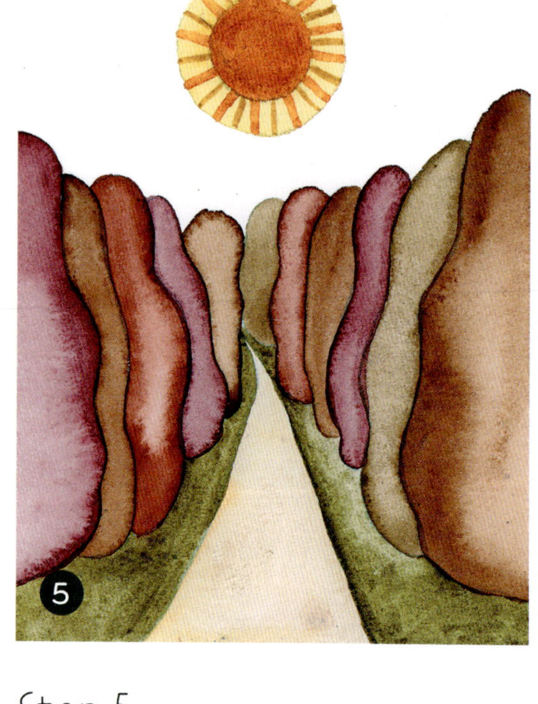

Step 4

Using your size 2 brush and Quinacridone Gold, paint the small inner circle of the sun. Then, with the same color, add a few thin lines between the inner and outer circles to suggest gentle rays. Now let's finish painting the remaining trees. Use Permanent Brown for the third tree from the left and the fifth from the right. Then, paint the second and sixth trees from the right with Raw Umber, using the same technique of outlining with pigment and blending inward with water. Let everything dry.

Step 5

Using Bohemian Green, paint the grassy areas on both sides of the path. Once that's done, add a few more delicate lines around the sun to enhance the ray effect. It's very important to let the watercolor dry completely before moving to the next step. This will keep the colors clean and the edges crisp where needed.

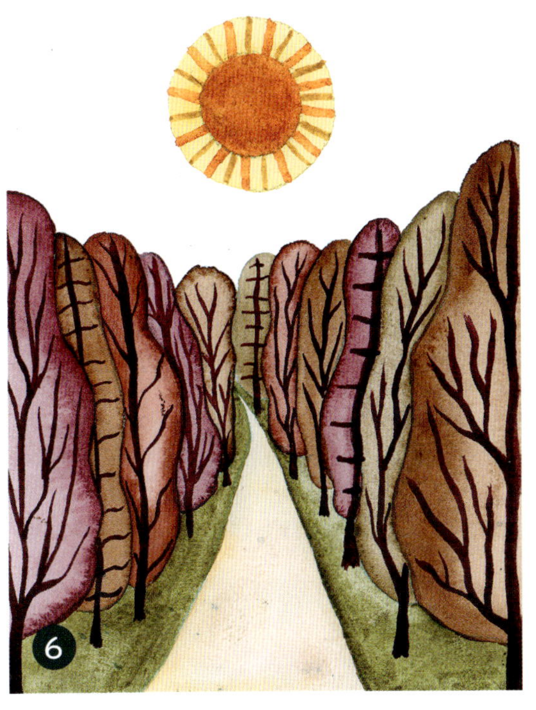

Step 6

Using the tip of your size 2 brush, load it with plenty of either Burnt Umber or Perylene Violet, and begin painting the branches of your trees. Use thin, gentle strokes to suggest natural shapes. I recommend starting each branch from the trunk at the base, near the grass, and painting upward toward the top of the tree, letting smaller twigs branch out along the way. You can refer to the example image for inspiration and guidance on how the branches look.

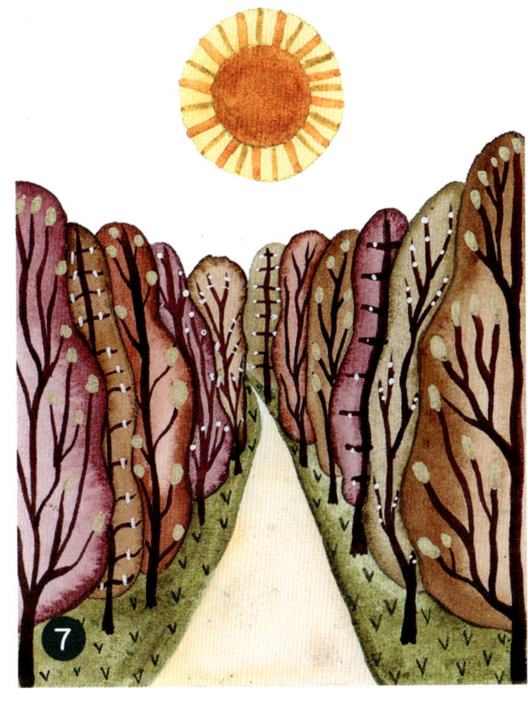

Step 7

Before we finish, let's add a bit of texture to the grass. Using Shadow Green, paint a few small leaves or strokes at the base of the trees to suggest scattered foliage and give the ground more depth.

Now it's time for the most fun and creative part: adding details that make the painting uniquely yours. Using gold and white gouache, add leaves to your trees with simple lines and dots. You can play with shapes like circles or flicks to suggest light and movement. This final step is personal and playful, so feel free to let your imagination guide you. There's no right or wrong, just enjoy the process and bring your golden woods to life.

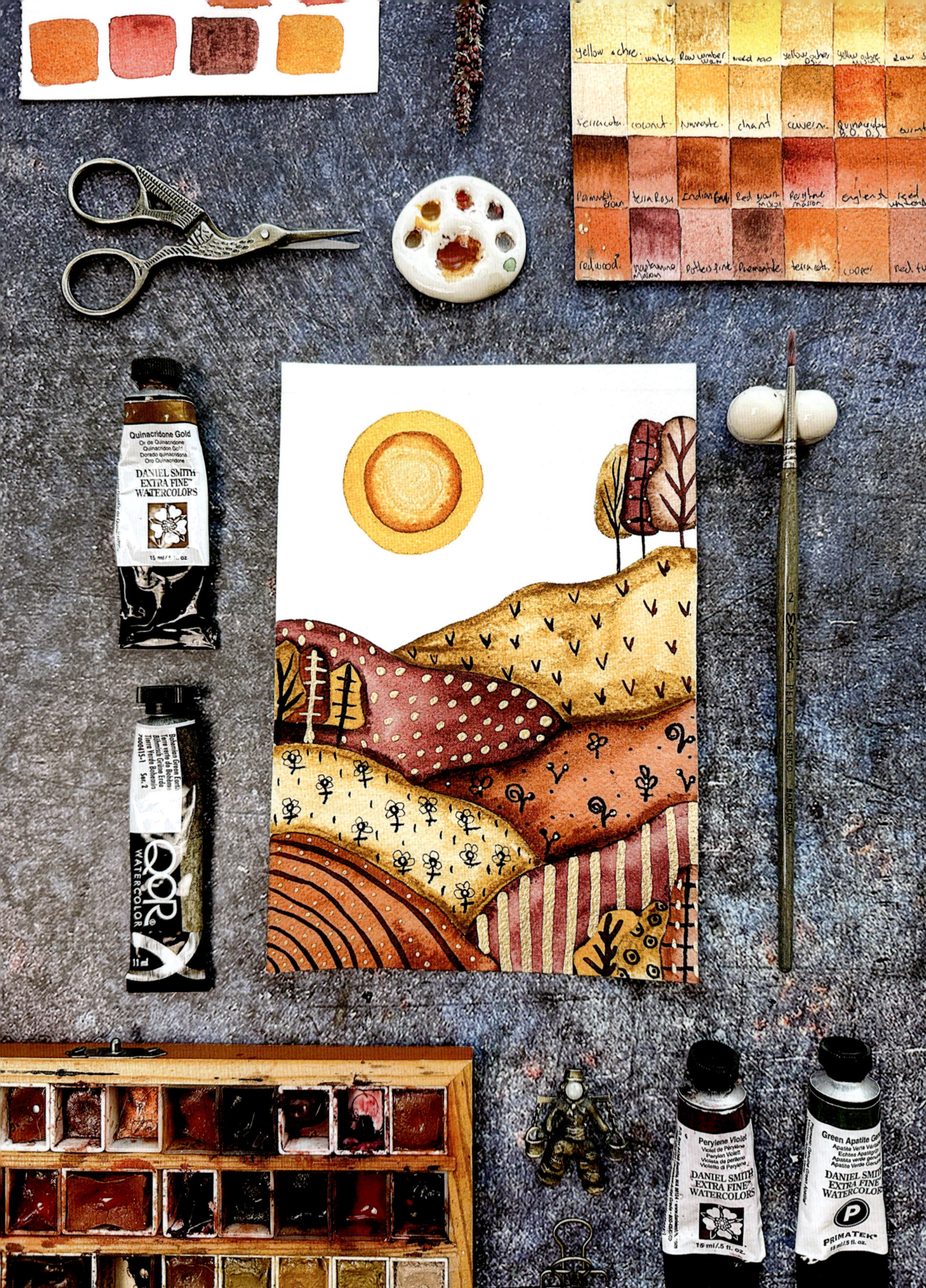

Whispers of Autumn

In this peaceful autumn scene, we'll paint a series of overlapping mountains, each one softly layered with unique textures and tones inspired by the changing season. Using a warm palette of earthy browns, golden hues, and deep violets, we'll add delicate trees dotting the hillsides and touches of gold to bring a hint of magic. A gentle, glowing sun will complete the sky, casting a warm light over the landscape. This exercise invites you to slow down and enjoy the quiet beauty of fall.

Materials

Paper size
5 x 7" (13 x 18 cm)

Brush
Size 2

Watercolors
Permanent Brown
Burnt Umber
Nickel Azo Yellow
Perylene Violet
Quinacridone Gold
Raw Umber

For details
Gold gouache
Size 12 fineliner

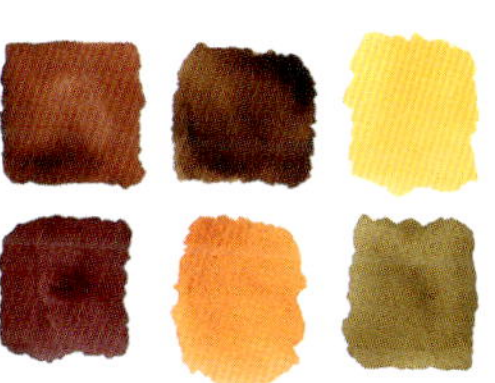

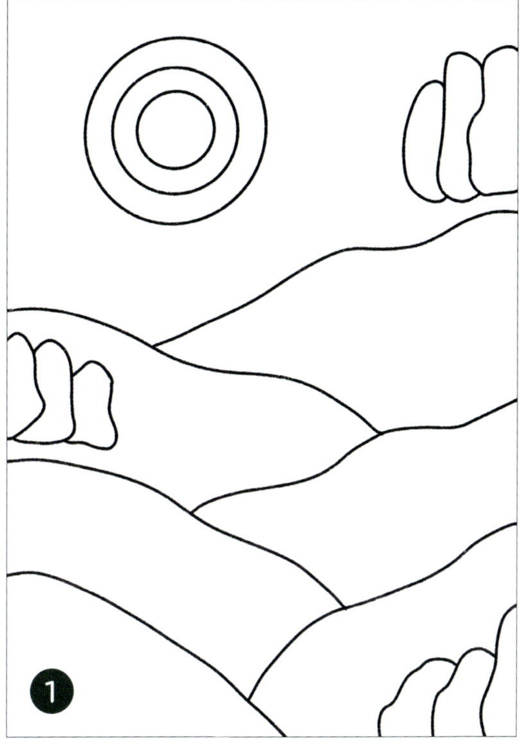

Step 1

Place your paper vertically. Lightly sketch the mountains stretching from one side of the page to the other. Start the first mountain from the left side and the next one from the right, and continue alternating sides until you have six small, overlapping mountains. In some of them, draw simple, uniform shapes to represent little trees. Then, in the upper part of the sky, sketch a large circle, followed by a medium circle inside it, and finally a small circle in the center. This will be your sun.

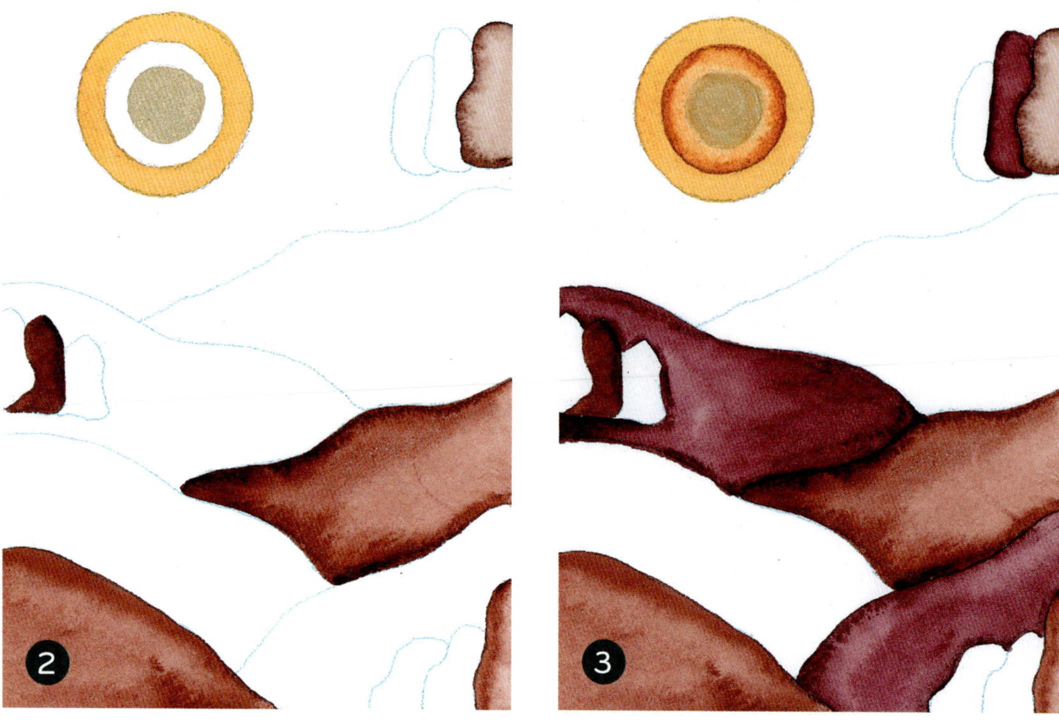

Step 2

Activate your paints with a bit of water. With Permanent Brown and your size 2 brush, paint the first mountain on the bottom left, as well as the fourth mountain. Then, paint the first tree on the bottom right and the second tree from the left. Paint the first tree on the top-most mountain with Burnt Umber. Next, use Nickel Azo Yellow to fill in the largest outer circle of the sun and gold gouache for the small center circle. Let everything dry thoroughly before continuing to the next step.

Step 3

With Perylene Violet, paint the second mountain from the bottom and the fifth mountain. Then, with the same color, paint the second tree on the topmost mountain.

Next, paint the middle circle of the sun using Quinacridone Gold. To do this, outline the circle with rich pigment and then rinse your brush. Using only clean water, gently pull the color inward to create a gradual wash effect (page 21). This technique will produce a soft gradient and add beautiful texture to the sun. Allow everything to dry completely before moving to the next step.

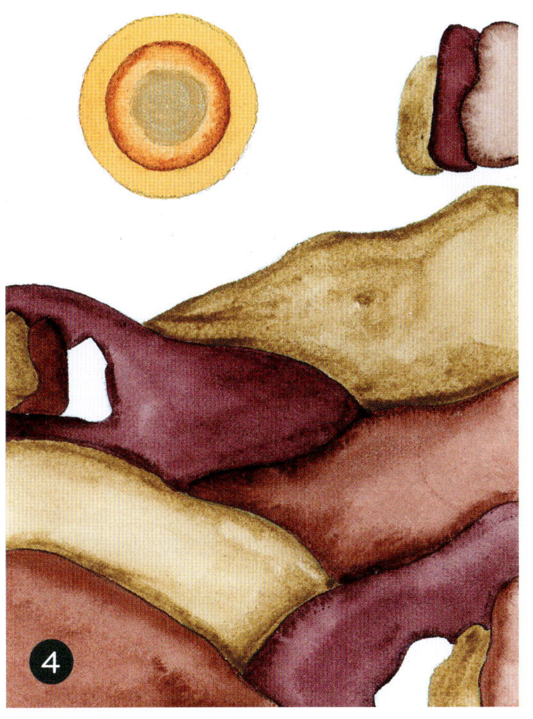

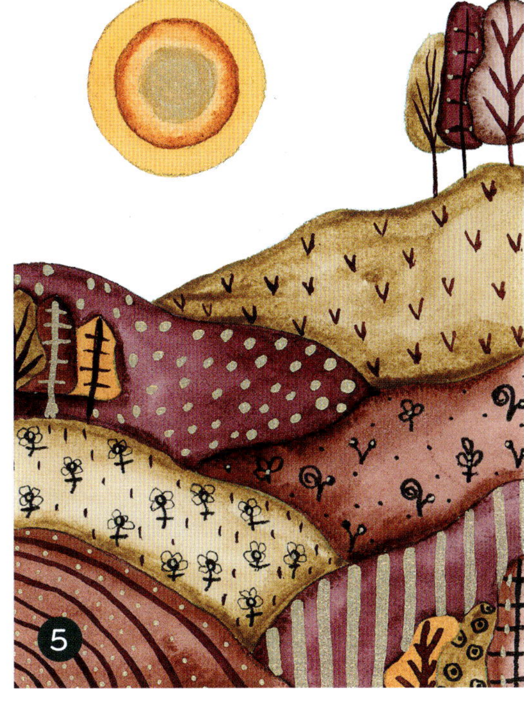

Step 4

Using Raw Umber, paint the third mountain from the bottom and the topmost mountain. With the same color, paint the second tree on the second mountain, the first tree on the fifth mountain, and the first tree on the top mountain. All these elements should be painted using this single color to maintain harmony across the scene.

Step 5

Using plenty of Perylene Violet, add details and branches. On the first mountain (bottom left), paint curved lines that stretch across the mountain, following its shape from side to side. With the same color, add branches to the trees that were painted with a different base color to create contrast and depth. Then, using gold gouache, add dots and lines across the mountains, and paint a few golden leaves on the trees. Finally, with your size 12 fineliner, draw small flowers on one of the mountains and some branches and leaves on another. Feel free to add extra details like golden dots or simple patterns on the mountains. Let everything dry completely to set the final details. Your charming landscape is now complete.

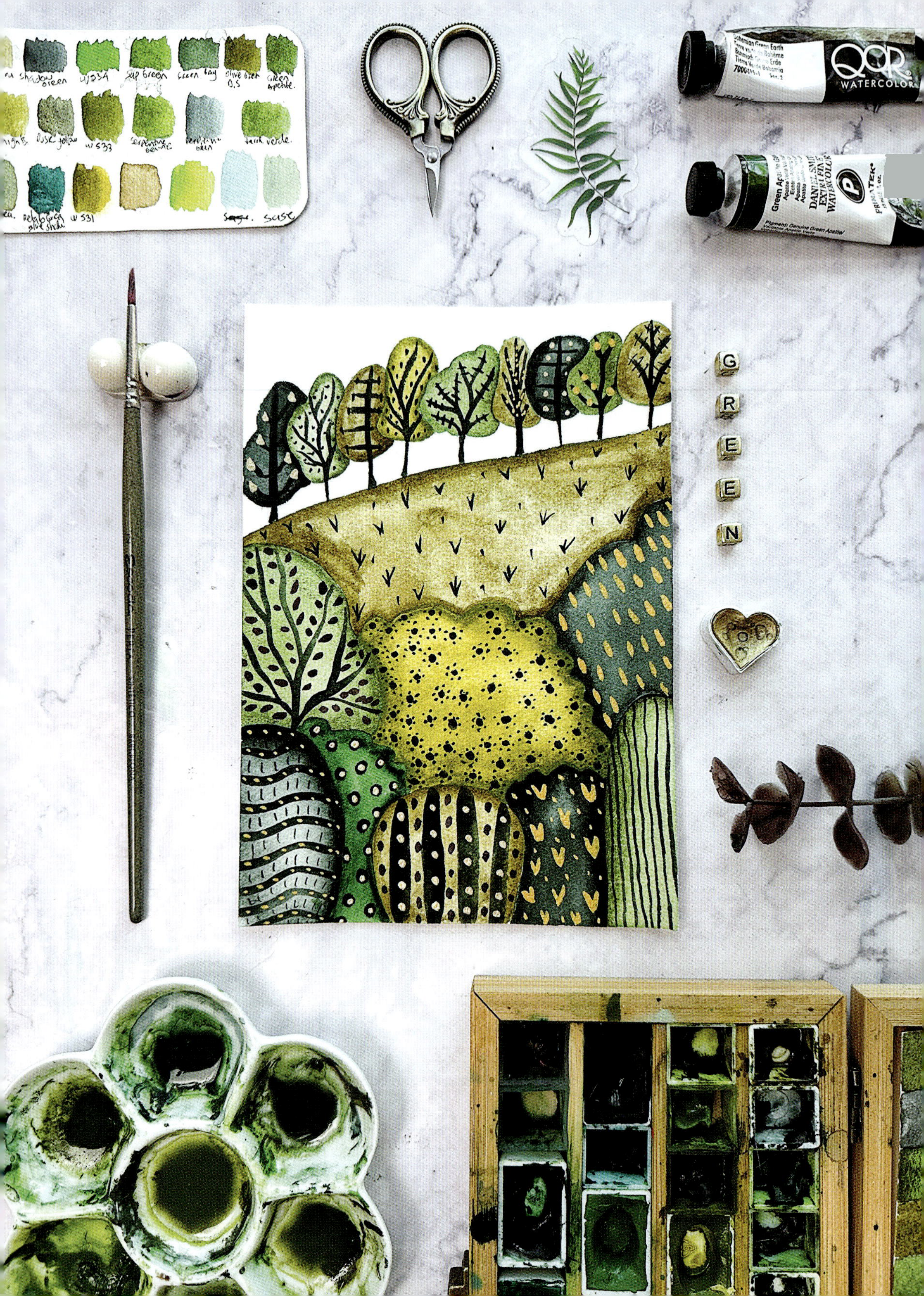

Magic in the Grove

This landscape invites you into a world of quiet wonder and rich texture. With every brushstroke of green, we create a sense of movement and harmony, like the soft rustle of leaves in a hidden grove. The golden touches scattered throughout offer little sparks of magic, while the distant trees and mountains hold the stillness of a peaceful afternoon. This exercise is a gentle reminder to slow down, observe, and find joy in the small, textured details of nature.

Materials

Paper size
5 x 7" (13 x 18 cm)

Brush
Size 2

Watercolors
Green Apatite
Shadow Green
Olive Green
Bohemian Green

For details
Gold gouache
Size 12 fineliner

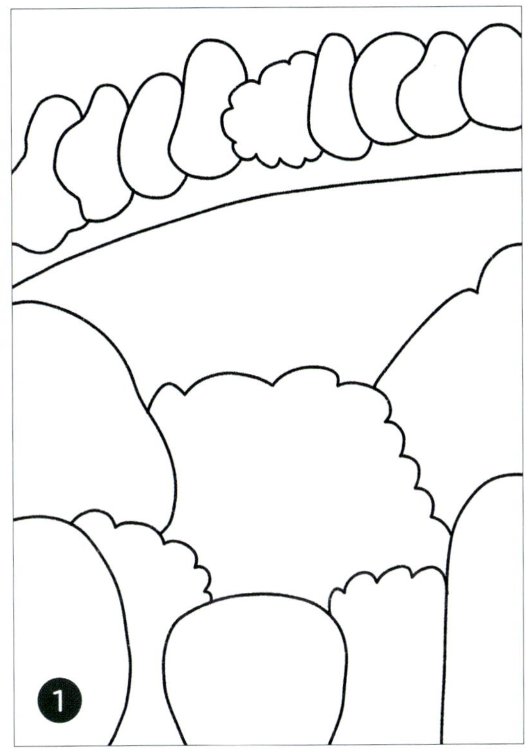

Step 1

Place your paper vertically. Lightly sketch the bushes. Start from the bottom of the page and work your way up, layering one bush over another. Their shapes can vary from oval to cloudlike as long as each one has its own distinct form. Continue drawing upward until just past the halfway point of the page. Once the bushes are complete, draw a gentle line above them stretching from one side of the paper to the other. This will be your mountain. On top of the mountain, sketch a row of trees side by side, each with a different shape to give a sense of natural variety.

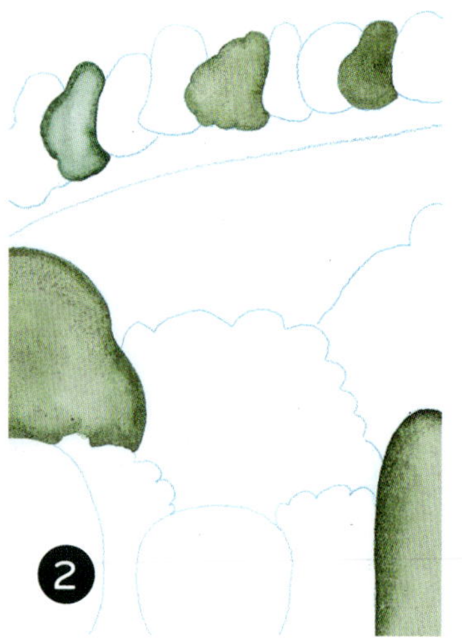 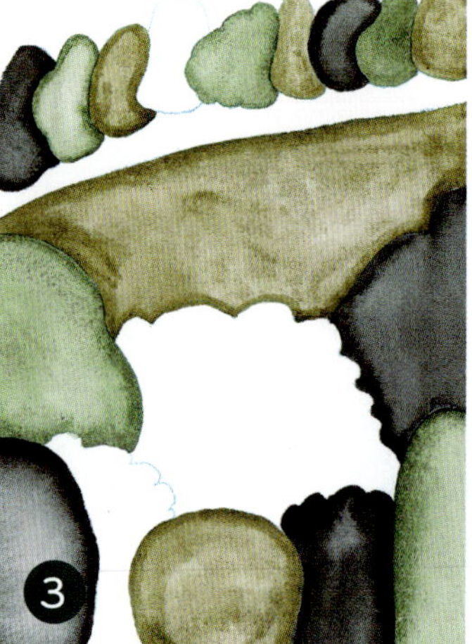 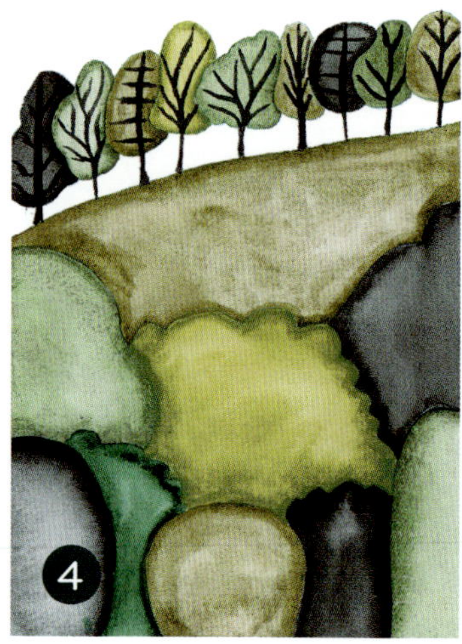

Step 2

Activate your paints with a bit of water. Using Green Apatite and your size 2 brush, paint one bush on each side of the page. Then, move to the top of the mountain and paint three trees. The key here is to select trees and bushes that are not directly next to each other; this creates visual balance and variation in your composition.

Note: Some of the bushes and trees can be painted using the gradual wash technique (page 21), where the edges are darker and fade toward the center, while others can be filled with a more uniform flat wash for contrast. This mix of approaches creates variety and texture. Let each shape stand out on its own and enjoy how this fresh green tone starts to bring your landscape to life. Allow everything to dry completely before moving to the next step.

Step 3

Using Shadow Green and Olive Green, paint most of the remaining trees and bushes. Avoid placing the same color next to itself—this will help keep each shape distinct and create a more dynamic landscape. Next, use Bohemian Green to paint the mountain and a few of the trees as well. Be sure to let each shape dry completely before painting the one beside it. This will prevent the colors from blending unintentionally and keep your edges crisp and clean.

Step 4

If the greens you have aren't enough to give each shape a unique color, feel free to mix small amounts of them together to create new, varied shades. Use these custom blends to paint the bushes in the center area of your composition. Then, load your brush with plenty of Shadow Green, and using just the tip of your brush, begin drawing the branches of the trees. Start each one from the trunk and extend it upward toward the top of the tree. From that main line, add smaller branches that branch out naturally, keeping each tree unique and balanced in its own organic way. Let your hand follow a gentle rhythm, as if the trees are whispering in the breeze.

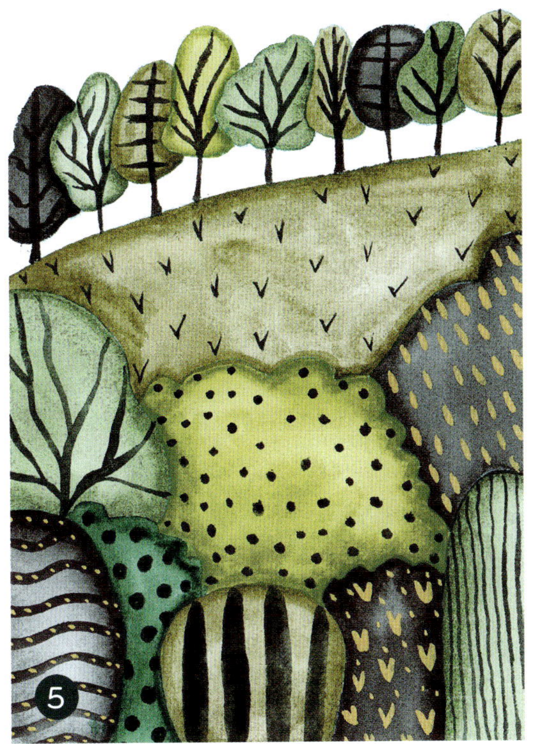

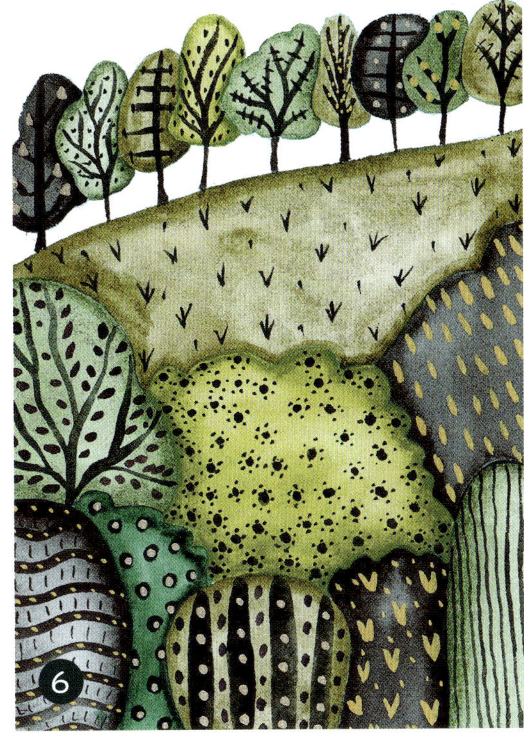

Step 5

To add texture to the foreground of your landscape, load your brush with plenty of Shadow Green. In each bush, paint a different pattern. The pattern can include waves, stripes, dots, leaves, branches, or circles. Let each one have its own unique character. For the mountain, use the same brush and pigment to paint small patches of grass by creating repeated V-shaped strokes. These details will start to bring your scene to life, adding movement and richness through variation and rhythm. With gold gouache and the tip of your brush, begin adding glowing details like hearts and dots to the foreground. Let everything dry.

Step 6

Add another layer of texture using gold gouache, the tip of your brush, and a size 12 fineliner. Paint over your first layer of patterns with new golden details such as little leaves, dots, hearts, and lines across your bushes and trees. These shimmering touches bring a sense of magic and warmth to your landscape, making it glow and come alive with light. You can also define the grass on the mountain and add extra details with your fineliner.

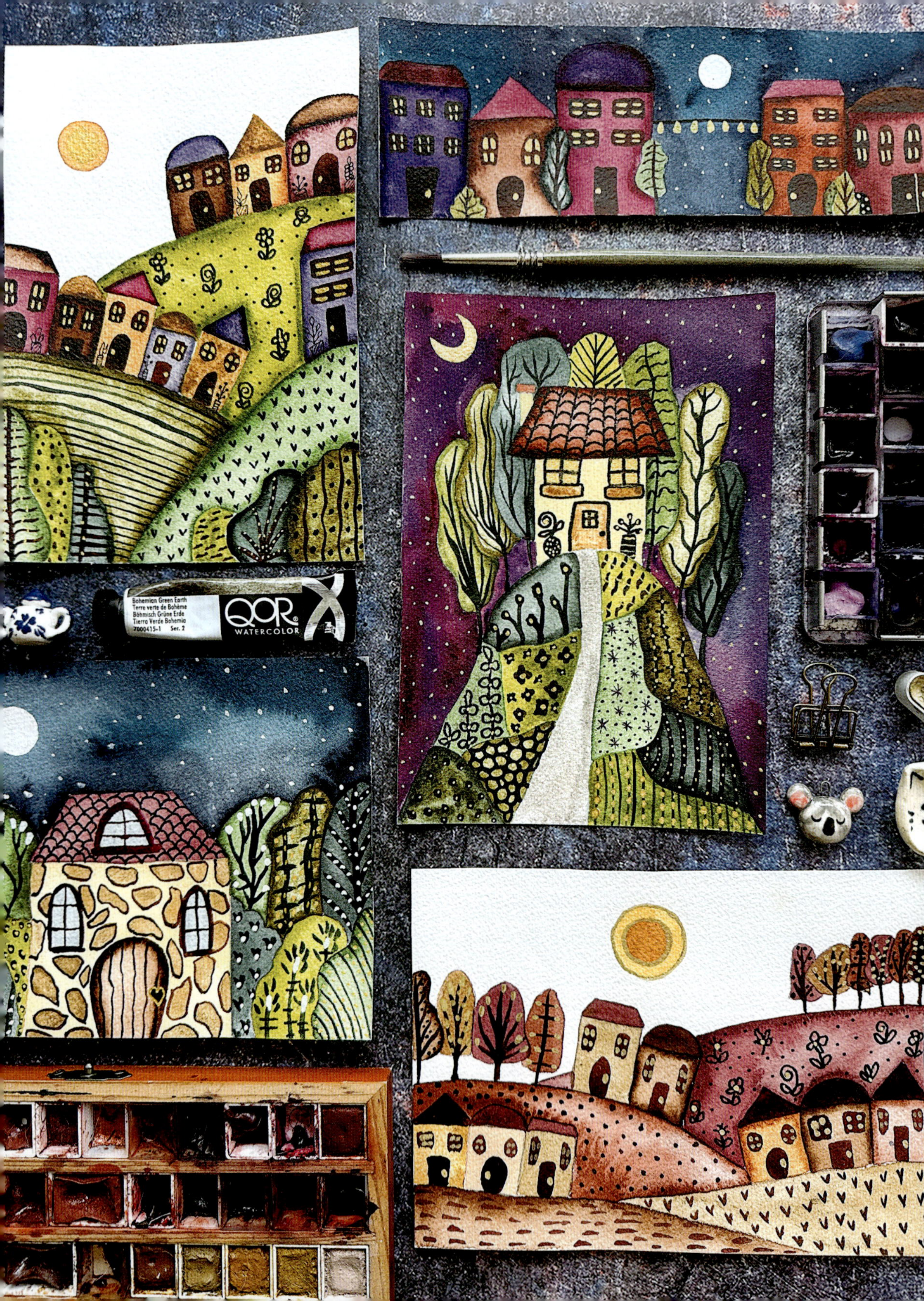
Bohemian Green Earth
Terre verte de Bohême
Böhmisch Grüne Erde
Tierra Verde Bohemio
7000415-1   Ser. 2
QoR
WATERCOLOR

Strolling in *Charming Villages*

There's a quiet kind of magic in wandering through a small village where cobblestone paths remember the footsteps of time, and flower-filled windows whisper stories of lives gently unfolding.

In this chapter, you'll stroll through sleepy mountain hamlets, forest cottages, and winding alleys painted in autumn gold. Every house holds a memory, every roof leans into the sky like a lullaby. You'll breathe in the scent of firewood, hear distant laughter from unseen porches, and feel the tender rhythm of life in places where the clock slows down.

These watercolor villages are not just scenes. They are invitations to rest, to dream, to remember that beauty lives in simplicity and that warmth often hides in the smallest corners.

Take a slow step forward and let your brush carry you home.

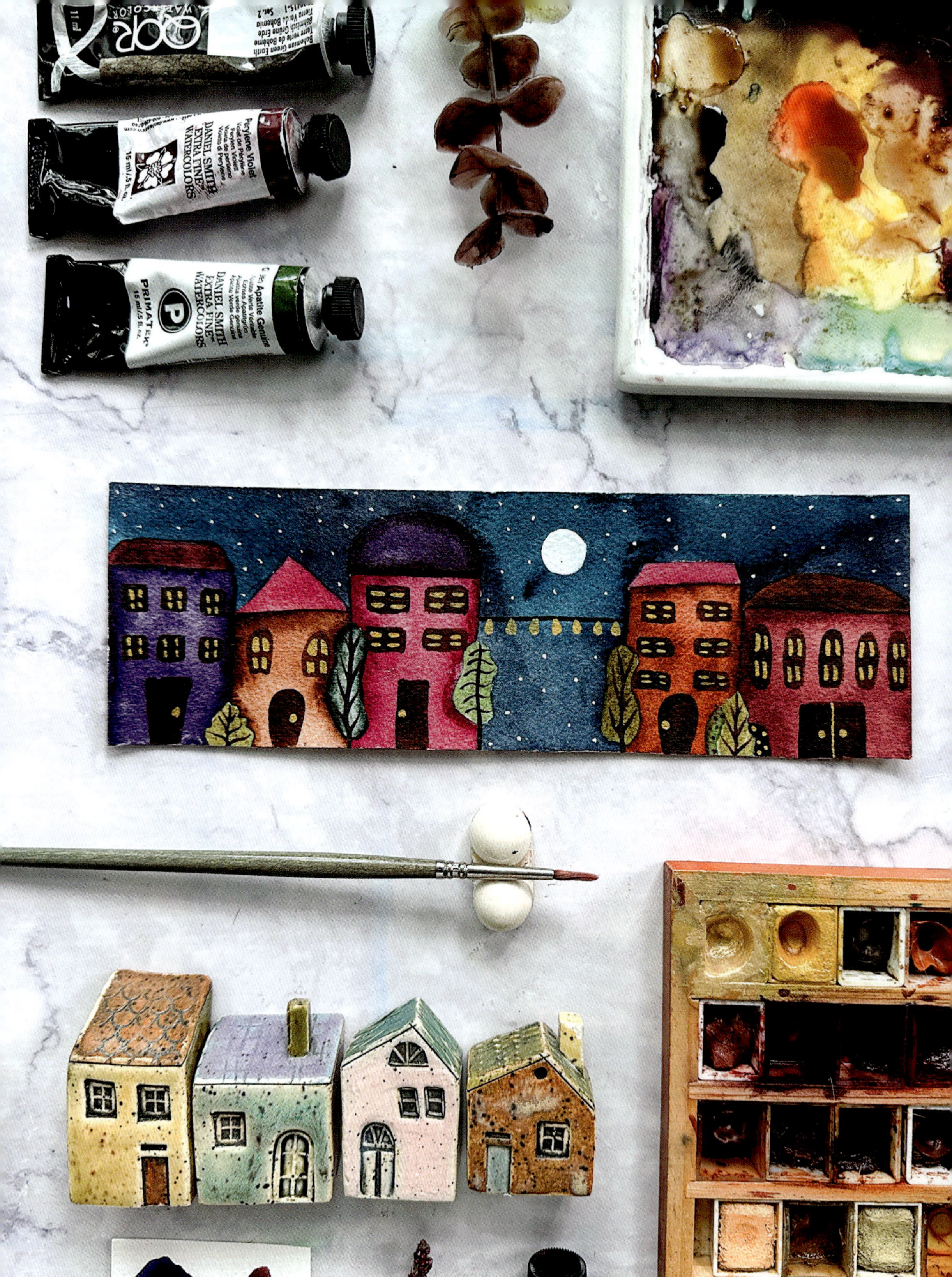

Old Town

This small, horizontal landscape painted in the shape of a bookmark, holds the quiet soul of an old village: timeless, gentle, and full of mystery. It invites you into a place where the night feels soft and alive, where silence wraps around you like a warm blanket. Each house seems to carry a story, and the deep shadows and glowing accents create a dreamlike calm. Above it all, a sky filled with tiny white stars casts a gentle hush over the rooftops. Painting this scene feels like stepping into a distant memory: peaceful, nostalgic, and filled with quiet wonder.

Materials

Paper size
2½ x 8" (6 x 20 cm)

Brush
Size 2

Watercolors
Violet
Quinacridone Lilac
Perylene Violet
Burnt Umber
Permanent Brown
Indigo

Turquoise
Green Apatite
Olive Green
Shadow Green
Bohemian Green

For details
Gold gouache
Size 12 fineliner
White gouache

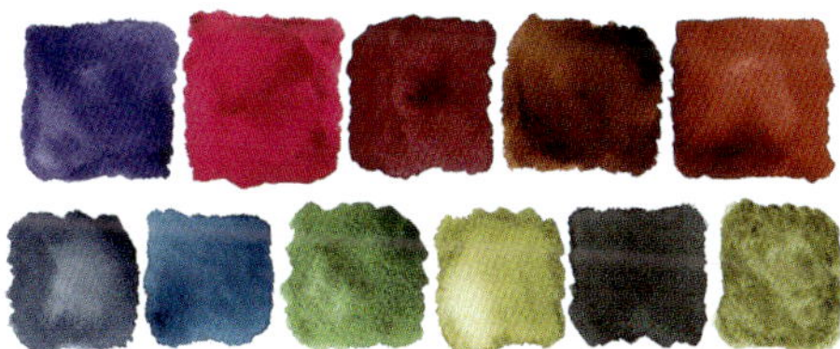

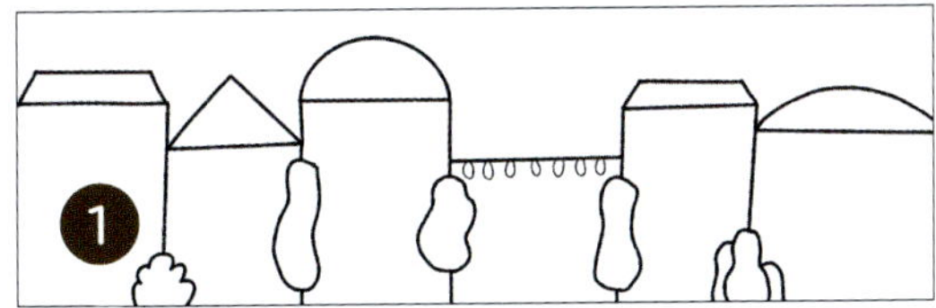

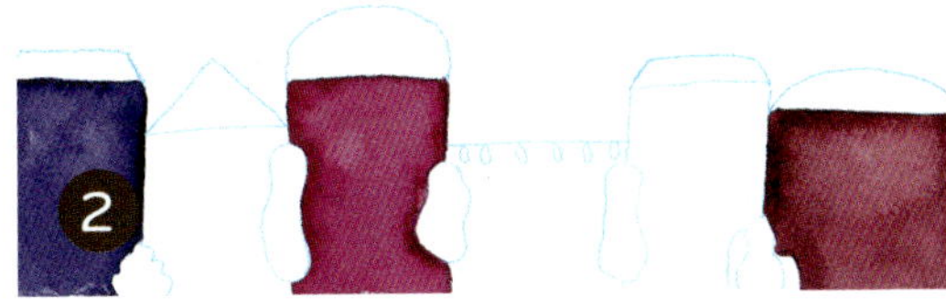

Step 1

Place your paper horizontally. Lightly sketch six rectangles in a row across the page, varying their height and width to give each building its own personality—just like in a real old village. Draw different rooftops on top of the first three rectangles and the last two. Leave the fourth rectangle without a roof—this space will hold a string of glowing lights that gently illuminates the village. To complete your sketch, add a few simple trees and bushes in the spaces between the buildings to bring a touch of nature and balance to the scene.

Step 2

Activate your paints with a bit of water. Then, paint the buildings using rich, warm tones. Color the first rectangle (from left to right) with Violet, the third with Quinacridone Lilac, and the sixth with Perylene Violet. Let each color settle into its space to create a dreamy, moody feel that matches the quiet night atmosphere. Allow everything to dry completely before moving to the next step.

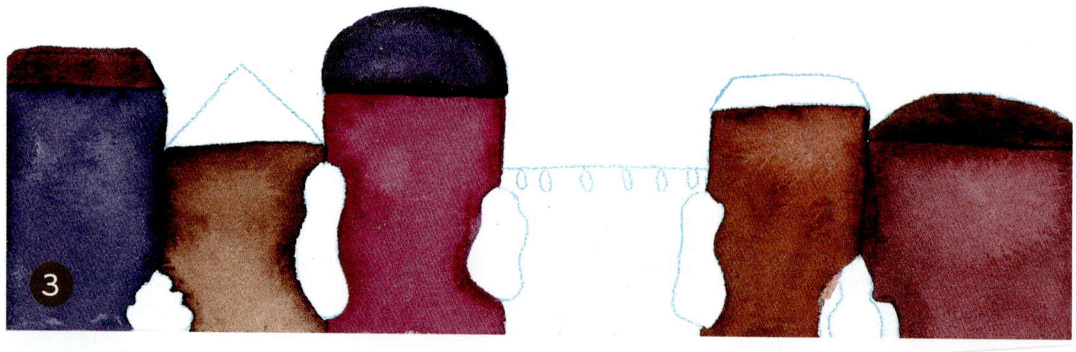

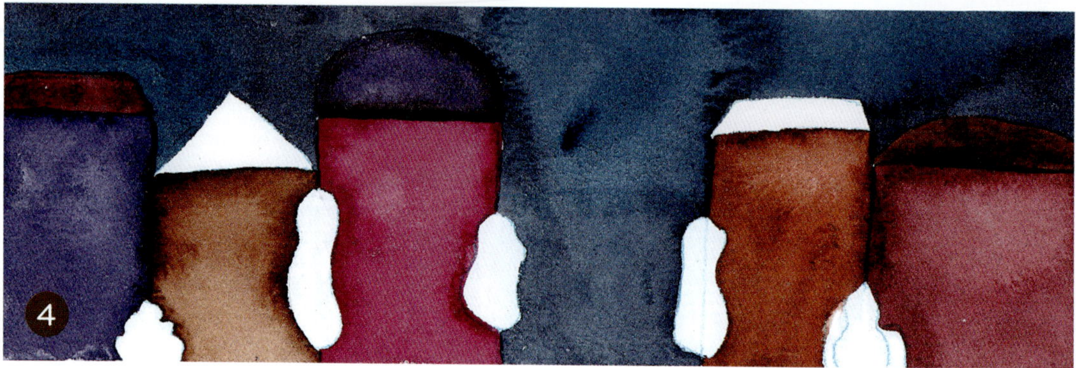

Step 3

Paint the second rectangle (from left to right) with Burnt Umber and the fifth with Permanent Brown. Once these areas are fully dry, paint the rooftops: Use Perylene Violet for the first house, Violet for the third, and Permanent Brown for the last one. Let all painted areas dry completely before adding rooftops or neighboring colors. This will keep the edges crisp and prevent colors from bleeding into each other.

Step 4

Wet the entire sky area with clean water. Then, apply a heavy amount of Indigo in some sections to create rich, dark areas of the night sky. In other sections, use only clean water, allowing the pigment to flow softly and create lighter spaces. While the surface is still wet, drop small touches of Turquoise into the lighter areas for a gentle glow and dreamy movement. This is the wet-on-wet technique (page 18). Keeping the surface evenly damp is the key to avoiding hard edges and achieving a smooth, even wash.

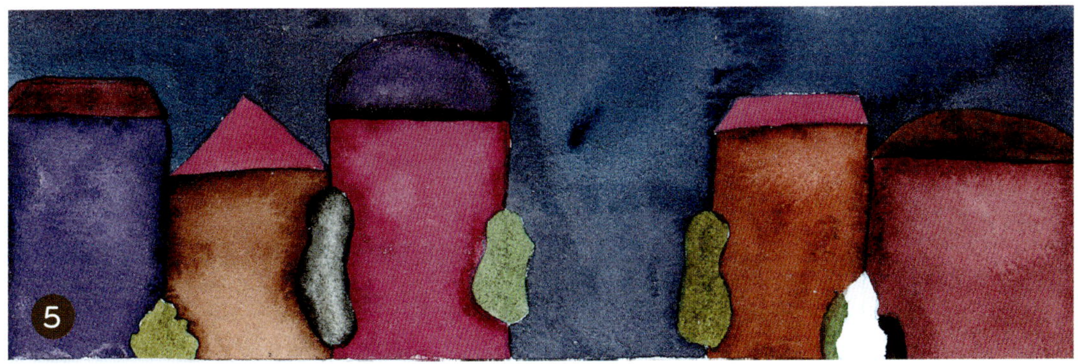

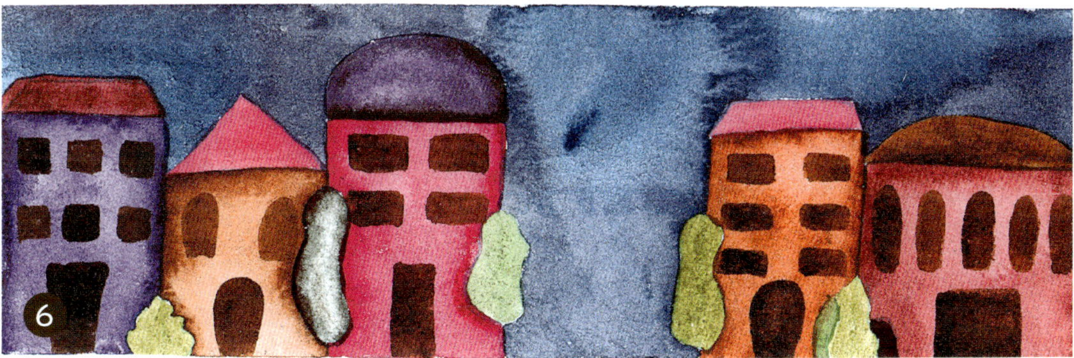

Step 5

Paint the trees and bushes nestled between each building. Use a different green for each one, choosing from Green Apatite, Olive Green, Shadow Green, and Bohemian Green (or your preferred greens). If two trees or bushes are right next to each other, paint only one at a time, and let it dry completely before moving to the one beside it. This will keep the shapes defined and prevent unwanted blending. At this stage, also paint the rooftops of the second and fourth houses (from left to right) with Quinacridone Lilac. Be sure the buildings are fully dry before adding the rooftops to maintain clean lines and soft contrast.

Step 6

Using a generous amount of Permanent Brown, paint the doors of your little houses and buildings with the tip of the brush. Feel free to choose rectangular, square, or arched shapes. Once the doors are completely dry, move to the windows, again using rectangles, squares, or arches. To finish, use Bohemian Green to complete the bush that was left unpainted.

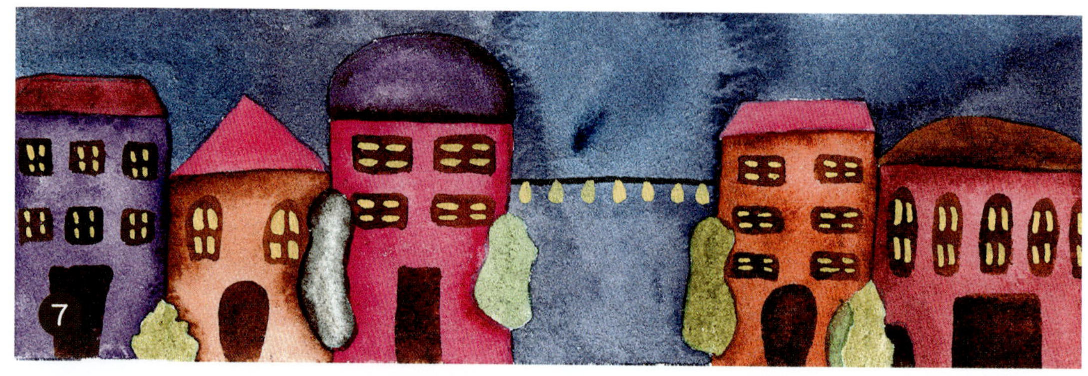

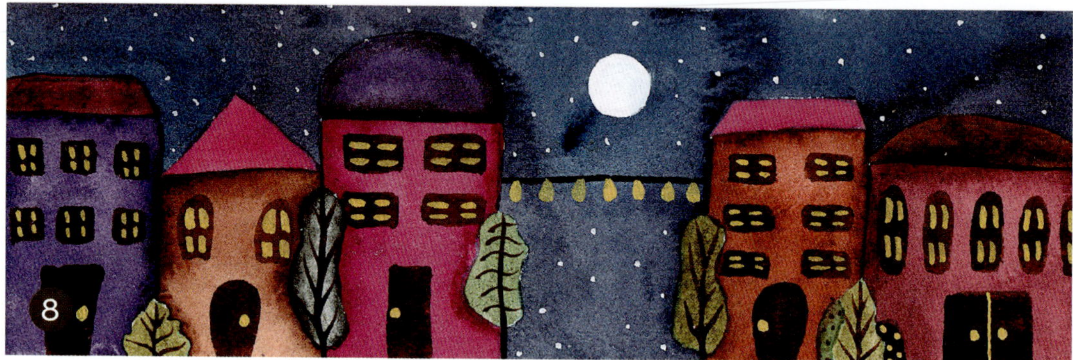

Step 7

Using gold gouache, paint small squares on the windows to suggest warm lights glowing inside your little houses and buildings—as if each one holds a story shining from within. Then, draw the wire that runs across the scene using the size 12 fineliner. Along this line, add hanging light bulbs with gold gouache, creating a string of lights that brings a magical and cozy touch to our night.

Step 8

With plenty of Burnt Umber and the tip of your brush, paint the branches of the trees and bushes. Start from the bottom and work upward: Begin with a main branch, then let smaller ones grow from it. Next, use white gouache to paint a small circle in the sky (just above the string of lights) that will become your moon. With the same white, scatter tiny dots across the sky to represent stars.

Then, with gold gouache, add shine by painting the door handles. You may also add golden details to the bushes if you like. Finally, once the moon is completely dry, apply a second layer of white gouache to make its glow even brighter. Your little old town under a starry night is now complete.

Little Villa in the Mountains

High up in the mountains, where the wind softly brushes the treetops, lies a little village born from a dream. The colorful houses rest gently on the peaks, as if trying to reach the sun, and everything around them breathes lush greens, warm earthy hues, and textures that whisper of time and nature's quiet magic.

This exercise invites you to wander through enchanted hills, to build with your brush a peaceful corner where every house tells a story and every stroke becomes a mountain's sigh.

Materials

Paper size
5 x 7" (13 x 18 cm)

Brushes
Size 4 and size 2

Watercolors
Green Apatite
Quinacridone Lilac
Nickel Azo Yellow
Raw Umber

Permanent Brown
Perylene Violet
Bohemian Green
Violet
Burnt Umber
Shadow Green
Olive Green

For details
Gold gouache
Size 12 fineliner

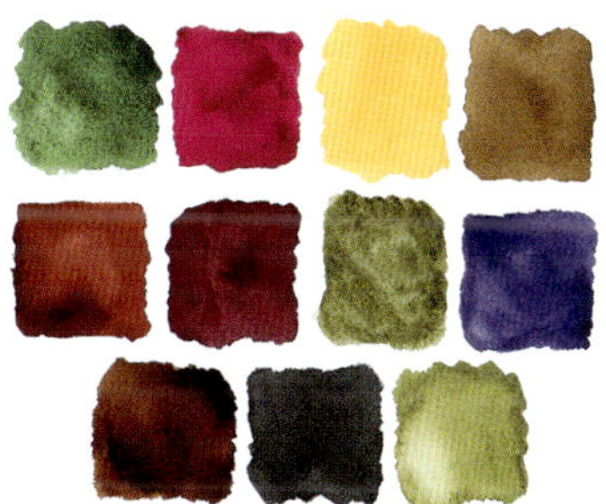

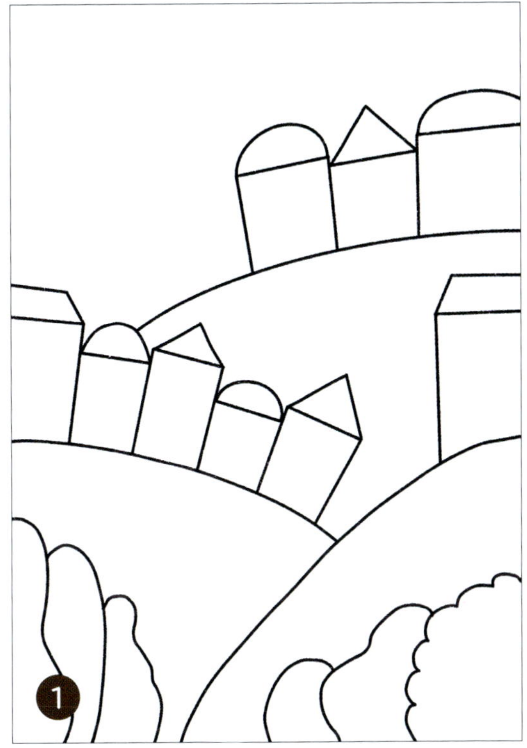

Step 1

Place your paper vertically. Lightly sketch your scene. In the lower corners, draw two sets of three bushes each, leaving a clear space in the center. From that central space, draw an arched line curving upward to the right. This will be your first mountain. Then, sketch a second mountain on the left that slightly overlaps the first.

At the top of this second mountain, draw five aligned rectangles, and place a triangle or semicircle on top of each one to form the rooftops of the houses. Next, add one more house at the top of the first mountain. Finally, above everything, draw one last curved line: the highest mountain, with three little houses sitting on its ridge. Be sure to leave a bit of space at the top of the paper to create a sense of open sky.

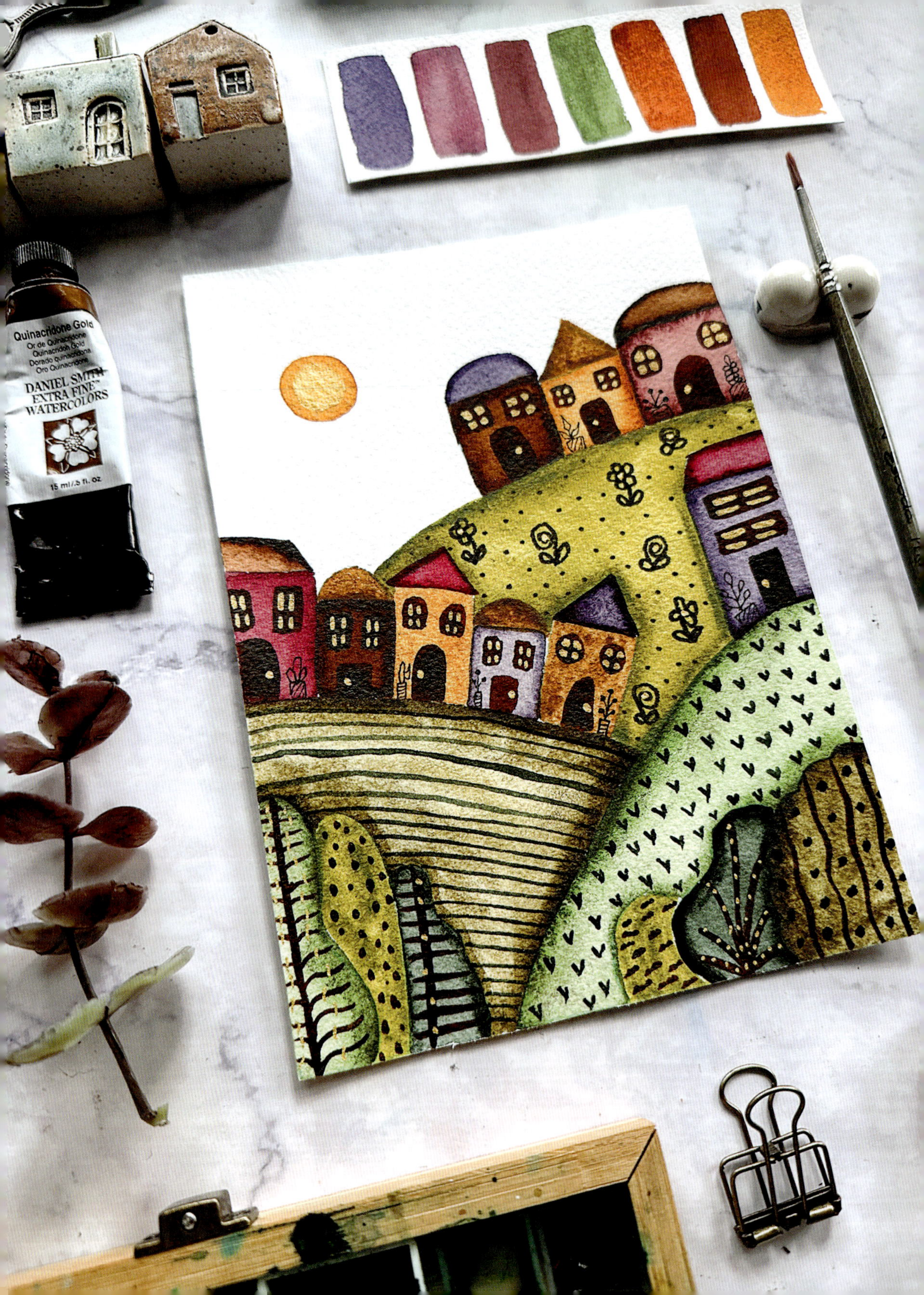

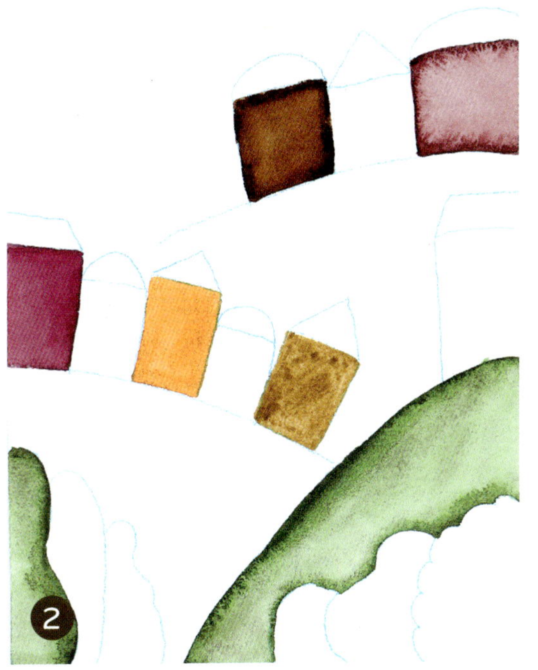

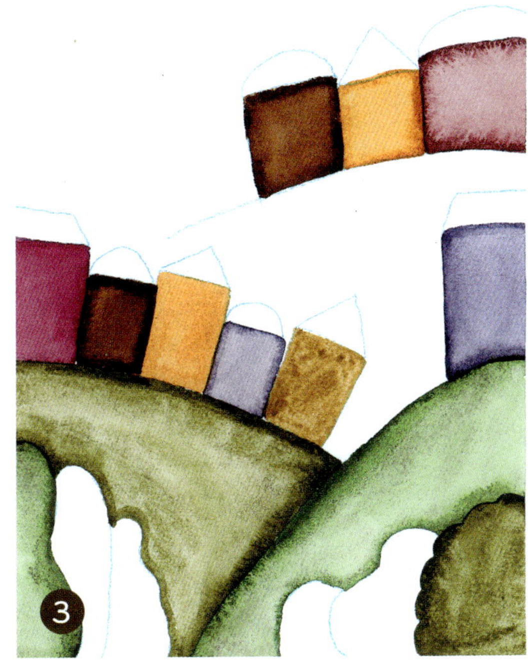

Step 2

Activate your paints with a bit of water. Using your size 4 brush, begin adding color to the scene. Start by painting the first mountain on the right, along with the bush on the left, using Green Apatite, which is a vibrant shade that brings the landscape to life. Next, paint the houses on the second mountain. Use Quinacridone Lilac for the first house (from left to right), Nickel Azo Yellow for the third, and Raw Umber for the fifth.

On the third and highest mountain, paint the first house on the left with Permanent Brown and the third house with Perylene Violet using the gradual wash technique (page 21). These rich colors will add character and variety to your little mountain village. Allow everything to dry completely before moving to the next step.

Step 3

Using Bohemian Green, paint the first bush on the right and the entire second mountain (on the left), adding freshness and depth to the scene. Let each area dry completely before moving to prevent unwanted color mixing.

Paint the house at the top of the first mountain with Violet. On the second mountain, color the second house with Burnt Umber and the fourth house with Violet. To finish this step, paint the middle house on the third mountain with Nickel Azo Yellow, bringing a warm, bright touch to the composition.

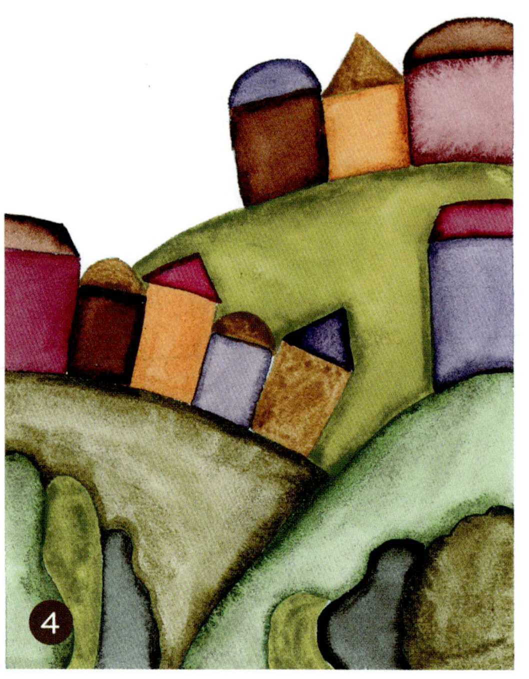 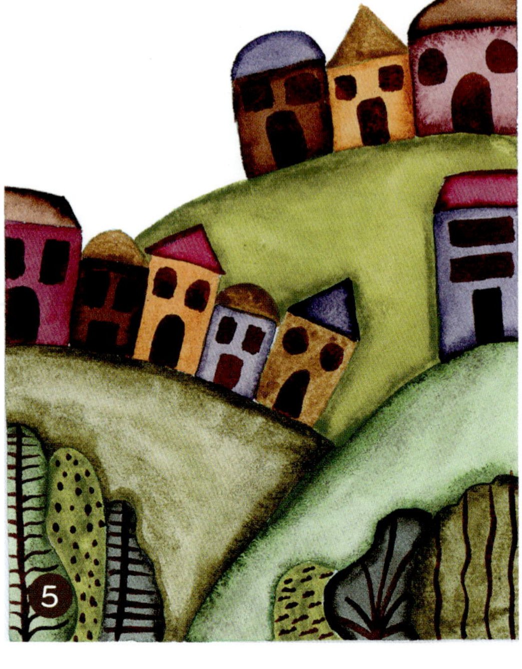

Step 4

With Shadow Green, paint the second bush from the right and the third bush from the left. Next, paint the rooftops. Use the same color palette as the facades but choose a different shade to create contrast. For example, if a house is Perylene Violet, paint its roof Quinacridone Lilac. This subtle variation adds richness and visual balance. Once the bushes and rooftops are completely dry, paint the remaining bushes with Olive Green, and use that same color to bring the final mountain to life.

Step 5

With a concentrated mix of Burnt Umber and the tip of your size 2 brush, paint the doors and windows of the houses using geometric shapes like rectangles, squares, and arches. These small details bring each building to life. Then, with the same color, add texture to the bushes by painting branches, lines, waves, and dots that suggest the natural variety of leaves and growth.

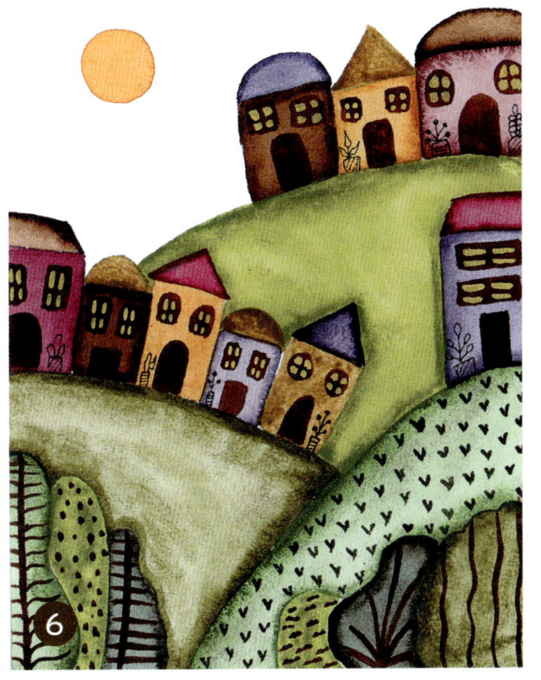

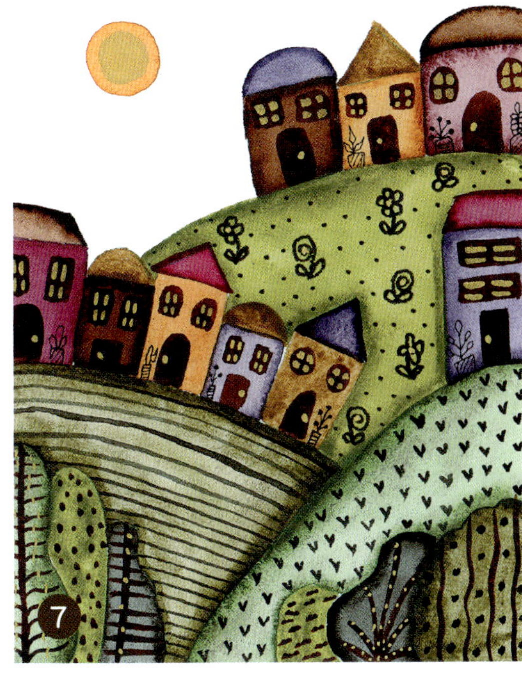

Step 6

With Shadow Green, paint small patches of grass on the first mountain by drawing two lines in a V shape. These blades of grass resemble tiny hearts, adding a sweet and organic touch to the scene. Next, with gold gouache, paint small squares on the windows to suggest the warm glow of lights coming from inside each home, as if each one holds a cozy story. Then, use Nickel Azo Yellow to paint a small circle in the sky, representing the sun and adding a warm, luminous touch to the atmosphere. Finally, with the size 12 fineliner, draw a few potted plants on the facades of the houses. Use the reference image for guidance—these plants might be cacti, leafy vines, or small flowers.

Step 7

Add the final details that bring your little village to life. With Shadow Green, paint gentle lines that follow the curves of the second mountain, giving it texture and a sense of natural flow. Next, using the size 12 fineliner, draw tiny flowers and dotted decorations on the third mountain, as if nature were quietly embellishing the landscape.

For the finishing touches, use the tip of your brush and a bit of gold gouache to place golden dots in the centers of the flowers and on the branches of the bushes, adding sparkle and movement—like they're catching the sunlight. Once the sun is completely dry, paint a small golden circle inside it to enhance its glow and make it shine with warmth. Your painting of the little village in the mountains is now complete.

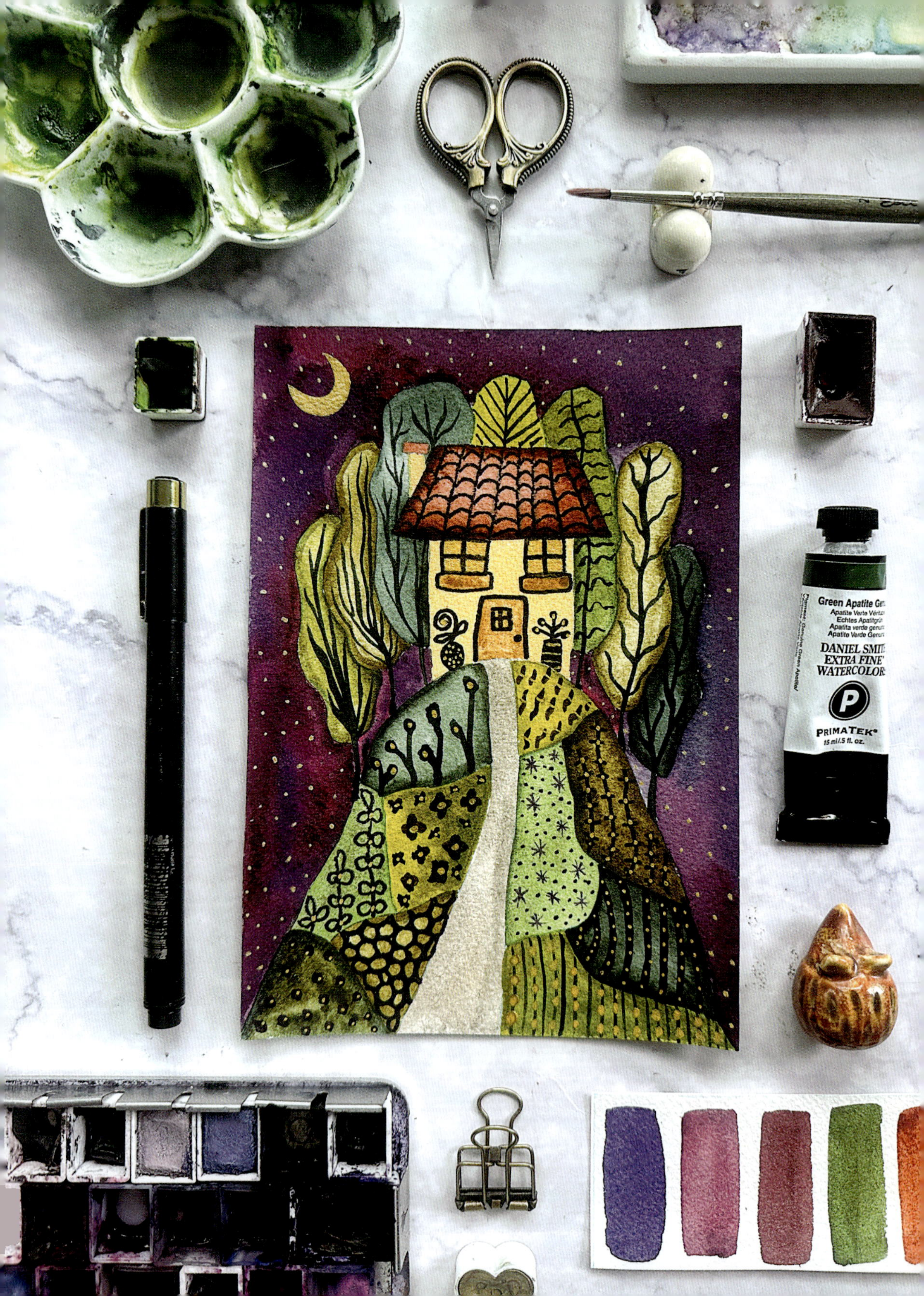

Dreamy Cottage

High atop a quiet mountain, a small cottage rests beneath a purple sky, where the moon glows gently and golden stars flicker like dreams. The air is cool, the trees stand like guardians, and everything seems to float in deep stillness.

In this exercise, we'll paint this serene corner of the world with soft strokes and airy tones, letting the watercolor lead the way. It's a moment to release control, welcome mystery, and enjoy the beauty of simplicity.

Materials

Paper size
5 x 7" (13 x 18 cm)

Brush
Size 2

Watercolors
Shadow Green
Olive Green
Bohemian Green
Green Apatite

Naples Yellow
Permanent Brown
Raw Umber
Violet
Quinacridone Lilac
Indigo

For details
Size 12 fineliner
Gold gouache

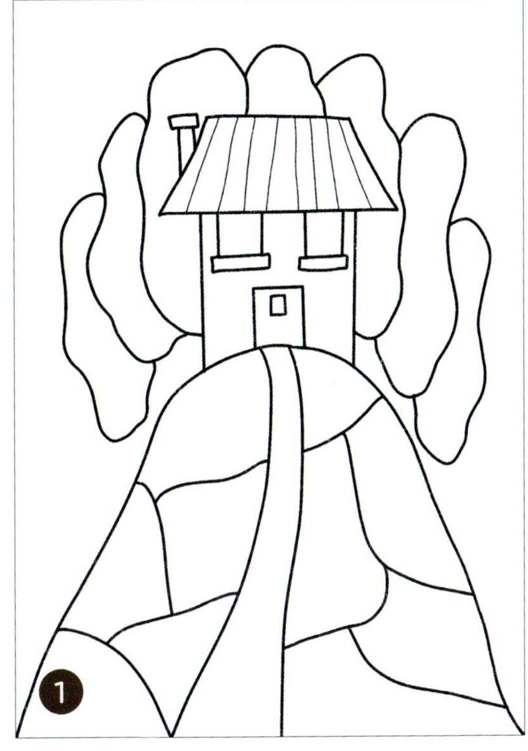

Step 1

Place the paper vertically. Lightly sketch a mountain that stretches from one side to the other, reaching slightly above the halfway point of the page. At the top, sketch a small cottage with a square for the main structure and a triangular roof. Add a few simple details—some lines on the roof to suggest shingles, a chimney, windows, and a centered door. From that door, begin a small path that gradually widens as it winds down to the base of the mountain. This path will divide the mountain into two sides. On each side, draw a few irregular sections that will later become bushes. Finally, behind the cottage, sketch seven trees with organic shapes, letting each one have its own personality.

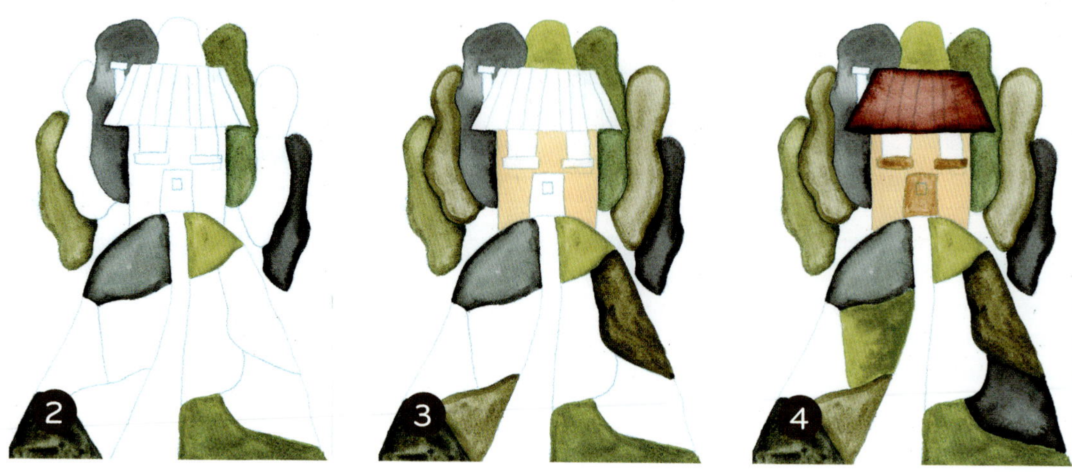

Step 2

Activate your paints with a bit of water. Using the size 2 brush and Shadow Green, paint the first and lowest bush on the left side of the mountain. Then, with Olive Green, paint the first and lowest bush on the right side. Now, move to the trees behind the cottage.

Using Olive Green, paint the first and fifth trees (counting from left to right). Then, with Shadow Green, paint the third and seventh trees. Be sure to let these areas dry completely before continuing. Taking your time here will help keep the edges clean and the transitions soft.

Step 3

Using Bohemian Green, paint the second bush (from bottom to top) on the left side of the mountain. Then, with Green Apatite, paint the fourth bush from bottom to top on the right side. For the trees, paint the second and sixth trees from the left with Bohemian Green, using the gradual wash technique (page 21). Paint the fourth tree with Olive Green.

Next, add a warm touch to the scene by painting the front of the cottage with Naples Yellow. Make sure everything is fully dry before moving on.

Step 4

With Olive Green, paint the fourth bush (from bottom to top) on the left side of the mountain. Then, with Shadow Green, paint the second bush on the right side. Next, paint the roof of the cottage with Permanent Brown. Apply plenty of pigment along the edges, then rinse your brush, and using only clean water, gently pull the color toward the center. This gradual wash technique (page 21) creates a soft lighting effect with beautiful variation.

With Raw Umber, paint the door of the cottage and the lower parts of the windows, adding warmth and depth with this earthy tone. Allow all these areas to dry completely before moving on.

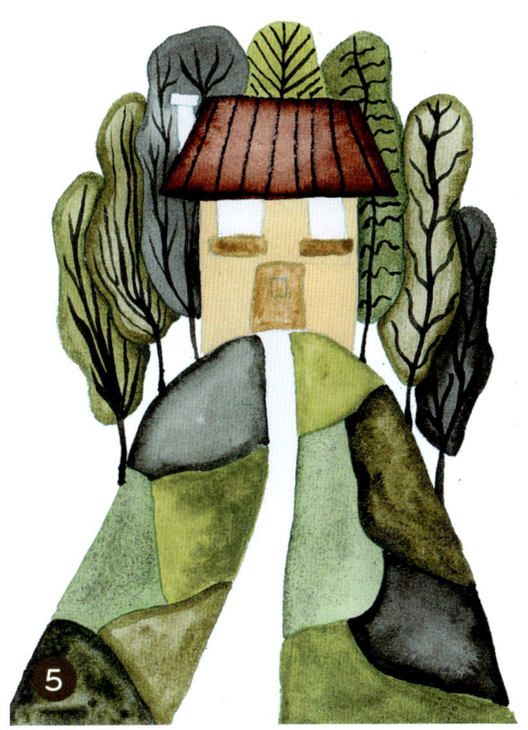

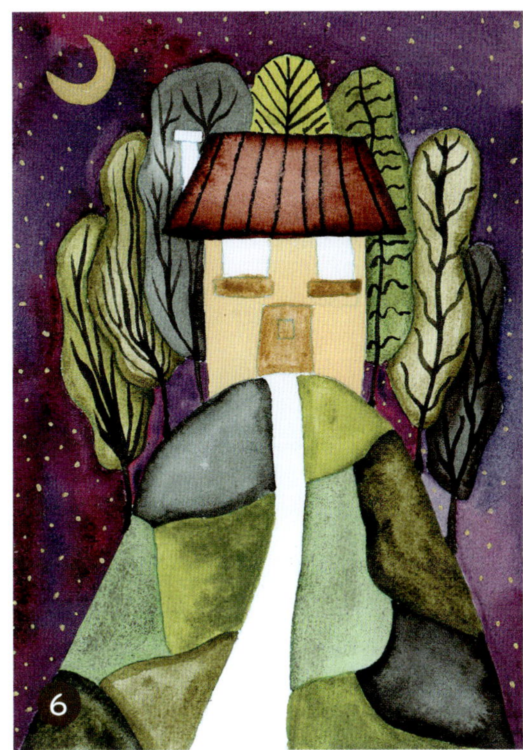

Step 5

Paint the final bushes. Use Green Apatite for the remaining bush on the left side and Bohemian Green for the last one on the right. Next, with well-pigmented Shadow Green and just the tip of your brush, paint the tree branches. Start from the main trunk and draw a line upward for the main branch. From there, add smaller branches that grow out organically. Let each tree be unique, with branches that differ in shape and direction. To finish, use the size 12 fineliner to draw lines on the roof, hinting at tiles with a fine, defined touch.

Step 6

Prepare plenty of Violet and Quinacridone Lilac ahead of time so you can work quickly and smoothly. It's important to keep moving during this step to avoid patchy drying. Start by applying Violet to the top of the sky. Then rinse your brush, and using only clean water, gently spread the color downward. Add Quinacridone Lilac in other areas and repeat the process, alternating the two colors. Let the pigments blend naturally, creating lighter and deeper tones—just like a soft, mysterious night sky.

Once the sky is completely dry, paint a crescent moon and tiny stars with gold gouache. These golden touches will be the final spark of wonder and delicate glow in your dreamy mountain night.

Step 7

Adding texture is your final and most special step. This last layer brings your painting to life. Load your brush with Shadow Green and add a second layer over the bushes: lines, flowers, branches, plants, asterisks, waves, dots, and circles. Let each bush have its own visual language.

While that dries, focus on the details of the house. Paint the chimney using Naples Yellow as the base color, and add Raw Umber to the top of the chimney to create depth and definition. Carefully, to avoid smudging any wet areas, use the size 12 fineliner to draw potted plants, window frames, the doorframe, and a small window right in the center of the door. You can also add soft waves along the roof to give it even more character.

For the final touch, use gold gouache to add a bit of sparkle. Paint the inside of the windows to suggest warm light glowing from within. Then, add small golden highlights on top of the textures you created in the bushes to give them a charming, magical glow. Finally, paint the path with Indigo diluted with lots of water (80-percent water and 20-percent Indigo). With these last touches, your painting is complete—a serene, dreamy place that seems to whisper quiet stories at dusk.

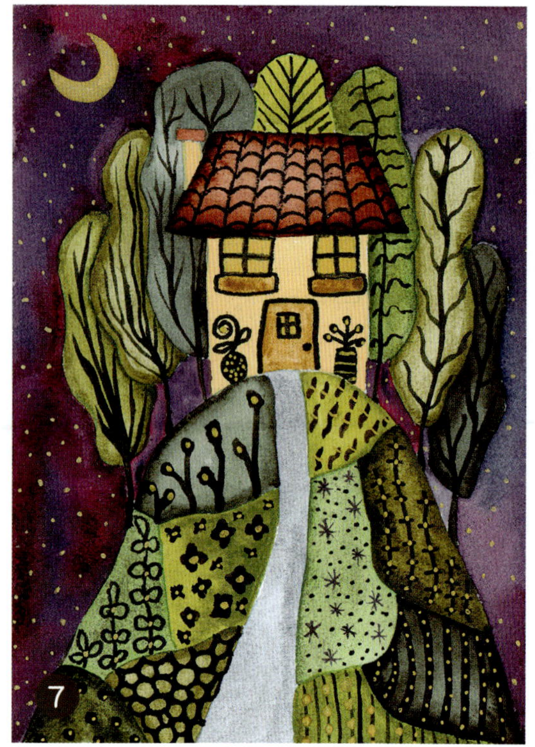

Falling into Fall

In this exercise, you'll paint a village surrounded by mountains, trees, and autumn textures. The palette is full of earthy tones, ochres, and golds that capture the warmth of the season beneath a soft, glowing sun. Each brushstroke connects you to the quiet of fall, the crisp air, the rustling leaves, and the golden light that invites stillness. This is a simple-yet-atmospheric scene, perfect for flowing with color and celebrating the beauty of change.

Materials

Paper size
5 x 7" (13 x 18 cm)

Brushes
Size 4 and size 2

Watercolors
Burnt Umber
Permanent Brown

Perylene Violet
Nickel Azo Yellow
Raw Umber
Quinacridone Gold
Naples Yellow

For details
Gold gouache
Size 12 fineliner

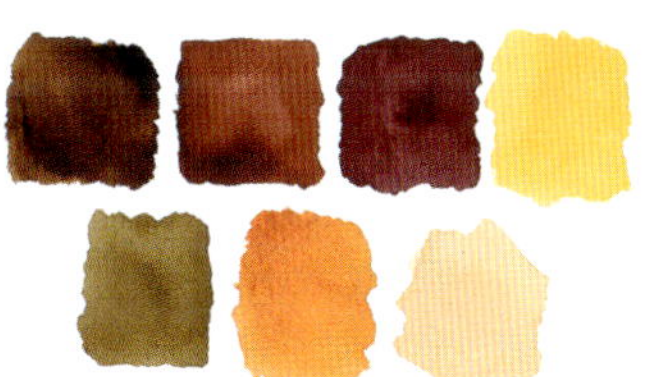

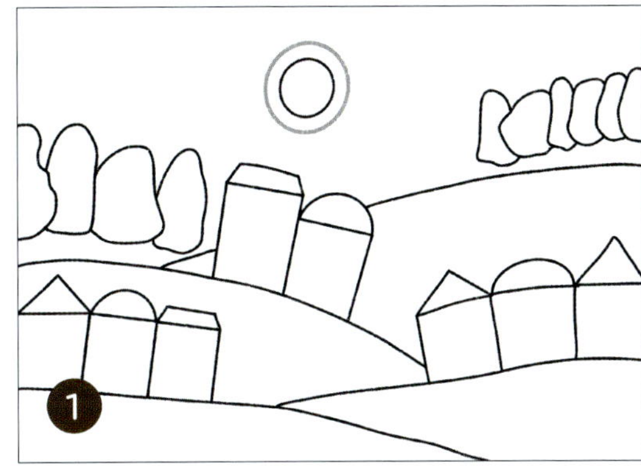

Step 1

Place the paper horizontally. Lightly sketch the landscape by drawing two small overlapping mountains, one coming from the left and the other from the right, slightly in front. On top of each mountain, draw three small houses: three rectangles with rooftops shaped like triangles or arches. Then, above those houses, draw another mountain starting from the left. In the center of this mountain, sketch two more houses, and at the beginning of the same mountain, add four tree shapes. From the right side, draw the final overlapping mountain. On top of it, sketch six smaller trees to create a sense of distance. In the center of the sky, draw a circle with a smaller circle inside. This will be our warm autumn sun.

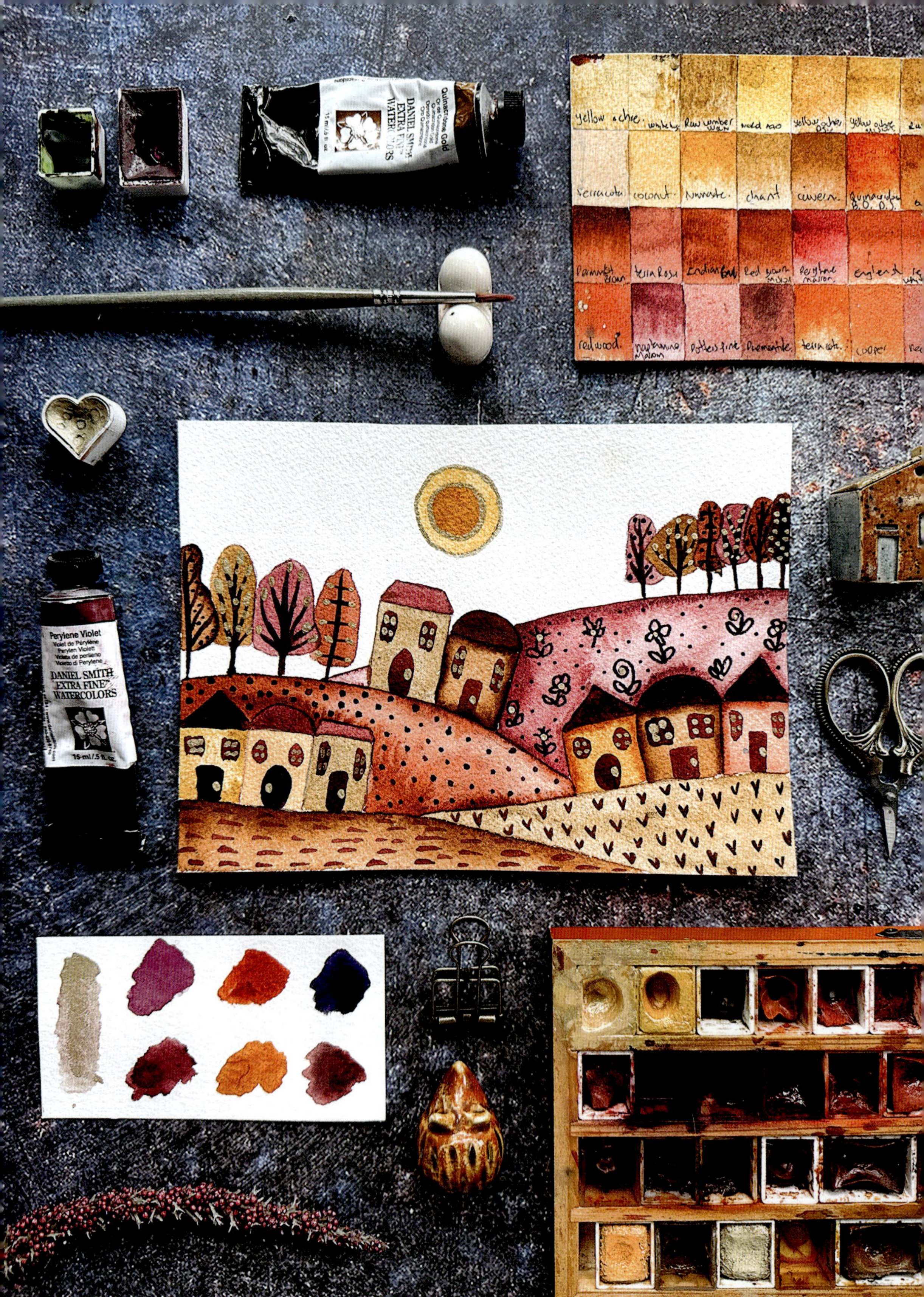

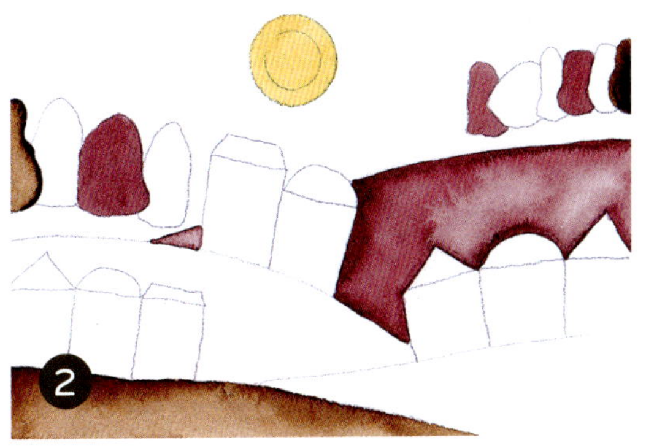

Step 2

Activate your paints with a bit of water. Using Burnt Umber and the size 4 brush, begin adding color to the composition. Paint the first mountain in the bottom left and the first tree from left to right. Then, paint the sixth tree from left to right on the upper right mountain with Permanent Brown.

Next, with Perylene Violet, paint the fourth mountain. Using the same color, paint the first and fourth trees (from left to right) above this mountain. Then, paint the third tree (from left to right) above the third mountain with the same shade. Finally, using Nickel Azo Yellow, paint the entire large circle we sketched in the sky; this will be our warm autumn sun.

Make sure to let each shape dry completely before painting next to it. This prevents the colors from bleeding into each other and helps keep each element crisp and defined. Patience here is key to achieving a clean and balanced result.

Step 3

Using Permanent Brown, paint the third mountain. Then, with the same color, paint the fourth tree from left to right on the third mountain, the first house on the right, and the fifth tree on the final mountain. Then, with Raw Umber, paint the first house on the left of the first mountain. Next, paint the second tree from left to right above this mountain. Finally, paint the second tree from left to right on the final mountain. To finish this step, paint the smaller circle inside the sun using Quinacridone Gold, adding a warm and glowing touch.

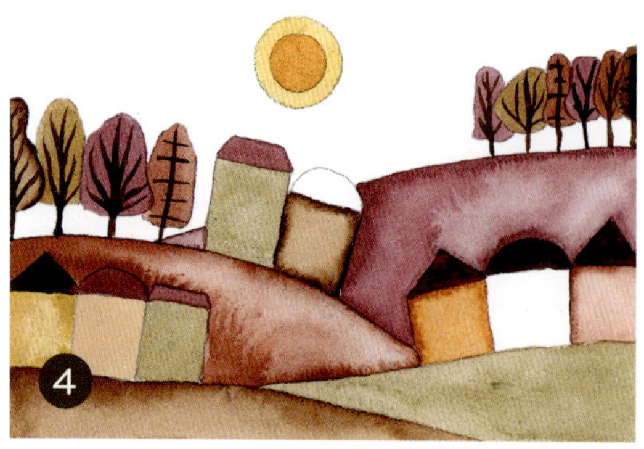

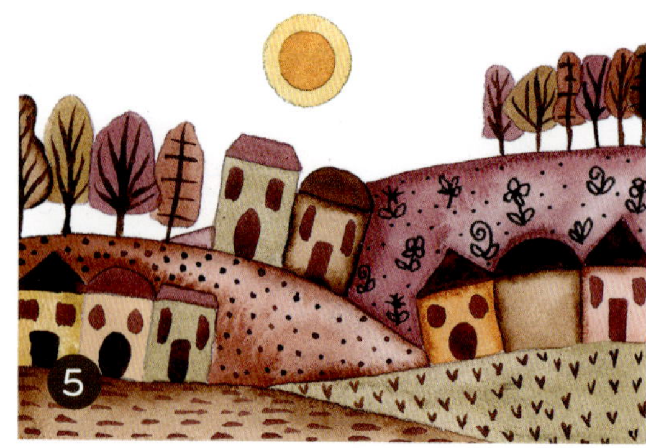

Step 4

Paint the second mountain using Raw Umber. Use the same color for the third house from left to right on the first mountain and the first house on the third mountain. With Naples Yellow, paint the second house on the first mountain. Then, using Quinacridone Gold, paint the third house from right to left on the second mountain, and then paint the second house on the third mountain with Burnt Umber.

Paint all but one of the roofs, alternating between Permanent Brown and Perylene Violet. Use the size 2 brush and highly concentrated pigment to create strong contrast.

With these same pigments, alternating between Permanent Brown and Perylene Violet, paint the tree branches. Start from the base and pull the size 2 brush upward to form the main branch. From there, let smaller branches grow naturally. Make each tree's branches unique to create a rich and balanced composition.

Step 5

Using Burnt Umber and the size 2 brush, paint the remaining house and roof. While these areas dry, begin adding textures to the mountains from bottom to top. On the first mountain, use highly concentrated Perylene Violet and the tip of the size 2 brush to paint horizontal lines. On the second mountain, paint small hearts, and on the third, dots all with the same pigment and brush.

For the final mountain, use the size 12 fine-liner to draw small flowers with stems and leaves. Fill in the spaces between the flowers with dots, creating a soft and rhythmic texture.

To finish this step, use concentrated Permanent Brown to paint small square windows on the facades of the houses. In the center of each house, draw a rectangle for the door or round the top for a more arched finish. Allow everything to dry completely before moving on.

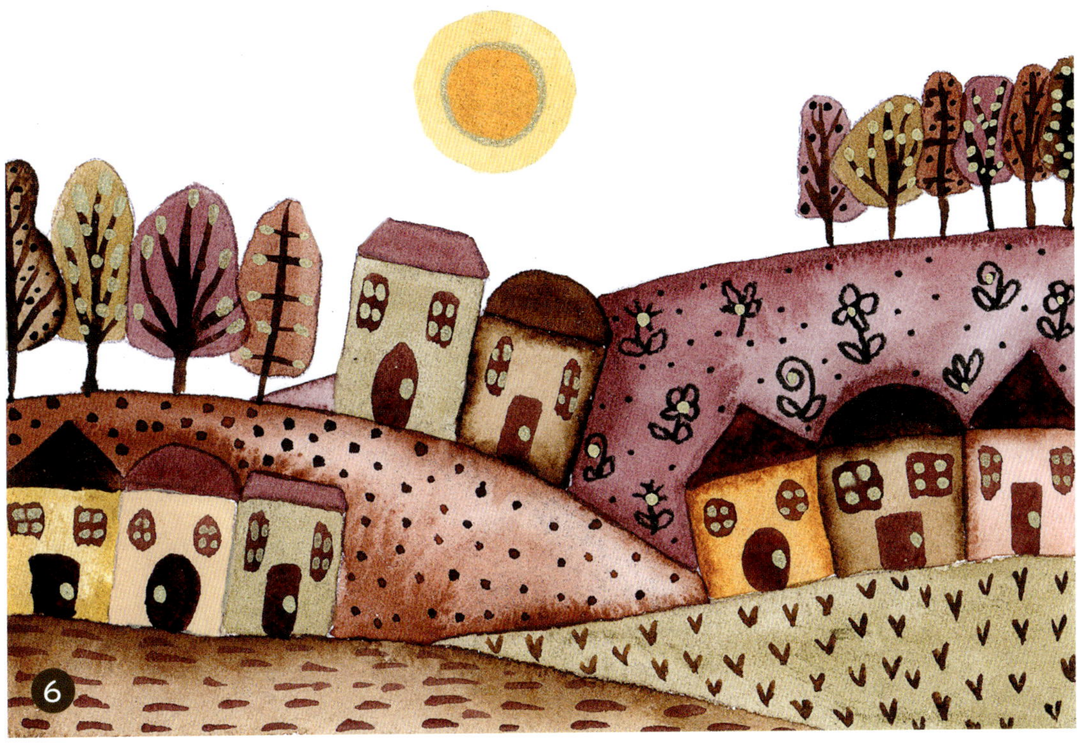

Step 6

To finish, add touches of gold gouache to bring sparkle and texture to your autumn village. With the tip of the size 2 brush, paint small golden dots on the tree branches, as if they were sunlit leaves. Next, paint tiny golden squares on the windows to suggest warm light glowing from within the houses. In the centers of the flowers on the last mountain, add small golden dots to bring them to life.

Finally, once the sun is completely dry, outline the inner circle with gold gouache to enhance its glow and make it the warm heart of your composition. With these final touches, your painting is complete—a peaceful, colorful landscape full of the quiet magic of fall.

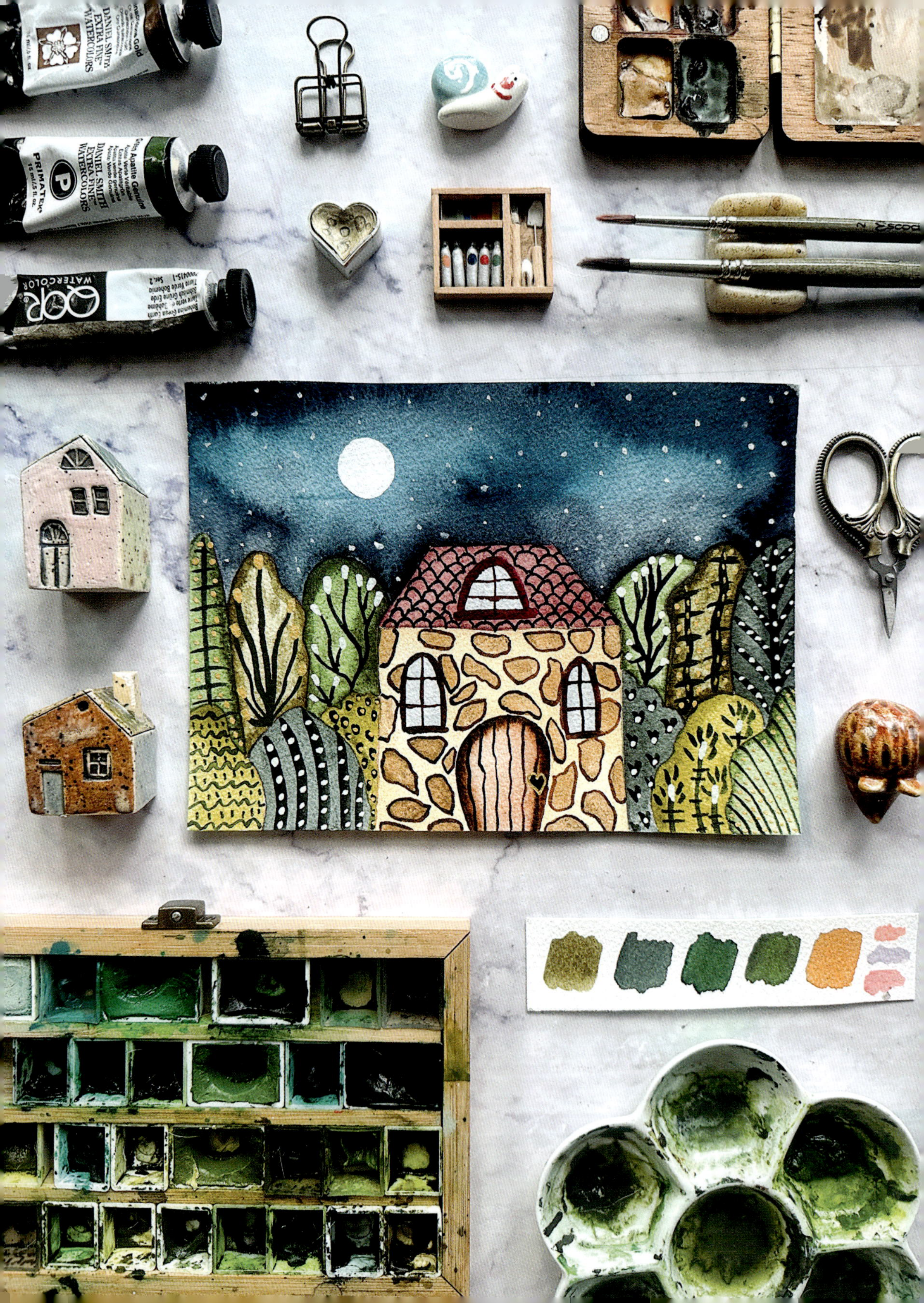

Stone House in the Woods

In this exercise, you'll paint a stone cottage nestled among trees, where each trunk and canopy is alive with textures and organic shapes. This scene is an invitation to explore playful patterns, layer delicate washes of green, and let the forest grow wilder with every brushstroke. The soft glow of a full moon illuminates the house and trees, creating a gentle contrast between light and shadow. With its whimsical details and dreamy atmosphere, this exercise encourages you to slow down, lose yourself in the rhythm of nature, and discover the quiet stories hidden in the forest night.

Materials

Paper size
5 x 7" (13 x 18 cm)

Brushes
Size 4 and size 2

Watercolors
Shadow Green
Perylene Violet
Burnt Umber
Indigo
Green Apatite

Naples Yellow
Olive Green
Turquoise
Raw Umber
Bohemian Green

For details
White gouache
Size 12 fineliner
Gold gouache

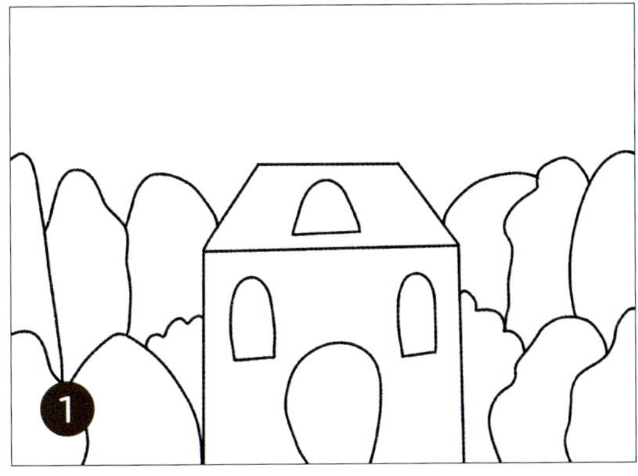

Step 1

Place your paper horizontally. Lightly sketch the base of the house (a square with a flat-topped triangle for a roof) in the center of the page. Sketch an arched door in the center and one arched window on each side. On the roof, add a small arched window. Next, fill the space on both sides of the house with uniform shapes to represent bushes and trees, as if the forest is surrounding the home. Leave a little less than half of the paper at the top free; this will be our space for the starry night sky.

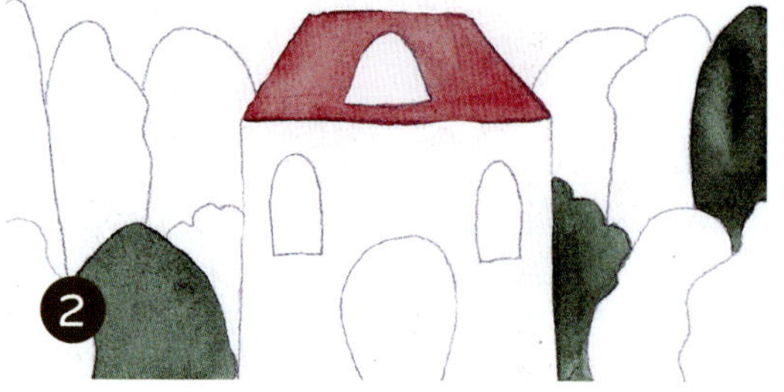

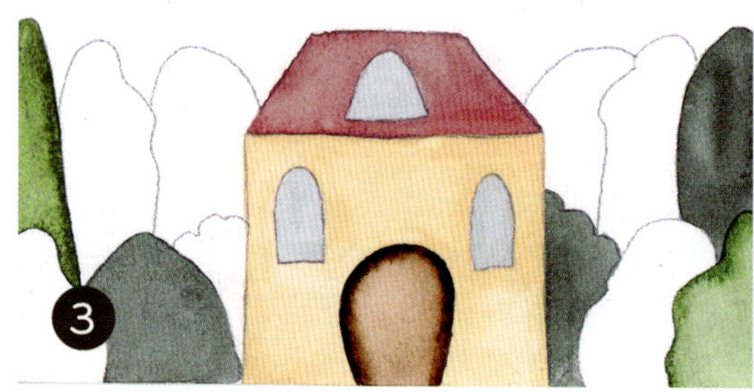

Step 2

Activate your paints with a bit of water. Begin adding color by painting three bushes with Shadow Green using the size 4 brush, making sure they are not directly next to each other. Then, with the same brush, paint the roof of the house with Perylene Violet. Be sure to let these areas dry completely before moving on so the watercolor doesn't blend unintentionally.

Step 3

Paint the door of the house with Burnt Umber using the size 2 brush, placing more pigment along the edges. Then, with a clean brush and just water, gently pull the color toward the center using the gradual wash technique (page 21) to create a soft lighting effect. Next, with a very diluted mix of Indigo (90-percent water and 10-percent Indigo) and the size 2 brush, paint all the windows to give them a soft, transparent wash. While the house dries, paint a couple of bushes on each side with Green Apatite. Once everything is completely dry, paint the facade of the house with Naples Yellow.

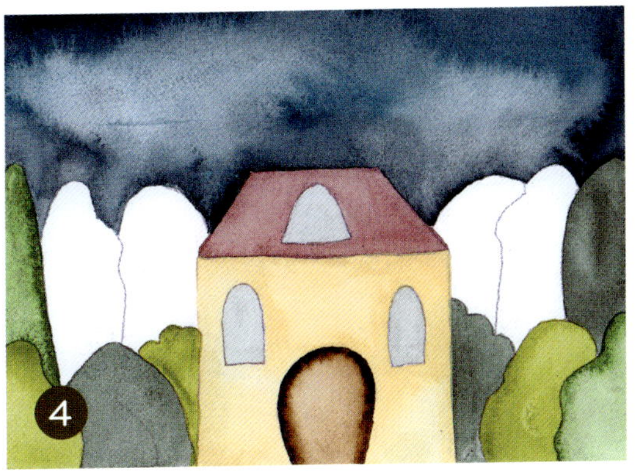 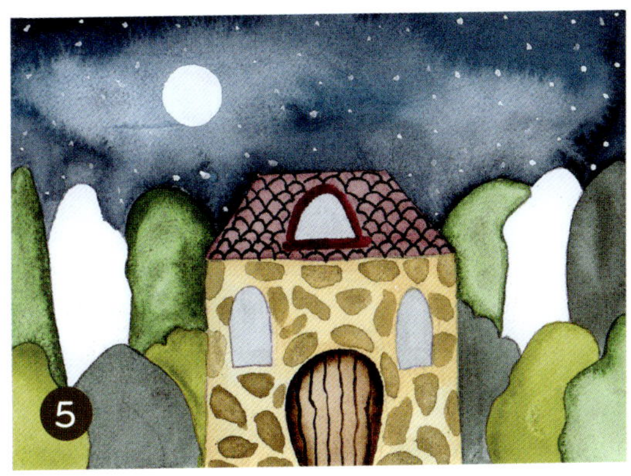

Step 4

With Olive Green and the size 4 brush, paint two bushes on the right side (leaving space between them) and one bush on the left. Keep them near the bottom edge so you can continue working without waiting for them to dry before starting the sky.

For the sky, prepare plenty of Indigo pigment. With the size 4 brush, apply it across the top of the page, and while the paper is still wet, blend the color downward with clean water—using the wet-on-wet technique (page 18). Then, add Turquoise to other areas of the sky with the same brush, applying the pigment and blending outward the same way. Work continuously while the paint is wet so the colors merge seamlessly, creating the rich, vibrant effect of a glowing night sky.

Step 5

Using Raw Umber and the size 2 brush, paint the stones of the house. Create irregular shapes, like cow spots, and fill the entire facade to resemble natural stone blocks. Then, with Green Apatite, paint one tree on the left and one on the right of the house to balance the scene. Next, use white gouache to paint a full moon in the sky. With just the tip of your brush, add small stars around it to complete the nighttime atmosphere.

Once the sky is completely dry, add final details to the house. Paint the frame of the small window on the roof and the wooden divisions on the door with Perylene Violet. When everything is fully dry, use the size 12 fineliner to draw the roof tiles, adding texture and definition to this architectural element.

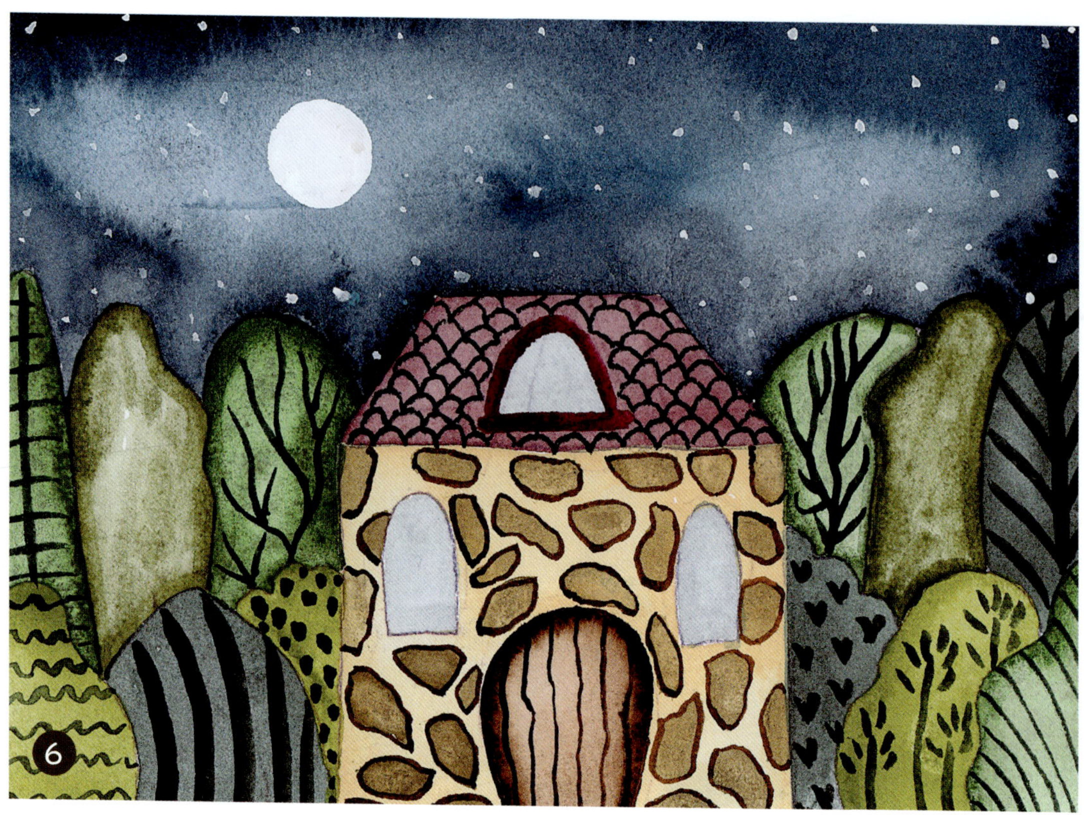

Step 6

Paint the remaining trees Bohemian Green. Allow them to dry completely before continuing. Then, add textures using Shadow Green to draw branches, leaves, dots, hearts, and lines, letting each tree develop its own rhythm and personality. With Burnt Umber, outline the stones of the house, gently marking the edges to give them definition and depth while keeping their natural look.

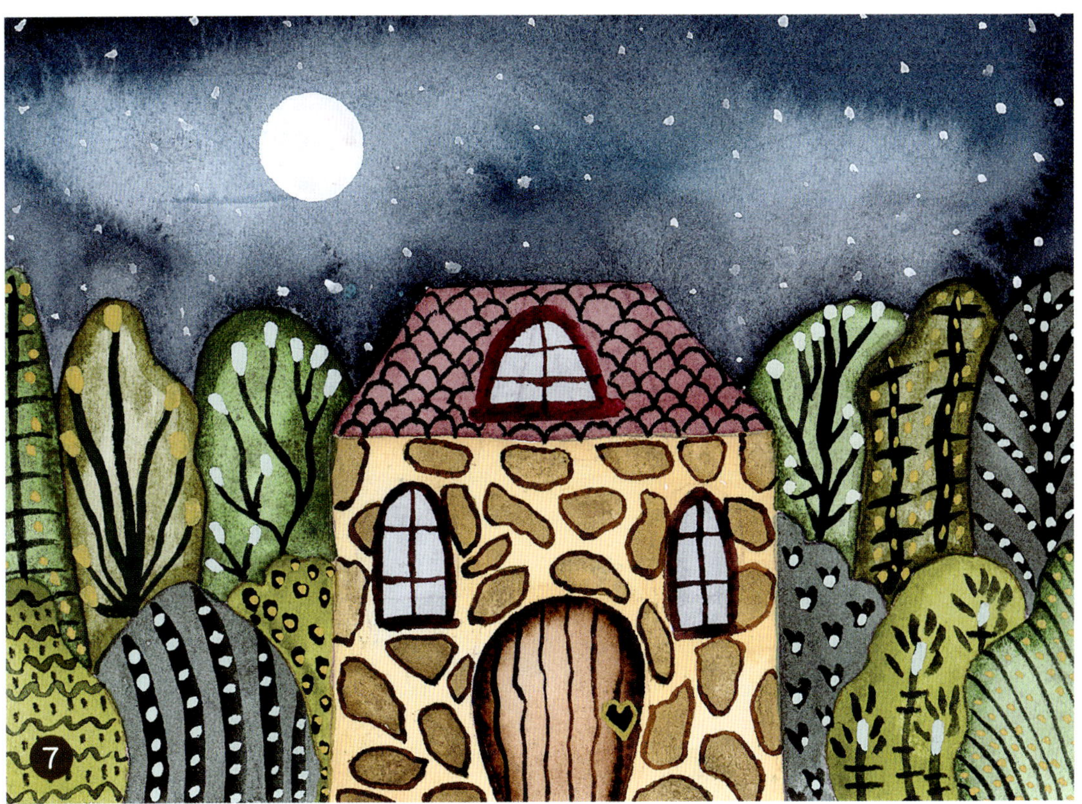

Step 7

Add the final details that bring charm and personality to the scene. With Perylene Violet, paint the window grilles and add a small heart-shaped door handle. Next, decorate the trees and bushes: Add small leaves and dots to the branches, and highlight areas of the bushes with touches of gold and white gouache. These details bring light, texture, and a bit of magic, making your nighttime forest come alive.

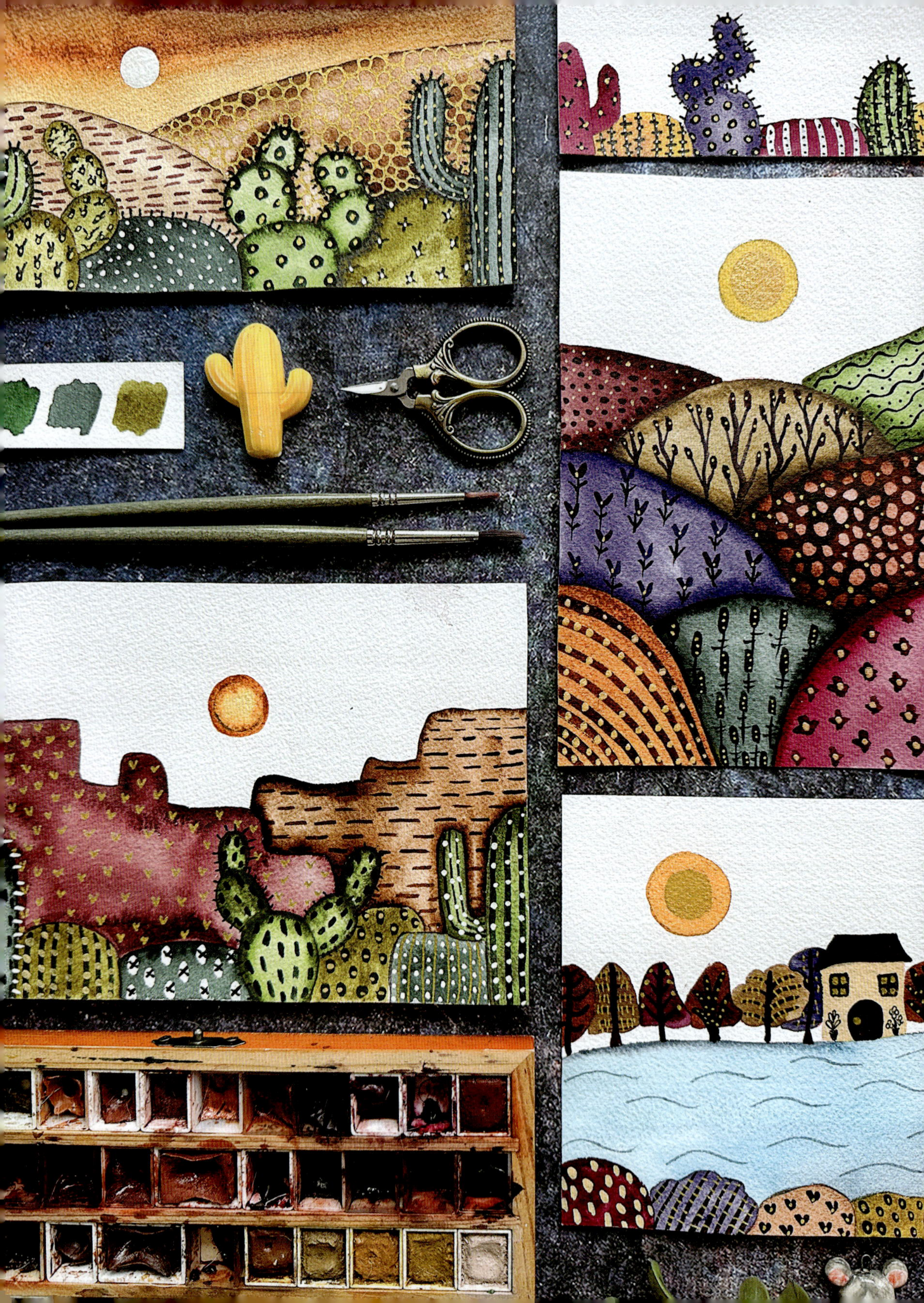

Chasing Sunsets

There are moments in the day when the sky turns into a blazing poem. As the sun says goodbye, it leaves behind a symphony of shadows, reflections, and colors born from the wildest imagination. In these landscapes, everything shifts. The mountains grow myster-ious, the lakes shimmer with dreams, and the land glows in liquid gold.

This chapter is a tribute to that magical moment when the day becomes memory. Through each exercise, we'll explore radiant skies, warm horizons, and scenes where light dances across water and stone. Here, every brushstroke is a luminous farewell and every color a whisper from the setting sun.

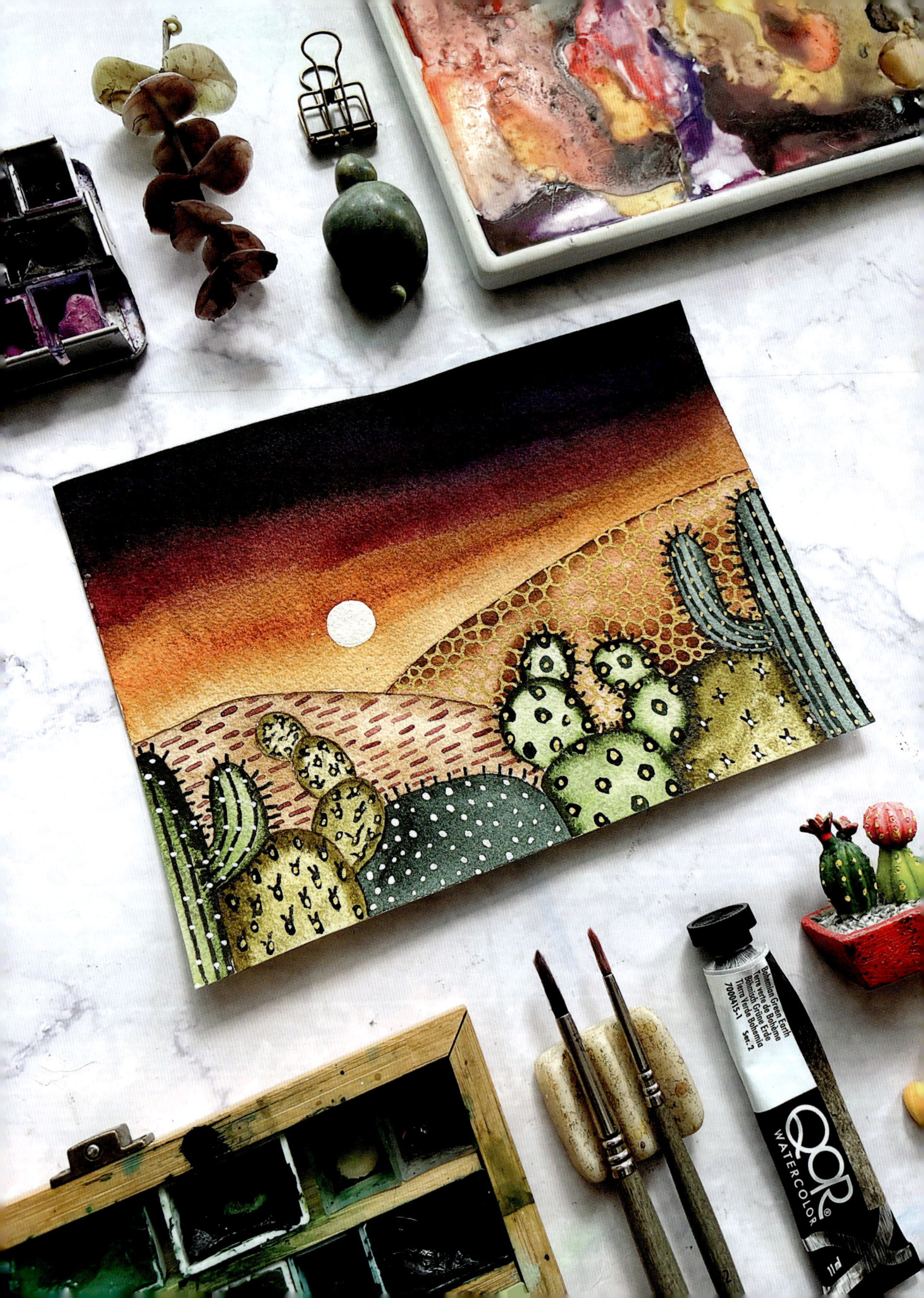

Shadows of the Sunset

Here, you'll paint a warm, peaceful landscape where the sky fades into a soft sunset gradient. Mountains stretch across the distance, while in the foreground, textured cacti rise in shadow, inviting us to explore their shapes. It's a play between light and darkness, between fading colors in the sky and bold silhouettes on the land. It's a simple-yet-powerful scene perfect for practicing contrast, gradients, and natural patterns.

Materials

Paper size
5 x 7" (13 x 18 cm)

Brushes
Size 4 and size 2

Watercolors
Indigo
Violet
Quinacridone Lilac
Quinacridone Gold
Bohemian Green
Green Apatite
Shadow Green
Olive Green
Burnt Umber
Raw Umber
Perylene Violet

For details
White gouache
Gold gouache
Size 12 fineliner

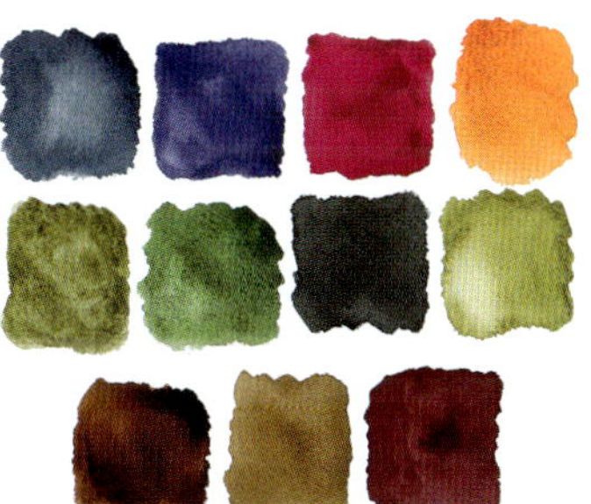

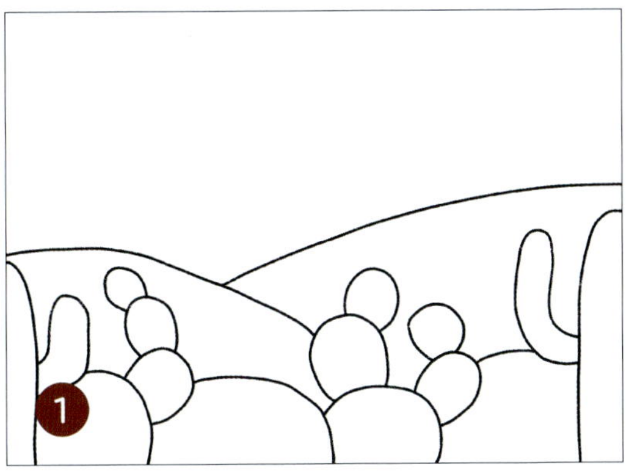

Step 1

Place your paper horizontally. Lightly sketch several cacti side by side across the foreground. Behind the cacti, draw two gently overlapping mountains to form the distant horizon. This step is just a guide—the details will come to life through watercolor.

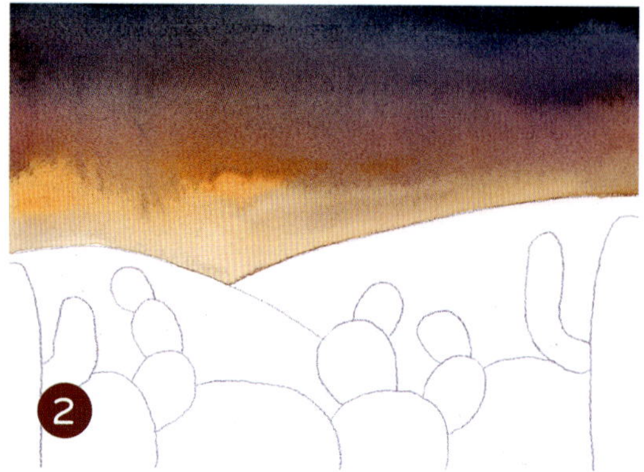

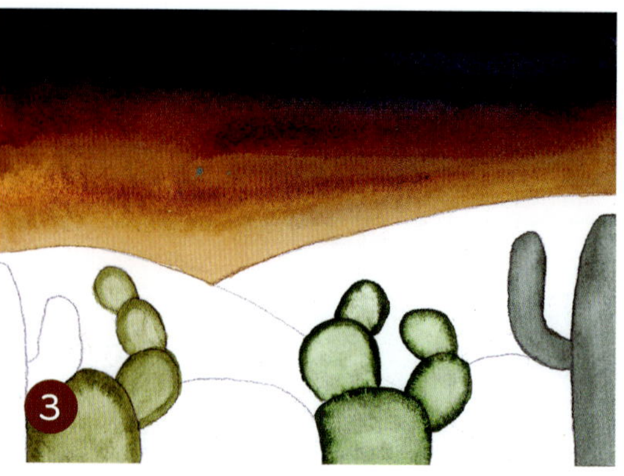

Step 2

We'll begin by painting the sunset sky. First, activate all the pigments you'll be using so they're ready to go, as this is a fast and continuous process. Using the size 4 brush, load it with Indigo and paint a thick horizontal line across the top of the sky. Rinse your brush, pick up Violet, and paint directly below the Indigo, placing the strokes close enough that the colors bleed into each other while still wet. Rinse again and apply Quinacridone Lilac as the next stripe, blending gently into the Violet. Finally, rinse once more, and paint the bottom portion of the sky with Quinacridone Gold, letting it merge naturally with the Lilac above. It's important to work quickly and without pauses so the paints remain wet and the transitions stay seamless—just like the shifting colors of a real sunset.

Step 3

With the size 2 brush, paint the second cactus from left to right with Bohemian Green, the fourth with Green Apatite, and the sixth with Shadow Green. Be sure to let each cactus dry completely before painting the one next to it to avoid any unwanted blending. You can also choose whether to paint your cacti with flat or gradual washes, depending on the look you want. Both options work beautifully.

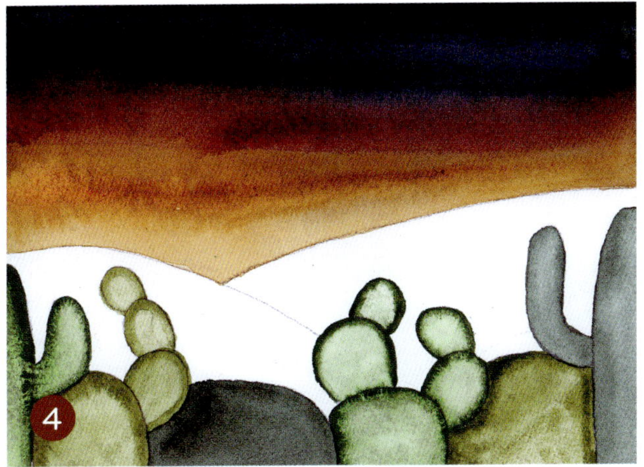

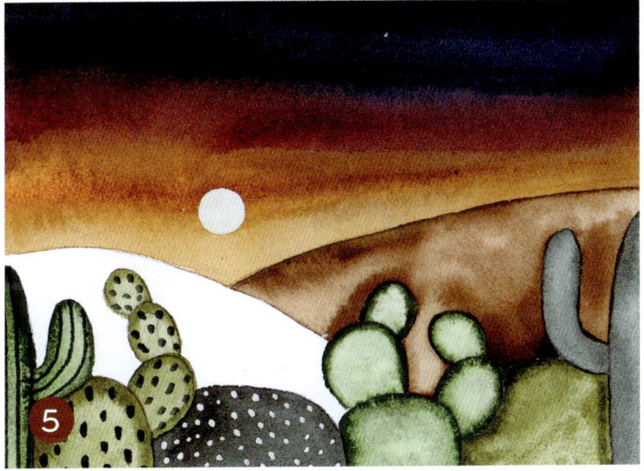

Step 4

Paint the remaining cacti from left to right: Use Green Apatite for the first cactus, Shadow Green for the third, and Olive Green for the fifth. Be sure to let each cactus dry completely before moving on.

Step 5

Paint the second mountain in the background with Burnt Umber, creating a warm and soft base. Then, add texture to the cacti.

On the first two cacti from left to right, use Shadow Green and the size 2 brush to paint lines and dots, giving them volume and depth. On the third cactus, add decorative dots with white gouache, creating a subtle-yet-striking contrast. Once the mountain and cacti are completely dry, use the white gouache to paint a small sun between the mountains, as if it's just about to set. This final touch gently connects the sky and the landscape.

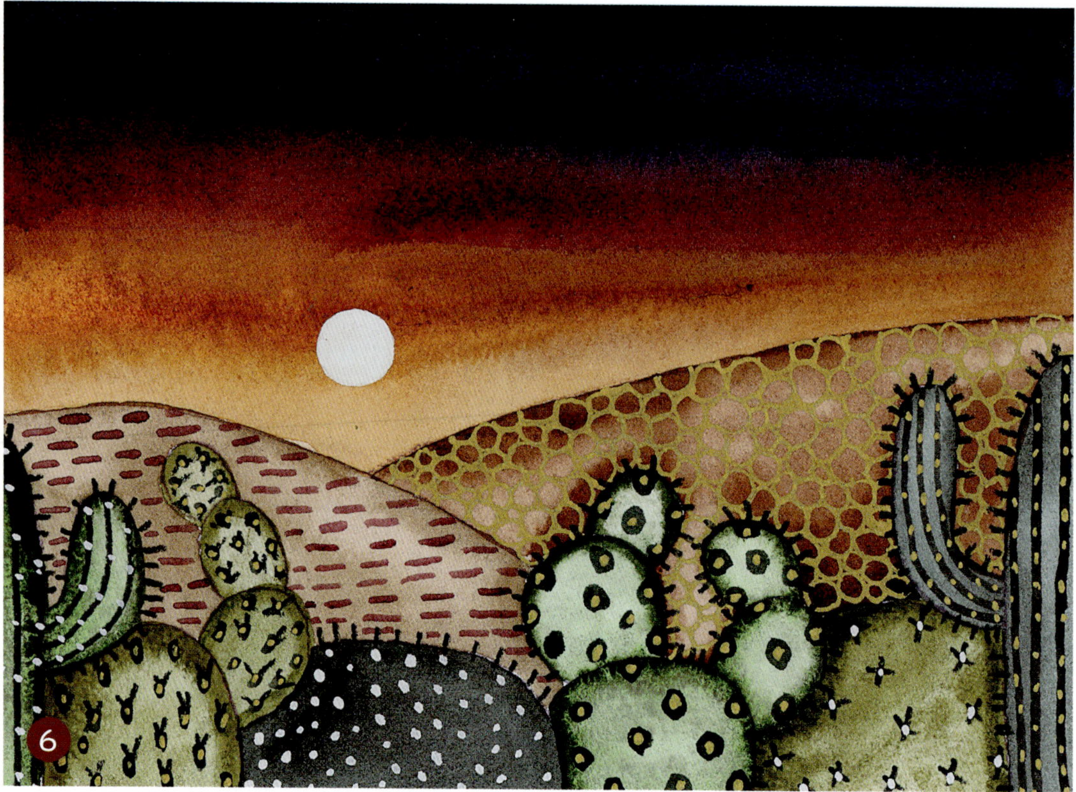

Step 6

Paint the first mountain in the foreground with Raw Umber, adding depth to the landscape. Once dry, on the same mountain, use Perylene Violet to paint subtle texture lines that enrich the surface and create contrast. Next, begin adding final textures throughout the painting. With gold and white gouache, create small dots, crosses, and lines across the sky, cacti, and mountains. With the size 12 fineliner, draw spines along the edges of the cacti to give them detail and character. These final touches are what truly bring the sunset to life . . . sparkling light, storytelling shapes, and a landscape full of calm and color.

Oasis of Color

In this exercise, the warm colors of the sunset come to life through the cacti themselves. Their shapes and tones carry the glow of the evening sky, so I chose to keep the background white to let those sunset colors shine even more. In this horizontal forest of cacti, color takes center stage. Cacti of various shapes and sizes stand like quiet guardians, wrapped in a vibrant palette that repeats and shifts across the landscape. It's a scene for play, for exploring harmony, and for letting watercolor flow without rules. A living oasis full of rhythm, texture, and light.

Materials

Paper size
2½ x 8" (6 x 20 cm)

Brushes
Size 4 and size 2

Watercolors
Quinacridone Lilac
Violet
Green Apatite
Nickel Azo Yellow
Perylene Violet

For details
Size 12 fineliner
White gouache
Gold gouache

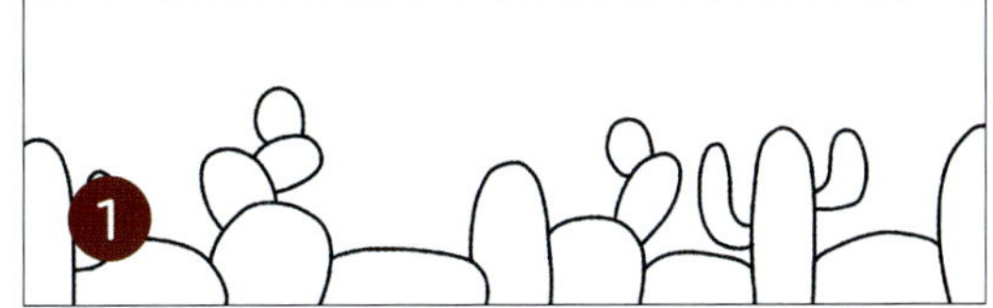

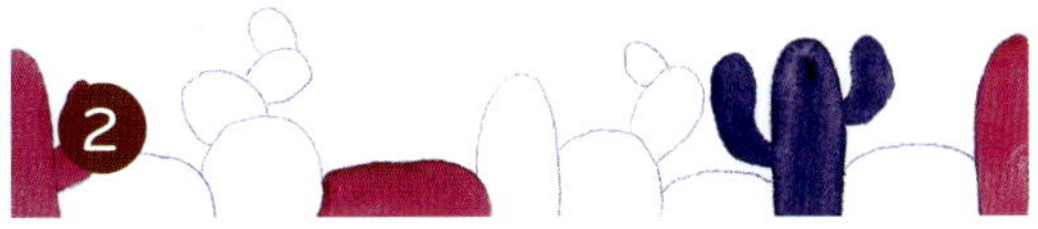

Step 1

Place your paper horizontally. Lightly sketch overlapping ovals across the page. These will be the base for your ten cacti spaced in a balanced way to build the horizontal forest. Don't worry about perfection—this sketch is just a gentle guide for the color to come.

Step 2

Activate your paints with a bit of water. Using the size 4 brush and working from left to right, paint the first, fourth, and tenth cacti with Quinacridone Lilac. Then, use the same brush to paint the eighth cactus with Violet. Be sure to leave space between wet areas and let each cactus dry before painting the ones beside it.

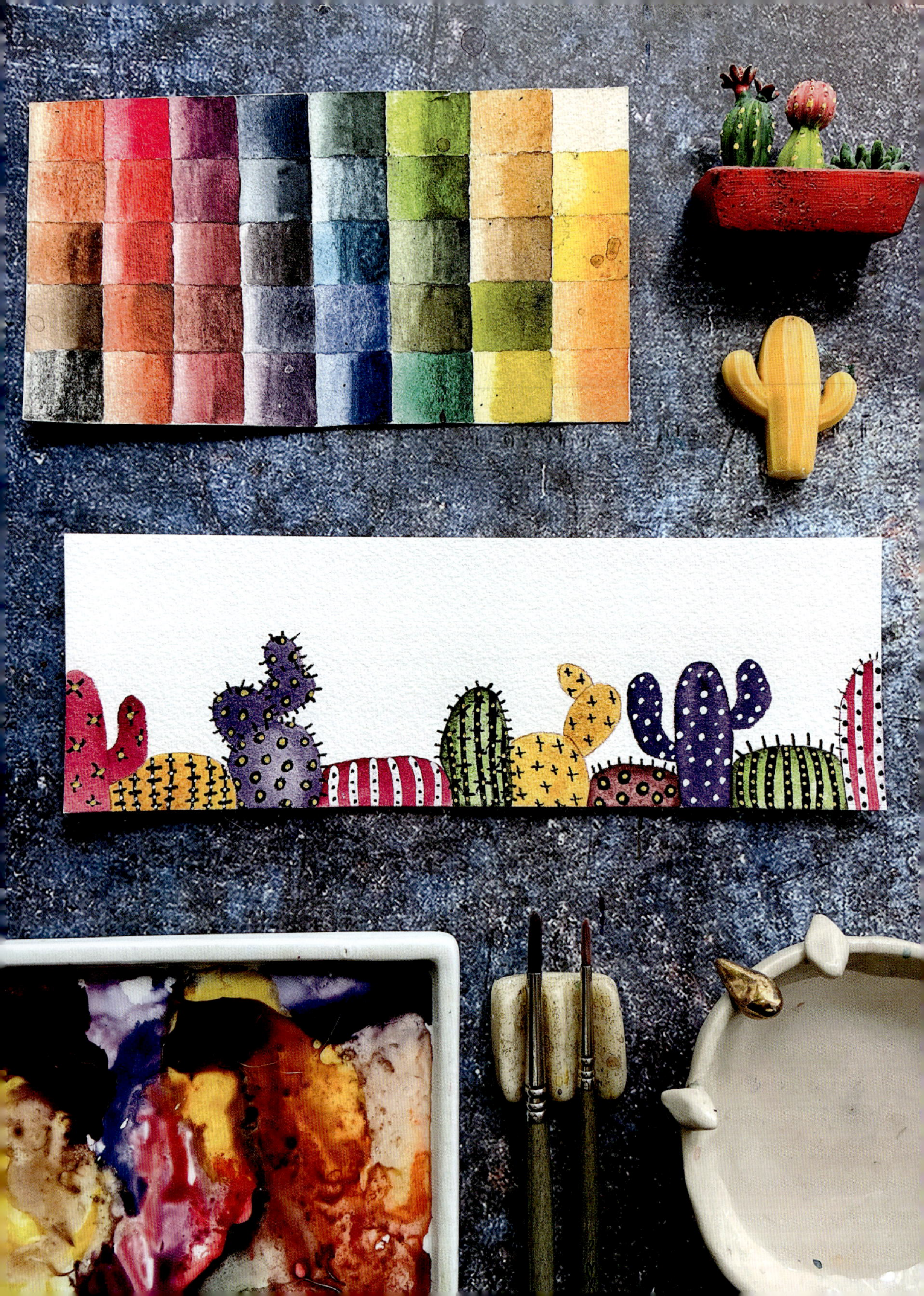

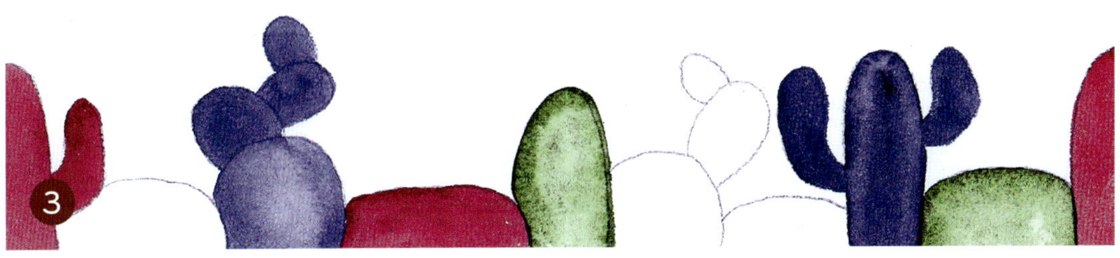

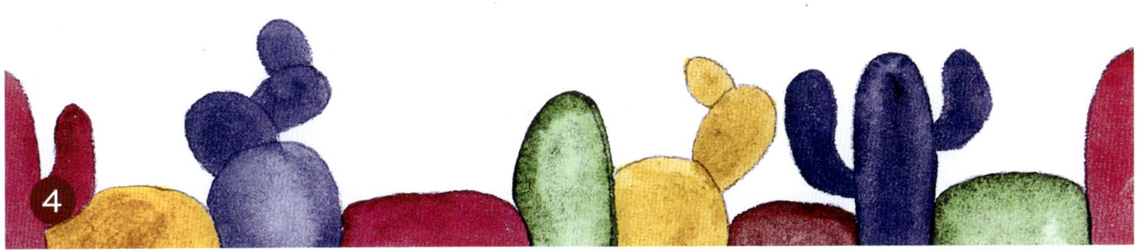

Step 3

Use Violet to paint the third cactus. If you prefer a softer look, you can dilute the Violet slightly to create a lighter wash. Then, use Green Apatite to paint the fifth and ninth cacti. Be sure to let this layer dry completely before moving on, to keep the shapes crisp and prevent any color bleeding.

Step 4

Paint the second and sixth cacti with Nickel Azo Yellow, bringing warmth and brightness into the composition. Once they are fully dry, paint the last cactus with Perylene Violet, adding a rich, deep contrast to the group.

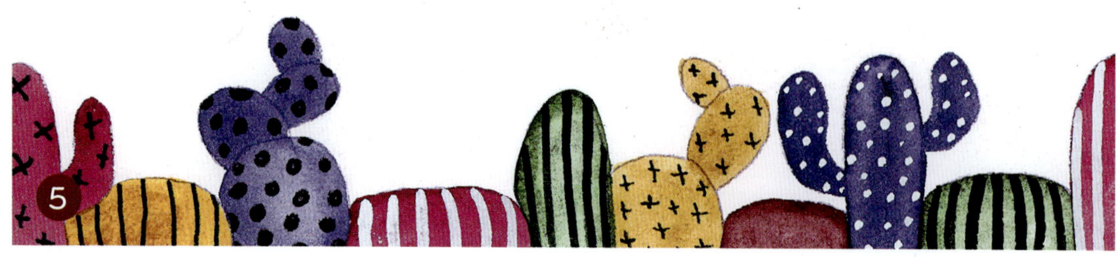

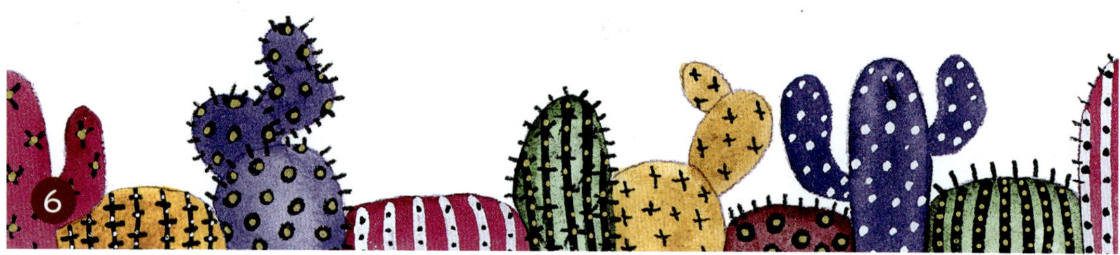

Step 5

Bring your cacti to life with the first layer of textures. Use the size 12 fineliner and white gouache with the size 2 brush to add crosses, lines, and circles across the surface of the cacti. Feel free to repeat or alternate the patterns to give each one its own personality and rhythm.

Step 6

Add the final details that bring contrast and character to the composition. Use gold gouache with the size 2 brush to paint dots, lines, or other small accents over some of the existing textures on the cacti. There's no need to cover all of them. Just choose a few to highlight with light. Then, with the fineliner, draw fine spines along the edges of some of the cacti. These simple lines complete the silhouette and add personality to each shape. With these final touches, your oasis of color is complete.

Land of Sun

In this exercise, we'll paint a landscape ruled by the sun. Along the horizon, a row of textured green cacti lines the desert floor. In the background, two square-shaped mountains rise like sleeping giants, bathed in the intense light of a blazing sun at the center of the sky. This is a space to explore contrast, play with bold shapes, and let the warmth of color guide you through this land where everything breathes sunlight.

Materials

Paper size
5 x 7" (13 x 18 cm)

Brushes
Size 4 and size 2

Watercolors
Perylene Violet
Bohemian Green
Green Apatite
Quinacridone Gold
Burnt Umber
Shadow Green
Olive Green

For details
White gouache
Gold gouache
Size 12 fineliner

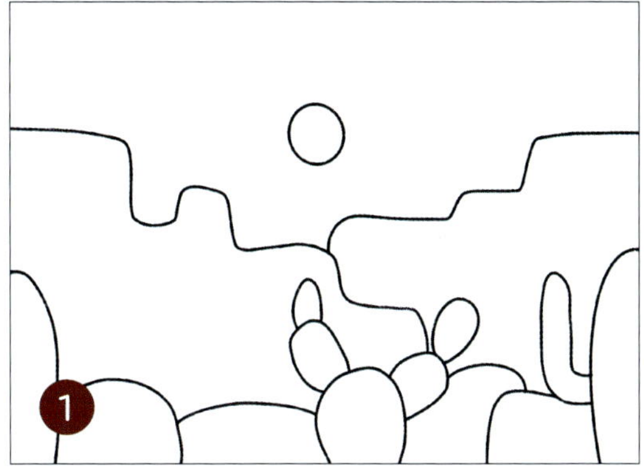

Step 1

Place your paper horizontally. Lightly sketch a row of overlapping ovals to represent the cacti. Distribute them from left to right, making sure to draw seven cacti in total across the bottom of the page. Behind this row, sketch two mountains with squared tops, evoking flat desert formations. At the top center of the page, draw a small circle—this will be our warm, glowing sun.

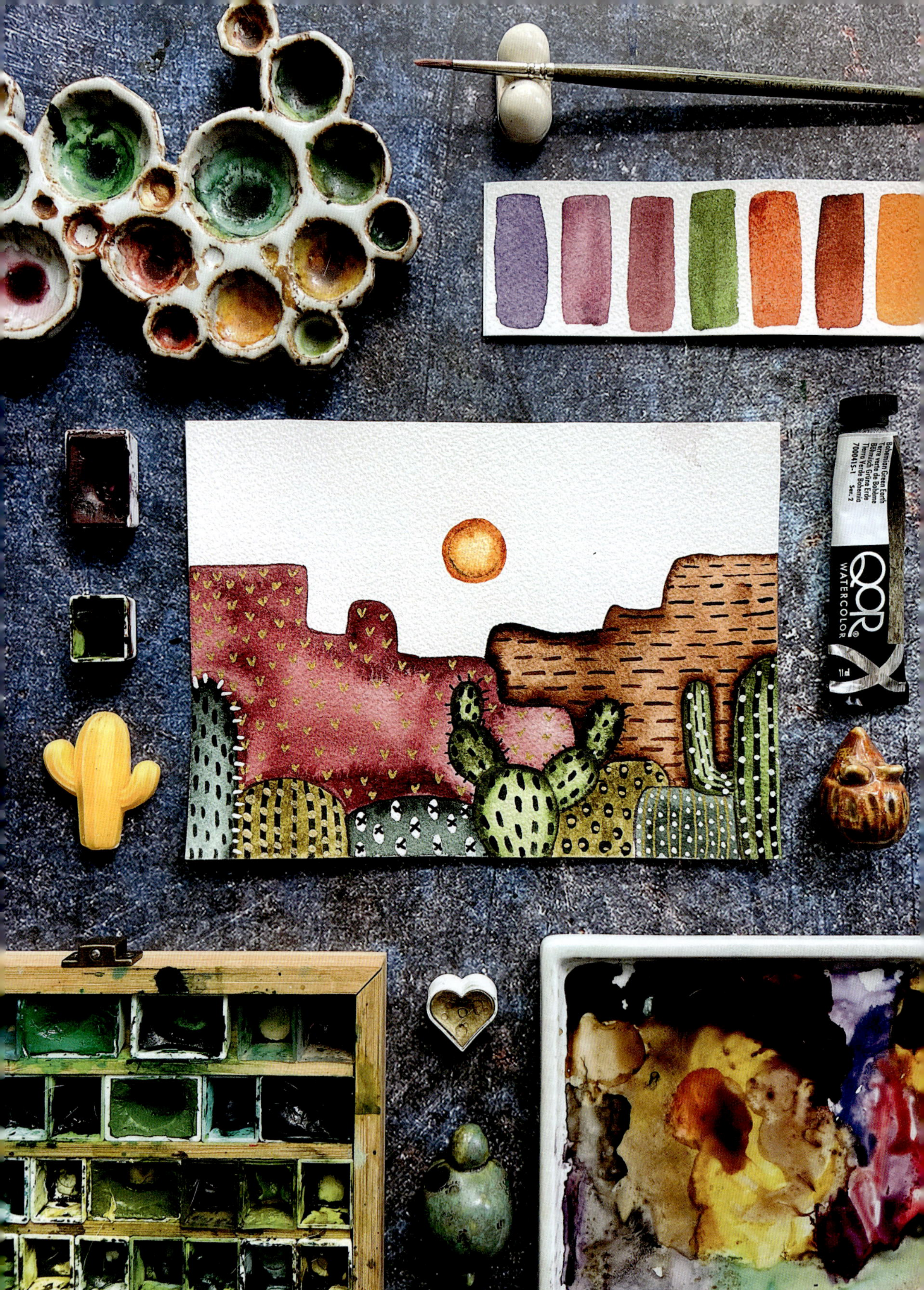

Step 2

Activate your paints with a bit of water. Then, using the size 4 brush, paint the first mountain on the left with Perylene Violet, applying the color evenly to cover the entire shape. Next, paint the fifth cactus from the left with Bohemian Green and the seventh cactus with Green Apatite. Paint the outer edge of the sun with a strong mix of Quinacridone Gold. Then rinse your brush and, using only clean water, softly pull the pigment inward to the center of the circle to create a radiant light effect. Be sure to let all areas dry completely before moving on so the shapes remain crisp and the colors don't blend unintentionally.

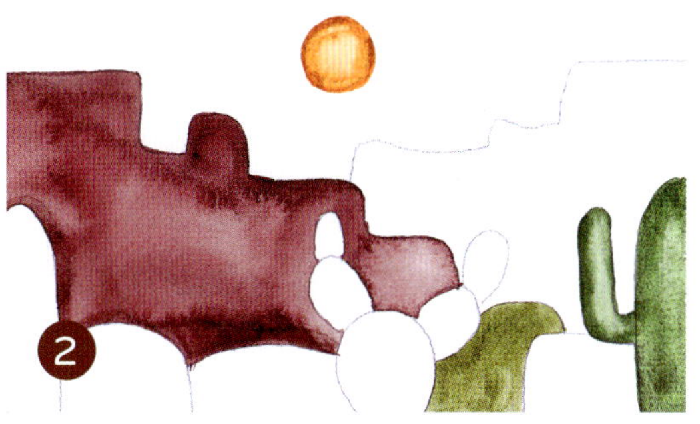

Step 3

Paint the second mountain using Burnt Umber, applying the color evenly. Then, using Shadow Green, paint the first and third cacti.

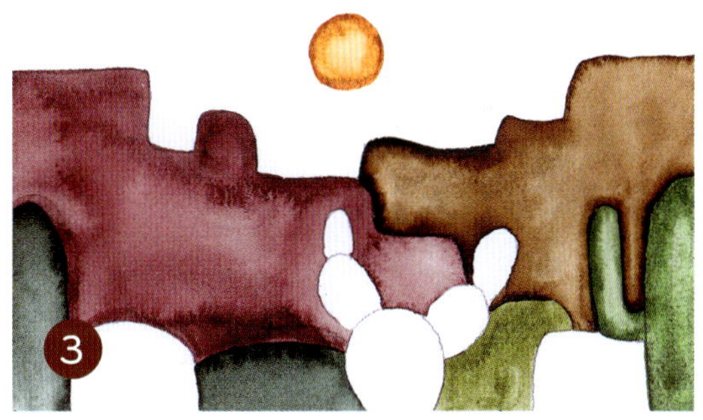

Step 4

Paint the second cactus Bohemian Green. With Green Apatite, and using the gradual wash technique (page 21), paint the fourth cactus. To do this, first paint the edges with a strong amount of pigment, then rinse your brush and, using only water, blend the color from the edges toward the center to create a soft, glowing transition. Finally, paint the sixth cactus Olive Green.

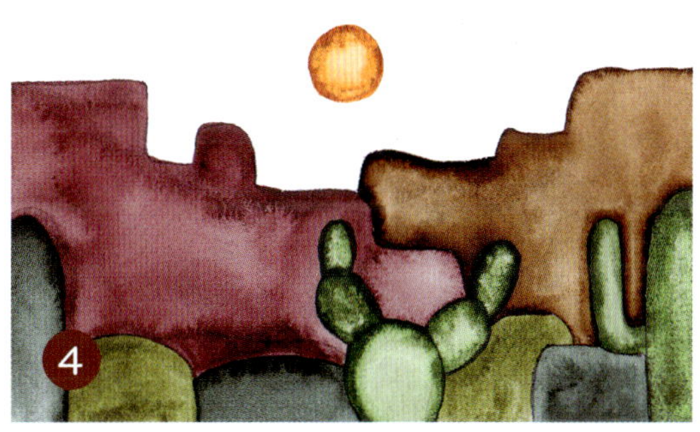

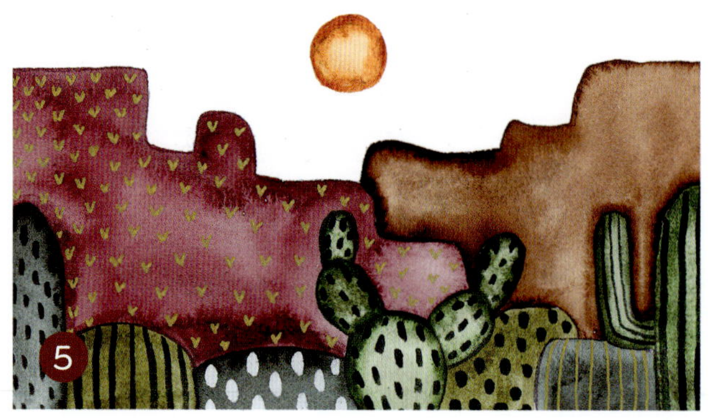

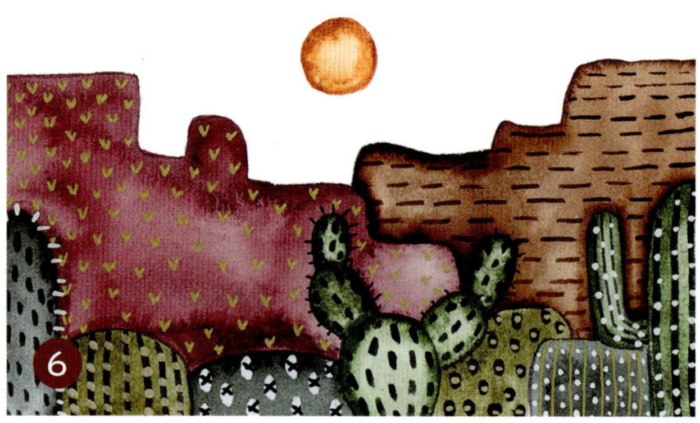

Step 5

This is where the magic begins. Using the size 2 brush, Shadow Green, and white and gold gouache, we'll create the first layer of texture on your cacti. Paint lines and dots in different shapes and sizes, giving each cactus its own visual rhythm. Then, using the tip of your brush and gold gouache, paint tiny glowing hearts on the surface of the first mountain, as if sunlight had left a trail of sparkle across the landscape.

Step 6

Once everything is completely dry, use concentrated Burnt Umber and the tip of your size 2 brush to paint small horizontal lines across the second mountain, evoking layers of rock or sand. Then, to add a second layer of texture to enhance the first, use a fine-liner and white and gold gouache with the size 2 brush to paint spines on some of the cacti, along with white and gold dots and small crosses to enrich the scene. With these final touches, your warm and radiant desert landscape is complete.

Lake of Dreams

Some landscapes feel like a deep breath, and this is one of them. A still lake holds the reflections of an autumn forest, while a small house peeks from between the trees, kissed by golden sunlight. Painting this scene is like stepping into a warm dream, where everything slows down and silence carries the light.

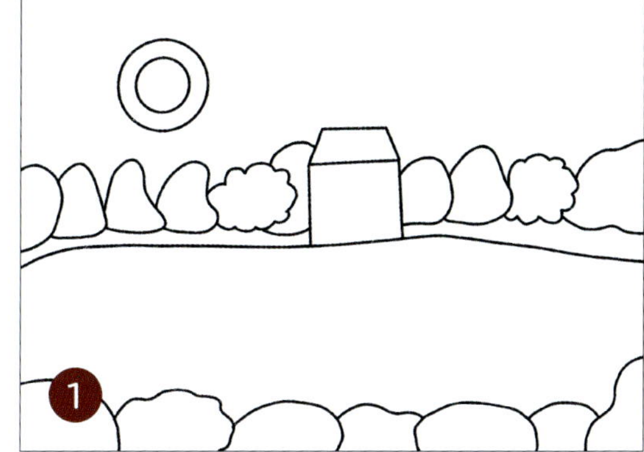

Materials

Paper size
5 x 7" (13 x 18 cm)

Brush
Size 2

Watercolors
Permanent Brown
Perylene Violet
Raw Umber
Burnt Umber

Turquoise
Indigo
Quinacridone Lilac
Violet
Nickel Azo Yellow
Quinacridone Gold
Naples Yellow

For details
Gold gouache
Size 12 fineliner

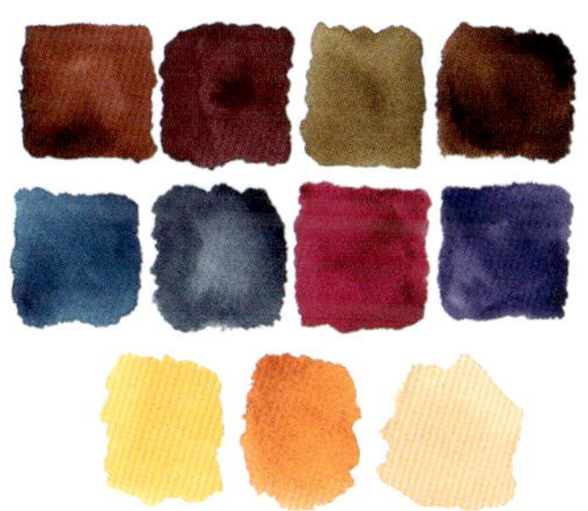

Step 1

Place your paper horizontally. Lightly sketch a row of overlapping oval-shaped bushes along the bottom of the page, from left to right. Above them, about halfway up the page, draw a gently wavy line to mark the shoreline of the lake. In the center of that line, sketch a small house with a square and a flat-topped triangle on top for the roof. Add small trees on both sides. Finally, in the sky above the house, draw a medium-sized circle with a smaller circle inside it. This will be our sun—a glowing heart of light above the forest.

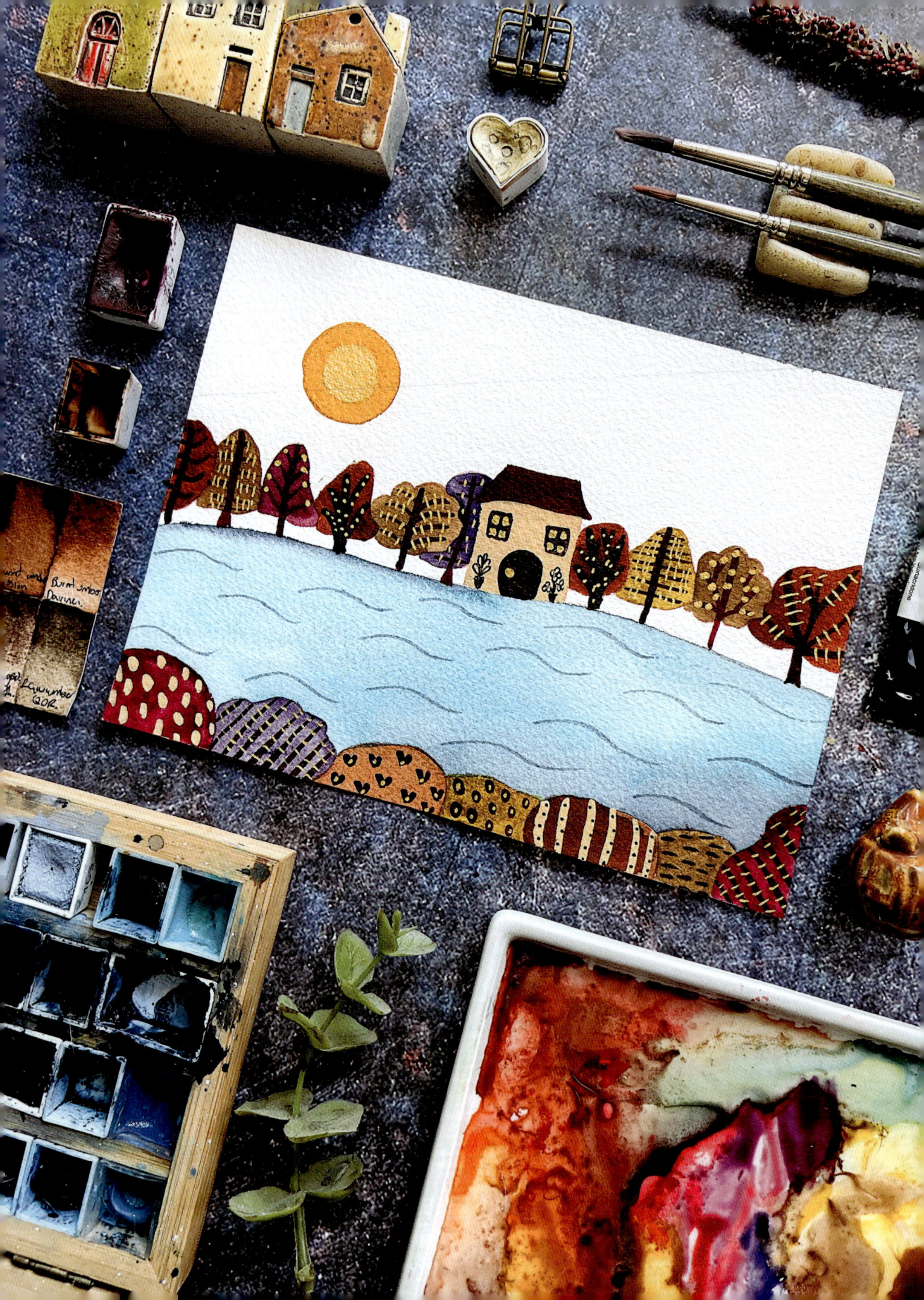

Step 2

Activate your paints with a bit of water. Then, using the size 2 brush and Permanent Brown, paint first, fourth, seventh, and tenth background trees, counting from left to right. In the foreground, use Perylene Violet for the first and last bush, Raw Umber for the third bush, and Burnt Umber for the fifth bush. Be sure to let each section dry completely before moving on to keep the colors clean and defined.

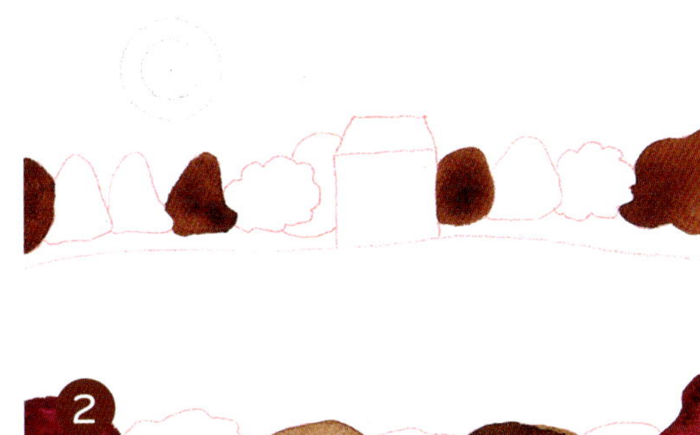

Step 3

Using Raw Umber, paint the second, fifth, and ninth background trees. Next, create a wash with 90-percent Turquoise and 10-percent water, and apply it evenly across the entire lake. While the paint is still wet, gently add small touches of highly diluted Indigo, especially around the edges and center of the lake, to create a soft texture and give the water some depth.

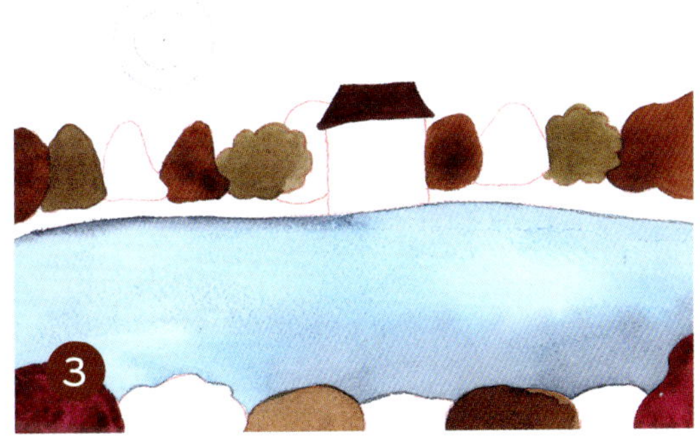

Step 4

Once the lake is completely dry, it's time to paint the remaining trees and bushes using Quinacridone Lilac, Violet, and Nickel Azo Yellow. Make sure not to repeat the same color on adjacent elements. This helps create contrast and visual rhythm throughout the composition. Then, with Quinacridone Gold, paint both circles of the sun, bringing warmth and light to the sky. Finally, paint the roof of the little house using concentrated Perylene Violet to add a deep, vibrant accent to the center of your landscape.

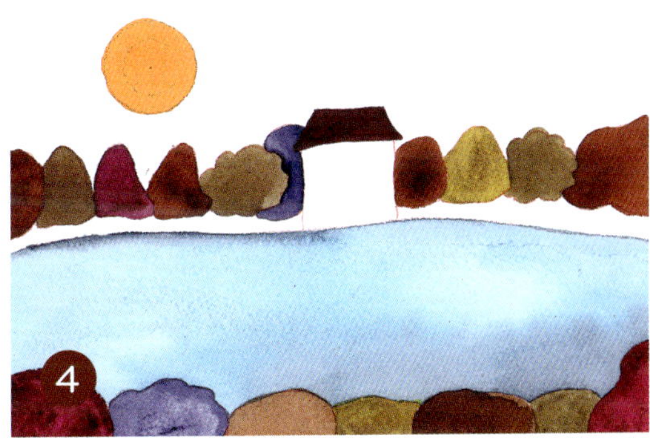

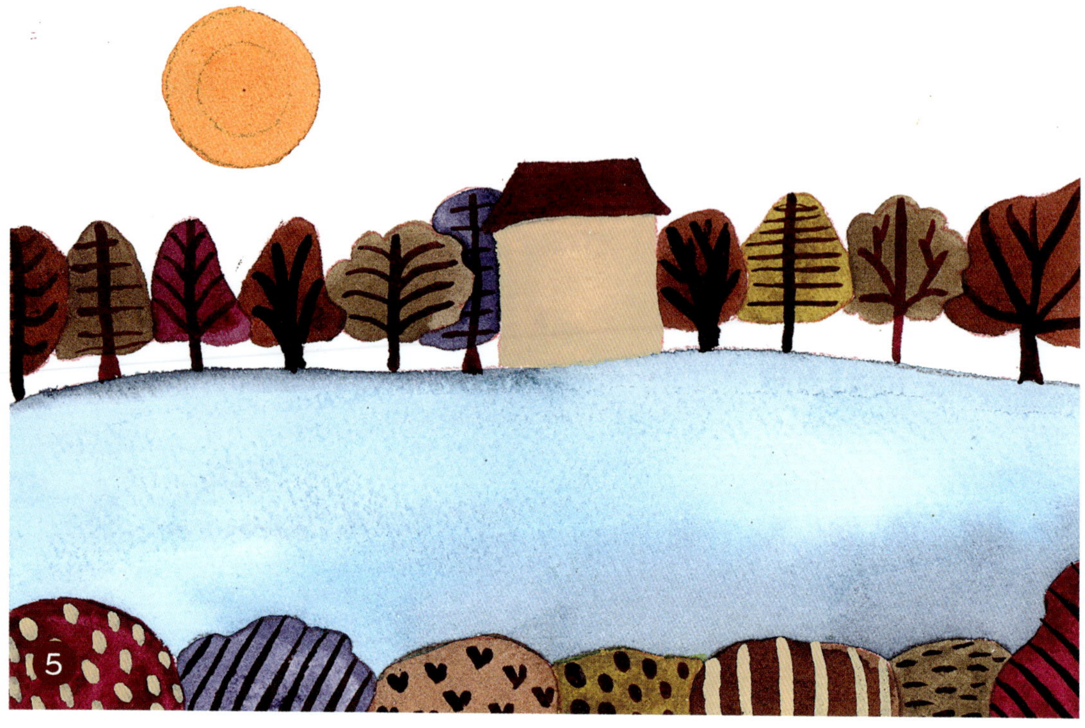

Step 5

Begin bringing your painting to life by adding the first layer of textures. Using Burnt Umber, paint branches on the trees, starting from the base and moving upward. Next, use Naples Yellow to paint the front of the little house.

To finish this step, make sure everything is dry, and then add texture to the bushes with Perylene Violet and gold gouache. Paint dots, lines, and tiny hearts, letting each shape add character and movement to the landscape.

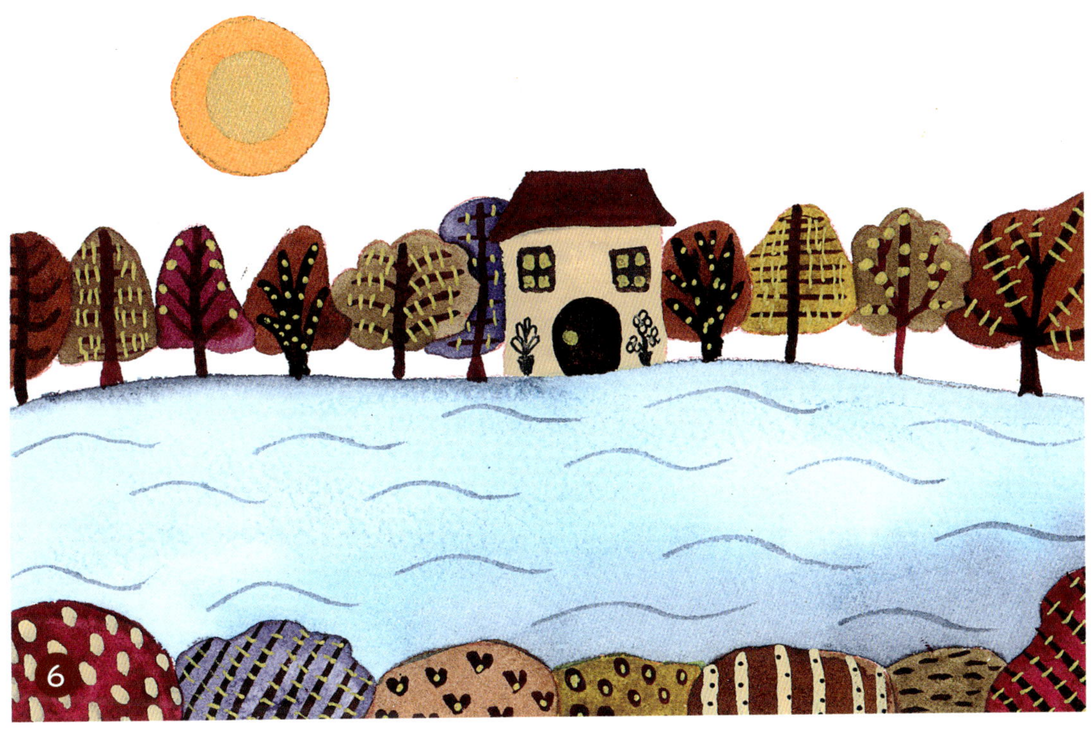

Step 6

Paint the door and windows of the house using Perylene Violet. While this layer dries, use gold gouache to add leaflike textures, dots, or fine lines on the trees. Then, add accents over the first layer of textures on the bushes, bringing depth and light to the scene.

Then, using your fineliner, draw two potted plants on the house's facade. With the tip of your brush and a touch of Indigo, paint gentle ripples across the lake to give the water subtle motion. Finally, use gold gouache to paint the inner circle of the sun, the glow inside the house's windows, and the door handle, ending the piece with warmth and wonder.

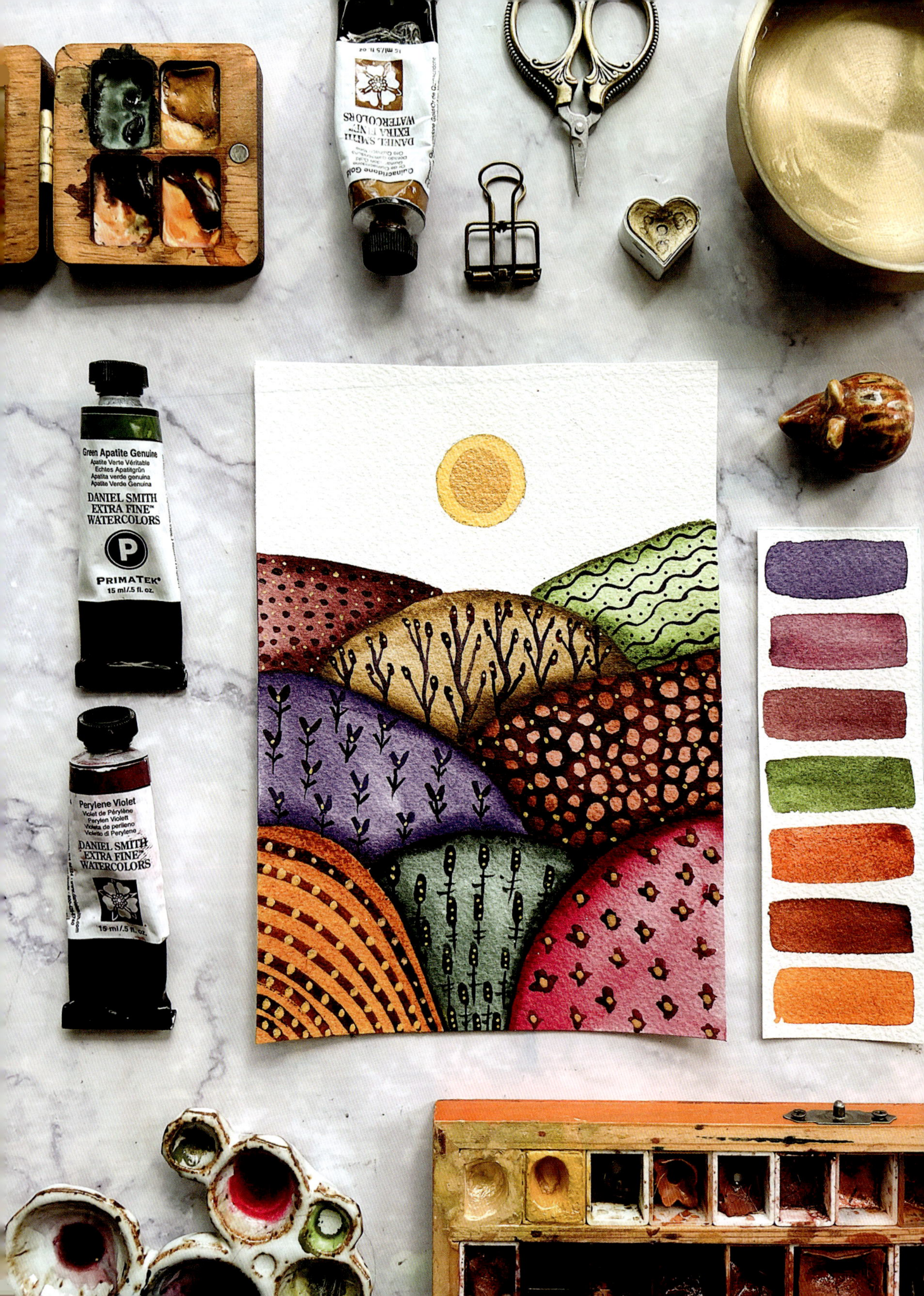

Mystical Mountains

Some landscapes feel like dreams made visible, where mountains don't just rise but whisper stories through their colors. In this exercise, we'll explore a world where every peak holds its own personality, where textures blend like drifting thoughts across the horizon, and where painting becomes a quiet ritual of wonder and discovery.

Materials

Paper size
5 x 7" (13 x 18 cm)

Brush
Size 2

Watercolors
Quinacridone Lilac
Violet
Green Apatite
Quinacridone Gold
Permanent Brown
Perylene Violet
Shadow Green
Bohemian Green

For details
Gold gouache
White gouache

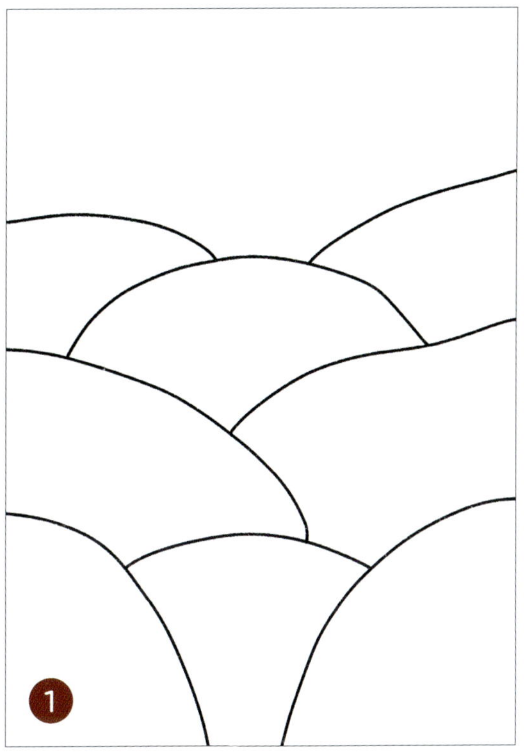

Step 1

Place your paper vertically. Lightly sketch a series of overlapping mountains, one behind the other, playing with different shapes and heights until you reach just above the halfway point of the page. These mountains will be the heart of our scene, so take your time shaping a silhouette that flows naturally.

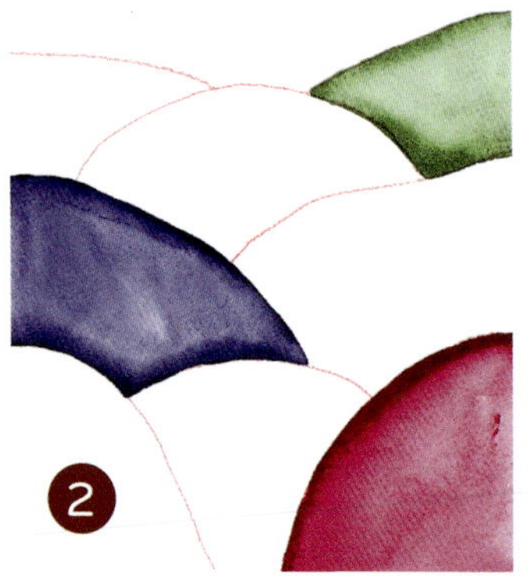 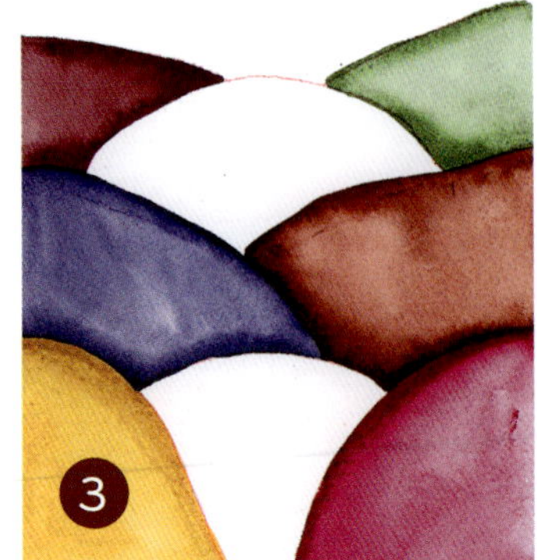 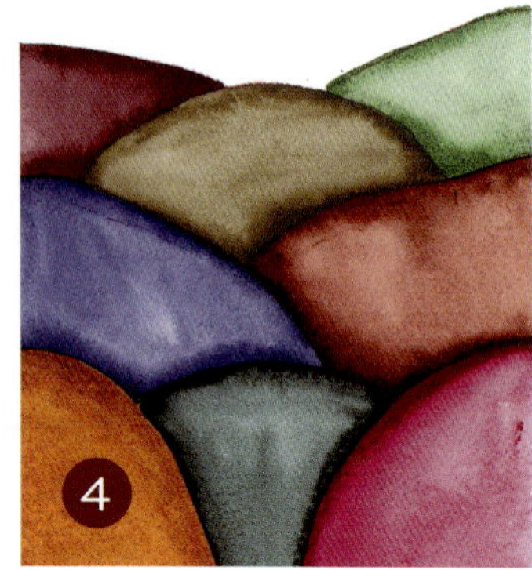

Step 2

Activate your paints with a bit of water. Paint the third mountain (from left to right) with Quinacridone Lilac, the fourth with Violet, and the eighth with Green Apatite. Let these layers dry completely before moving on so the colors remain crisp and don't bleed into each other.

Step 3

Continue painting the mountains, making sure each layer dries well to keep the edges crisp and clean. From left to right, paint the first mountain with Quinacridone Gold, the fifth with Permanent Brown, and the sixth with Perylene Violet.

Step 4

From left to right, paint the second mountain with Shadow Green and the seventh with Bohemian Green. Let these areas dry completely before continuing to the next step.

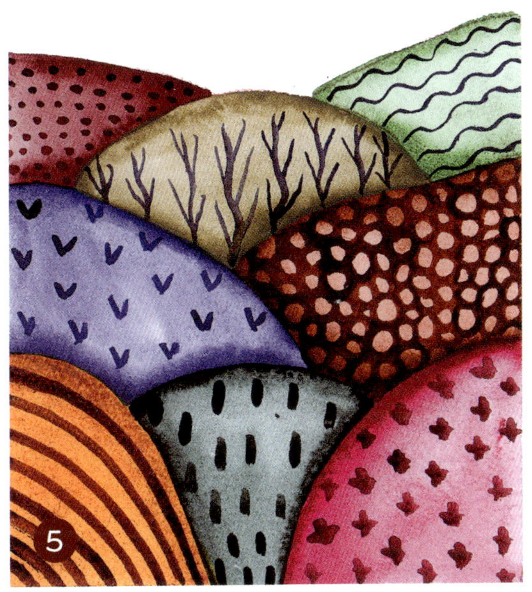
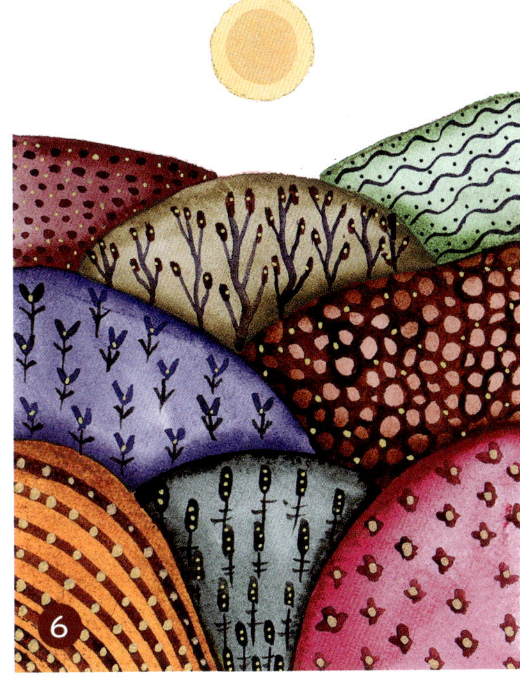

Step 5

Using highly pigmented Perylene Violet and Violet, and the tip of your size 2 brush, begin adding the first layer of textures to your mountains. Paint lines, crosses, hearts, branches, waves, and dots . . . changing the patterns on each mountain to create a scene full of movement and personality. This step is an invitation to play with your brush and let each mark tell its own story.

For the fifth mountain, apply a flat wash of color over the entire shape. Instead of covering it completely, leave small dots unpainted so the lighter base layer shines through. This negative space creates the effect of scattered highlights across the mountain, giving it both texture and a luminous quality without adding extra paint on top.

Step 6

Now enhance the first layer of textures using gold and white gouache. Paint leaves on the branches, dots along the waves, and small highlights across the patterns to make them stand out. Be sure your mountains are completely dry before applying these details so the colors remain crisp. These luminous touches bring light and magic to the scene, completing your mystical peaks with a glowing golden finish.

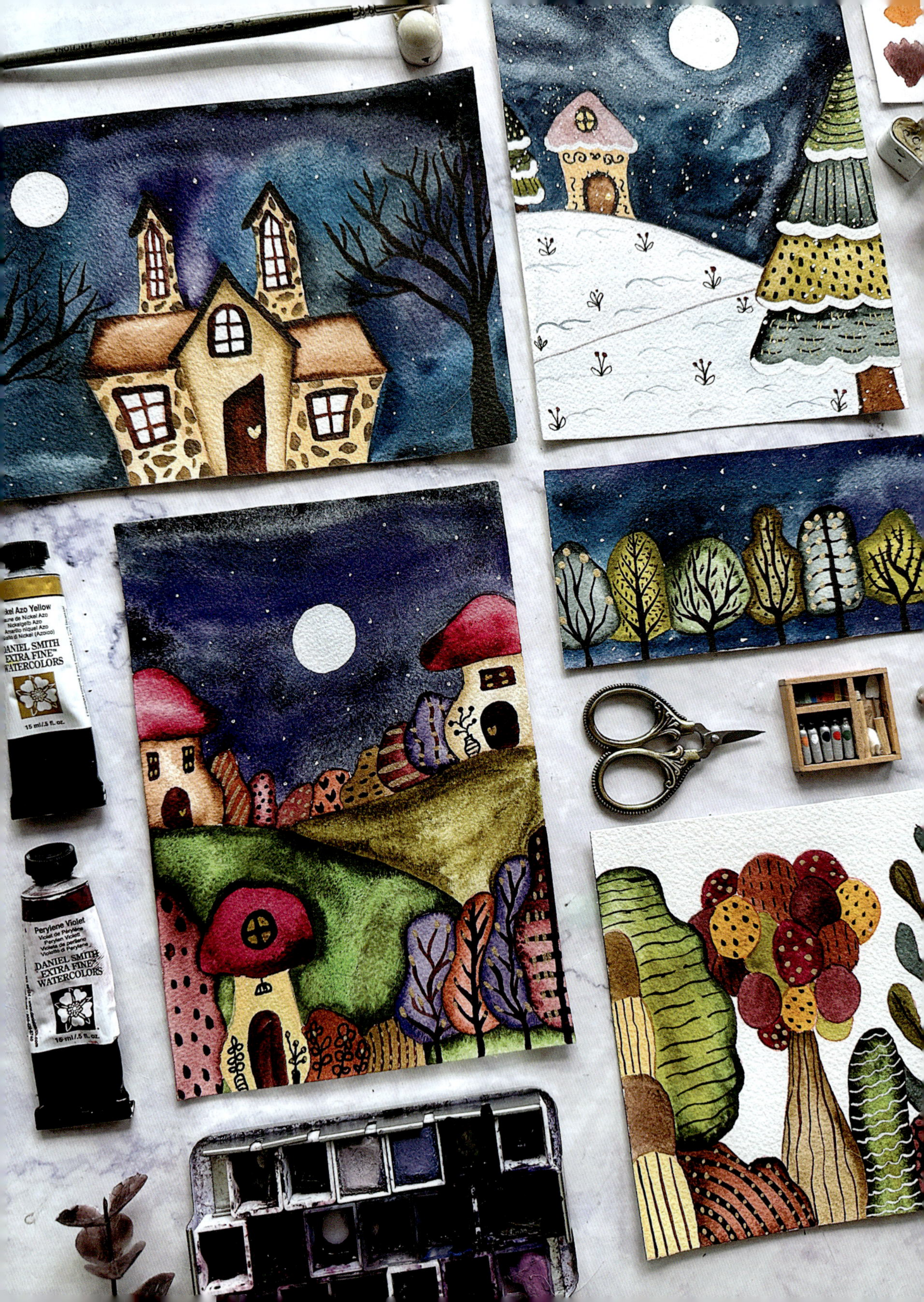

A Touch of
Magic

There are places that don't exist on any map yet live vividly in the depths of our imagination: forests glowing with starlight, jungles whispering secrets through their leaves, haunted houses hiding in shadows, and mushroom villages straight out of a fairy tale. This chapter invites you to leave the ordinary behind and step into landscapes where magic feels entirely real. Through each brushstroke, we'll wander through worlds where nature and fantasy intertwine, evoking wonder, curiosity, and the sweet nostalgia of daydreaming.

Grab your brushes. The journey begins where reason ends. That's where magic begins.

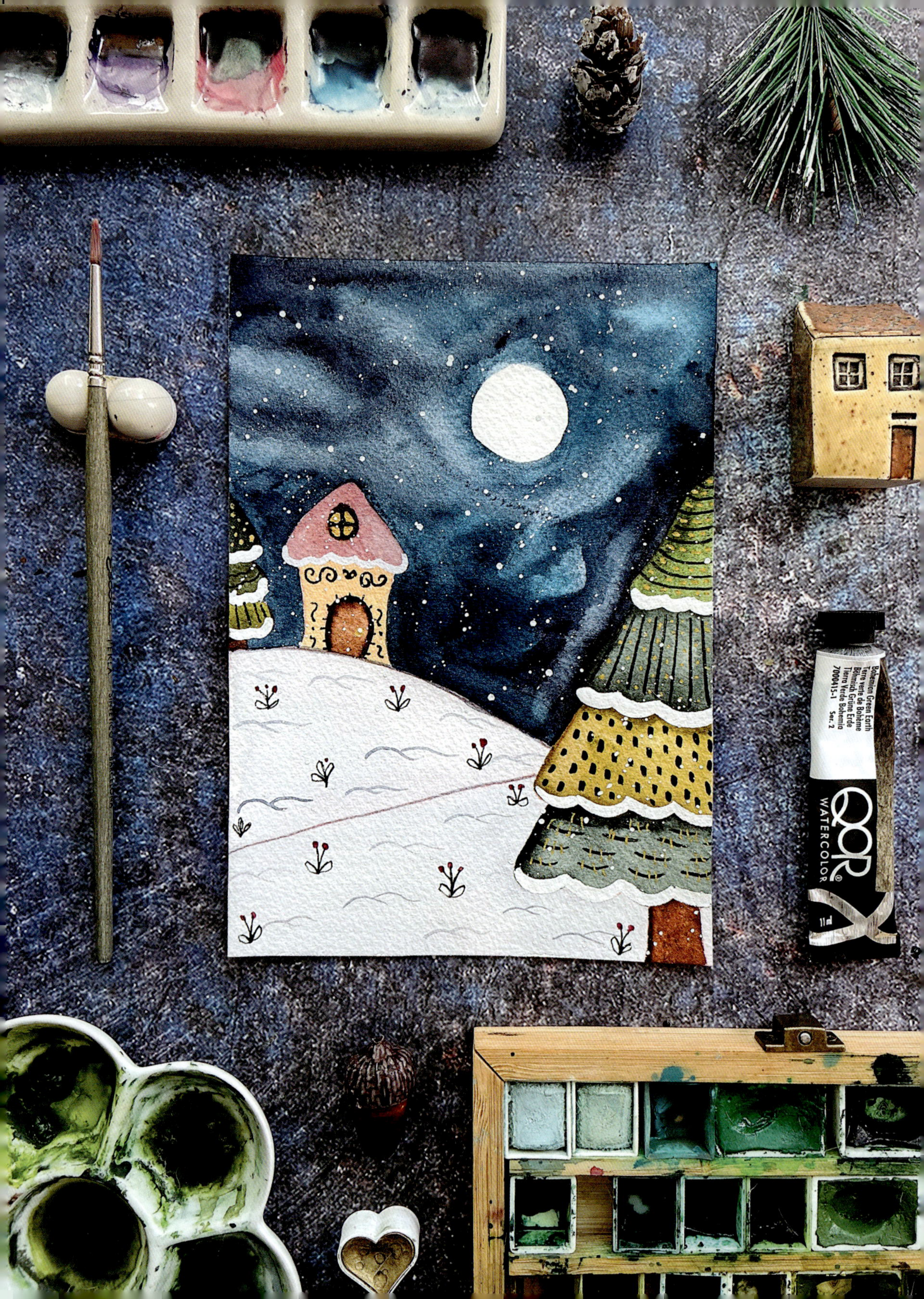

Winter Wonderland

In this quiet scene, winter covers everything with its soft white cloak. The mountains rest beneath the snow, a lone pine stands tall, and at the top, a little house keeps the warmth of home amid the frozen hush. We'll paint a snowy night sky, gently falling flakes, and a full moon casting light over this serene landscape. It's an invitation to embrace stillness, contrast, and the quiet beauty of winter.

Materials

Paper size
5 x 7" (13 x 18 cm)

Brushes
Size 4 and size 2

Watercolors
Indigo
Green Apatite
Naples Yellow
Shadow Green
Olive Green
Burnt Umber
Turquoise
Quinacridone Lilac

For details
Size 12 fineliner
Gold gouache
White gouache

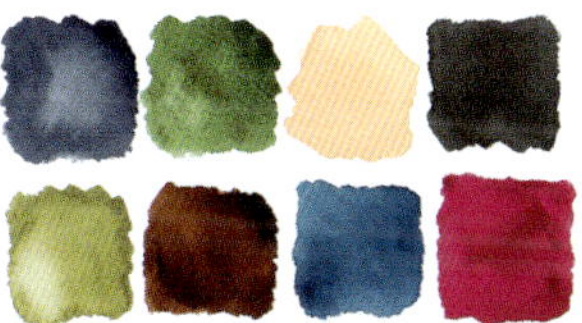

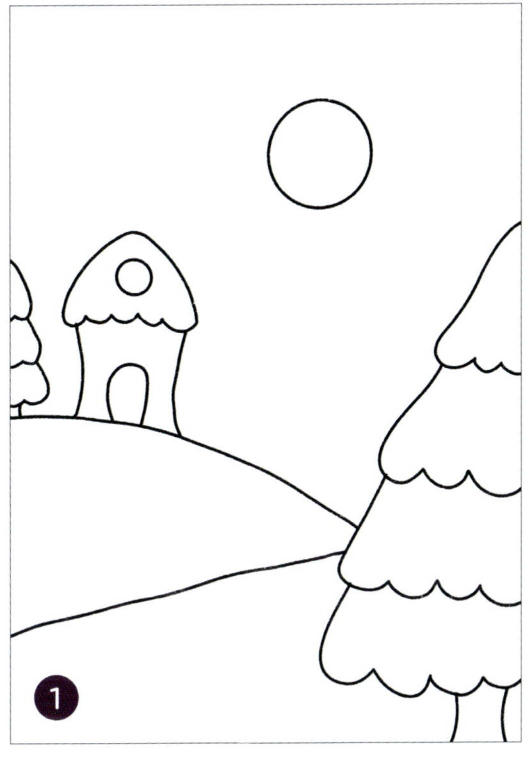

Step 1

Place your paper vertically. Lightly sketch a large pine tree on the right side of the page. Begin slightly above the center and build layered branches that widen as they move downward, leaving space for the trunk at the bottom. Next, draw a mountain that starts near the base of the pine and stretches toward the left. Above it, sketch another mountain that crosses back from left to right, finishing again near the pine. On this top mountain, toward the left, draw a small pine, and beside it, a tiny house with a roof, a window, and a door. Finish the sketch by drawing a circle in the center of the sky that will be our full moon, casting light over the snowy stillness.

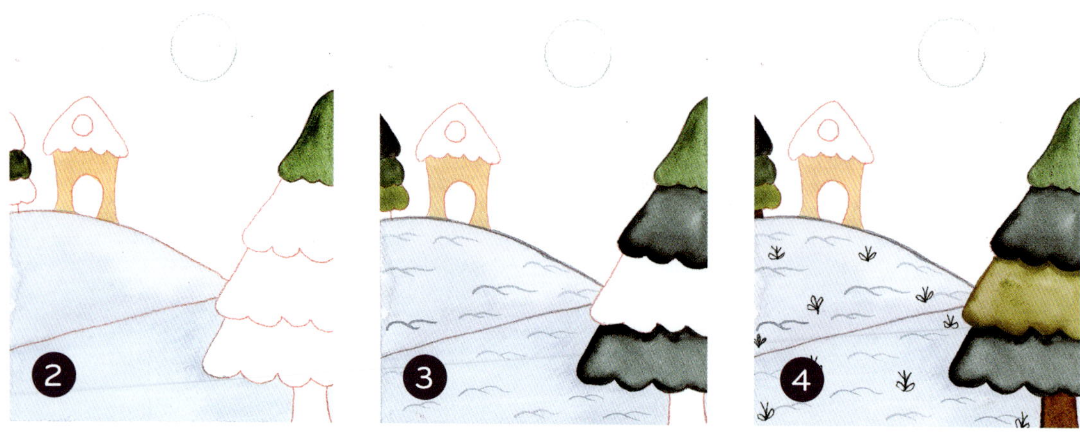

Step 2

Activate your paints with a bit of water. Prepare a mix of 90-percent Indigo and 10-percent water. With the size 4 brush, paint the two snowy mountains that create the base of your scene. Using the size 2 brush, paint the tip of the large pine tree and the middle section of the small pine sitting on the mountain with Green Apatite. Once the mountains are fully dry, gently paint the facade of the house with Naples Yellow, adding a warm accent to contrast the cool winter tones.

Step 3

From top to bottom, paint the middle and bottom sections of the large pine tree Shadow Green. For the small pine, use Shadow Green for the top half and Olive Green for the lower half, creating a gentle variation in tone. Then, using the tip of your size 2 brush and a light value of Indigo, paint soft, wavelike strokes on the mountains to add movement and texture, as if the wind had danced across the snowy slopes.

Step 4

Paint the final section of the main pine using Olive Green, completing its lush shape. Then, use Burnt Umber to paint the trunks of both pine trees. With your fineliner, draw small leaves and twigs peeking out from the mountains. These subtle details help bring the winter scene to life.

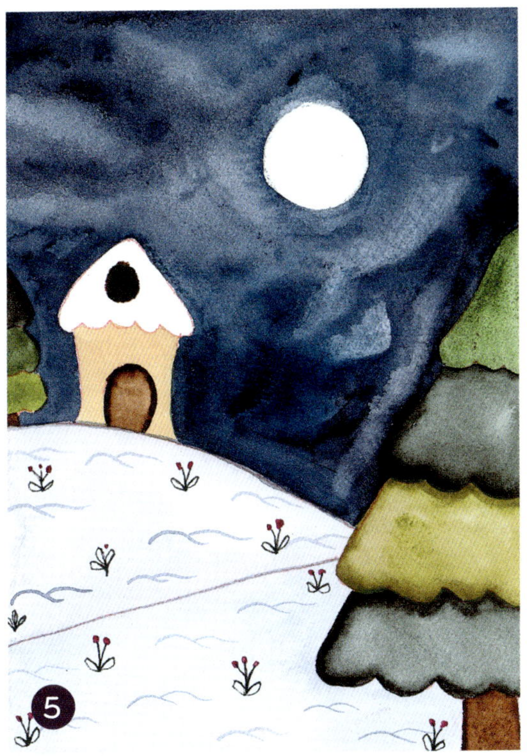 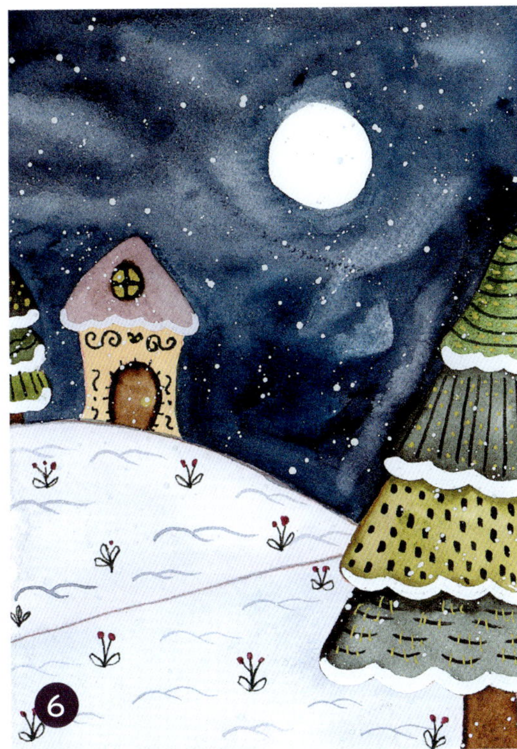

Step 5

Using your size 4 brush and Indigo and Turquoise, paint the sky with alternating brushstrokes, allowing the two colors to softly blend. In some areas, blend with water to create a dreamy, diffused effect. The most important part is to work quickly so the watercolor doesn't dry before the entire sky is finished. This helps avoid harsh edges or stains. Switch to your size 2 brush and paint the door and window Burnt Umber. Then, on the twigs and leaves emerging from the snow, add tiny dots of Quinacridone Lilac at the tips, like delicate winter blooms peeking through the frost.

Step 6

Mix 20-percent Quinacridone Lilac and 80-percent water, and use it to paint the roof of the cottage, creating a soft hue that blends beautifully with the winter sky. With Shadow Green and the tip of your size 2 brush, add textures to the pine trees—lines, dots, and waves that bring their branches to life. Then, with the fineliner, draw small decorative details on the cottage facade. Next, use gold gouache to paint the warm glow of the lights inside the cottage windows and to add subtle details and textures to the trees. Finally, paint the lower edges of each pine tree section with white gouache to suggest snow resting gently on the branches. With the same paint, splatter (page 22) tiny white specks across the scene to mimic falling snow, wrapping this winter wonderland in a soft, magical hush.

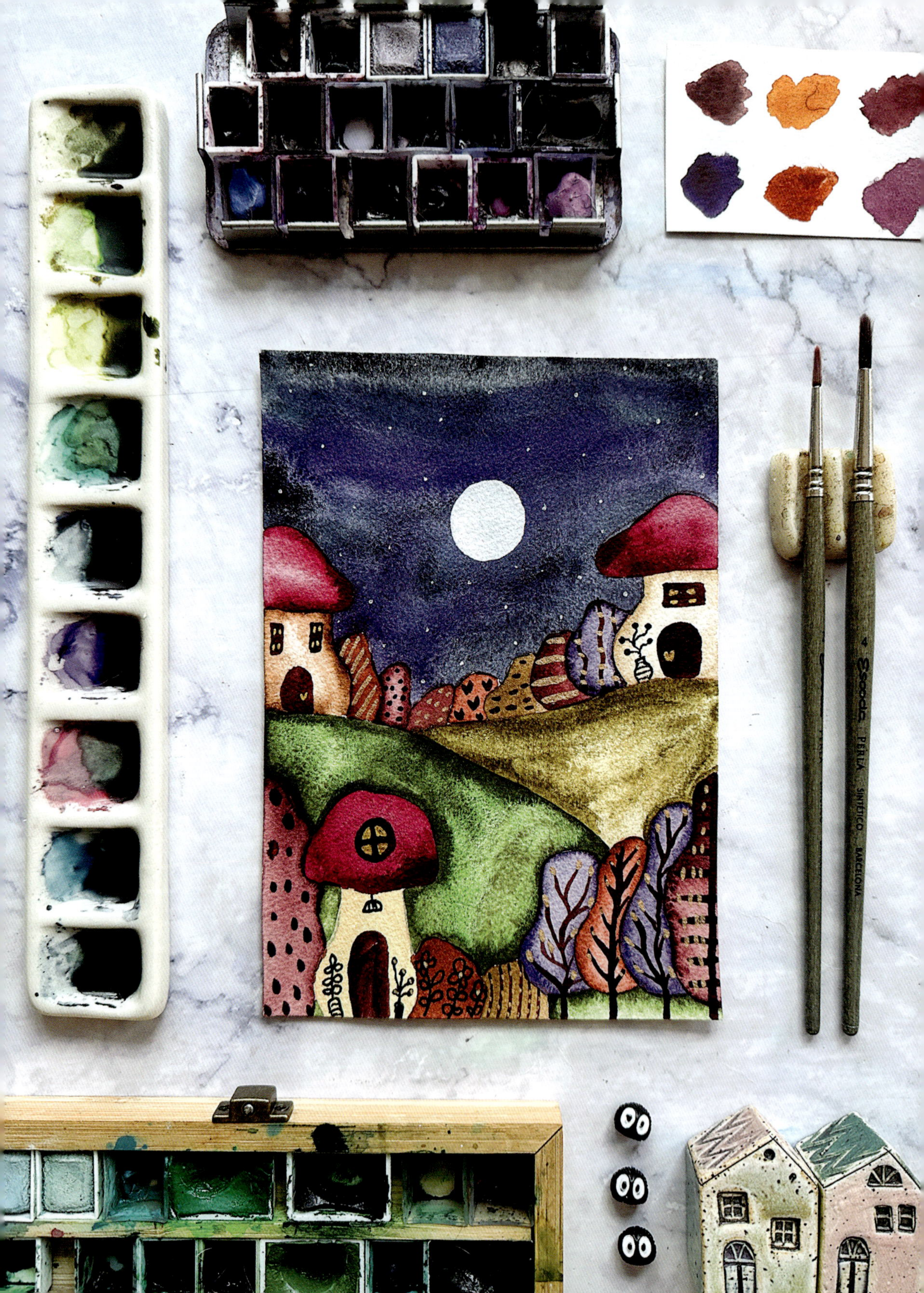

Mushroom Village

Tucked between cozy hills and autumn trees lies a tiny village where rooftops are mushroom caps and golden windows glow in the night. A full moon watches from above, casting gentle light on this enchanted forest scene, where every detail whispers warmth and wonder. In this exercise, we'll bring to life a magical landscape filled with earthy tones, textured bushes, and whimsical mushroom houses tucked beneath the stars.

Materials

Paper size
5 x 7" (13 x 18 cm)

Brushes
Size 4 and size 2

Watercolors
Indigo
Violet
Green Apatite
Naples Yellow

Burnt Umber
Raw Umber
Perylene Violet
Permanent Brown
Bohemian Green
Quinacridone Lilac

For details
White gouache
Gold gouache
Size 12 fineliner

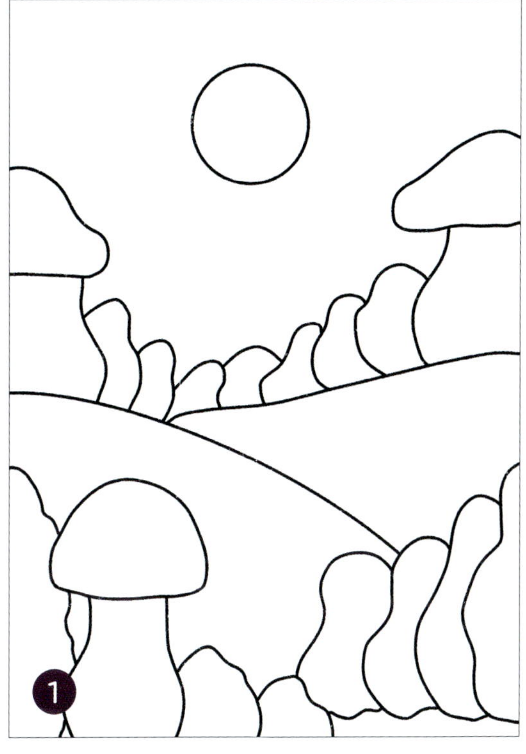

Step 1

Place your paper vertically. Lightly sketch a row of bushes at the bottom of the page. In the center, sketch a little mushroom-shaped house. Then, add a few trees around it to complete the foreground. Above this area, draw a mountain from left to right, and over it, a second line from right to left to create an overlapping mountain. At the top of each mountain, draw a mushroom house—one on the left and one on the right—and connect them with bushes along the slope. In the middle of the sky, draw a circle that will be our full moon.

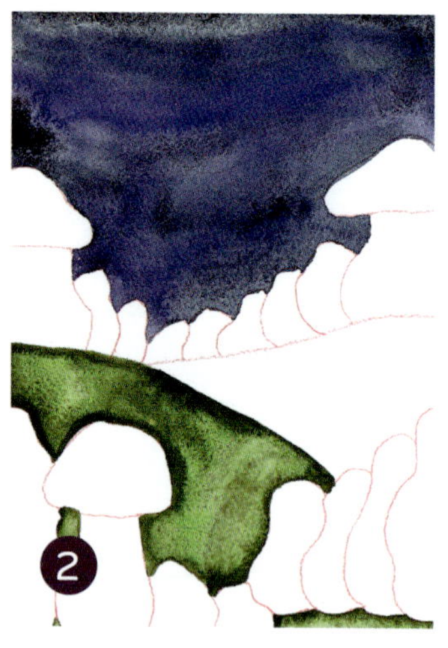 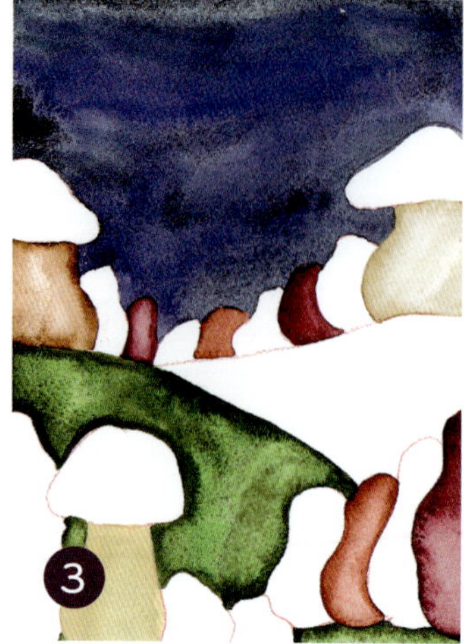 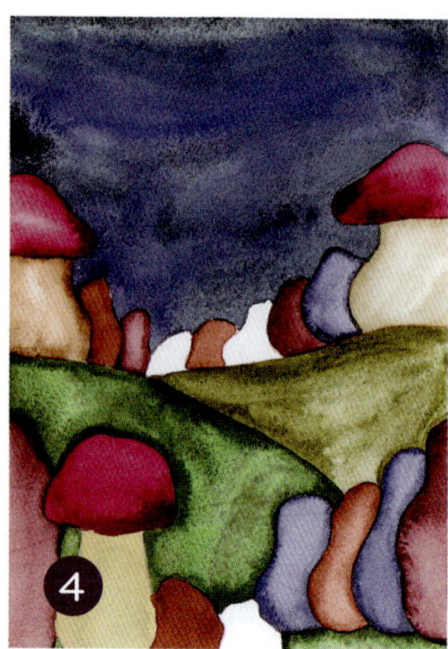

Step 2

Activate your paints with a bit of water. With the size 4 brush, paint the night sky using the wet-on-wet technique (page 18) with Indigo and Violet. Apply broad strokes, alternating between the two colors, and leave some areas lighter to create soft contrasts like drifting clouds. Work quickly to keep the surface wet so the colors blend smoothly and avoid patchy drying. Let the sky dry completely before moving on. Next, paint the mountain on the left with Green Apatite.

Step 3

Once the sky is completely dry, begin painting the facades of the mushroom houses and some of the surrounding bushes using the size 2 brush. For the facades, apply soft, warm tones like Naples Yellow, Burnt Umber, and Raw Umber to create a gentle contrast against the night sky. For the bushes, use rich autumnal colors like Perylene Violet and Permanent Brown, building a cozy and vibrant foundation for our little enchanted village. To keep the colors crisp, paint every other bush first, and let them dry completely before painting the ones next to them.

Step 4

With your size 2 brush, paint the second overlapping mountain in the background Bohemian Green. Then, with Quinacridone Lilac, paint the mushroom rooftops, adding a magical touch under the moonlight. Continue with the trees and bushes using Violet, making sure not to place the same color side by side. (This helps create a balanced and visually rich composition.)

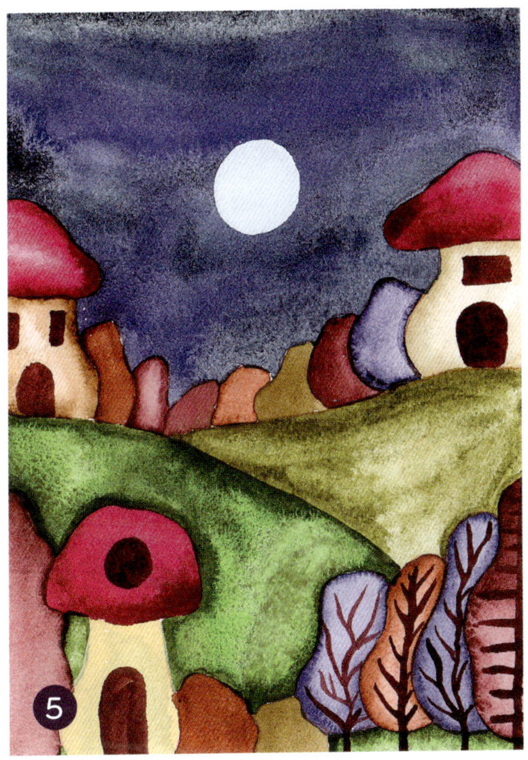 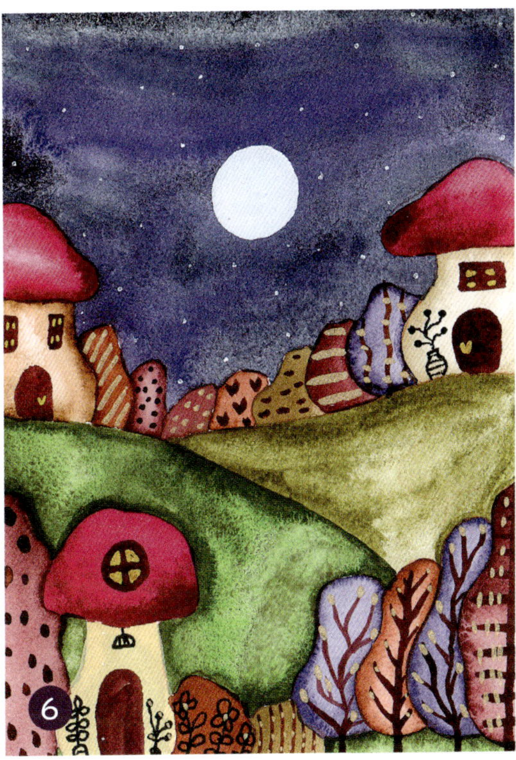

Step 5

Finish painting the remaining bushes using Raw Umber. With Permanent Brown, add detail to the little houses by painting the doors and windows, and use the same color to draw the tree branches. To complete this step with a magical accent, paint a glowing full moon in the center of the sky with white gouache, casting light over the entire scene.

Step 6

With gentle touches of gold and white gouache, we awaken the magic in our tiny village: Windows glow warmly and door handles shimmer with golden light while tiny white stars glisten in the night sky. Use the tip of your size 2 brush to weave the poetry of the forest textures that whisper, crafted with dots, lines, hearts, and waves in Permanent Brown, Perylene Violet, and gold gouache. As if the branches dreamed of fireflies, sprinkle golden dots upon them. And to complete this enchanted corner, draw little potted plants on the houses with your fineliner . . . quiet details full of soul.

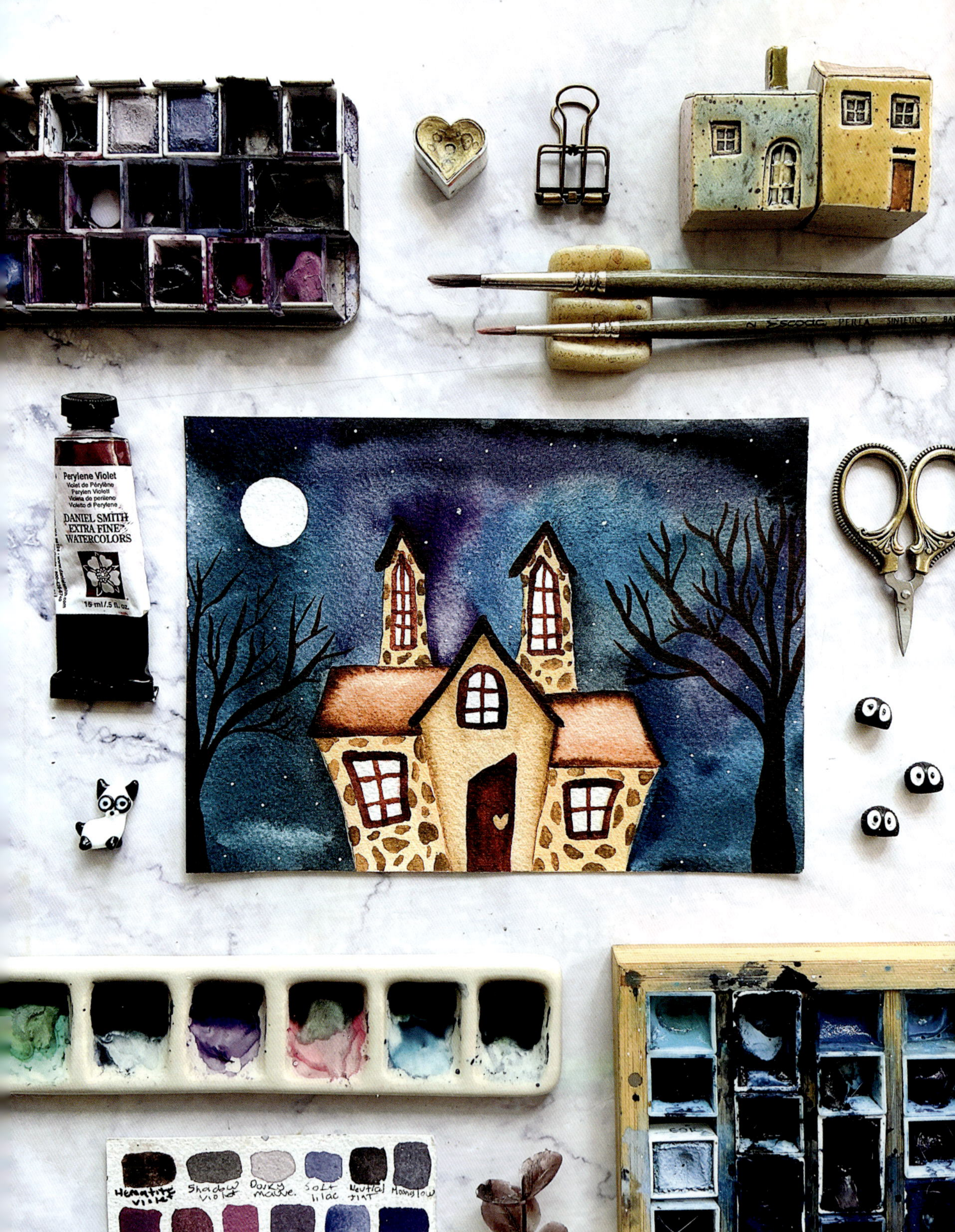

Hematite Violet
Shadow Violet
Dusky mauve
Soft lilac
Neutral Tint
Moonglow
Rose Utlamanne
Dusk Pink
Morgan violet
Amethyst
Ultramarine violet
Violet
Lavender
Bright
Mineral
Quinacridone lilac

Spooky House

Deep in the forest, where bare trees stretch their limbs like whispers in the wind, stands a mysterious house. Its solitary silhouette holds ancient secrets beneath a starry sky, while the full moon casts a silvery glow over the landscape. This exercise is a tribute to the mystery and beauty of the unknown, where each brushstroke conjures a haunted tale, a forgotten corner, a home of shadows and dreams.

Materials

Paper size
5 x 7" (13 x 18 cm)

Brushes
Size 4 and size 2

Watercolors
Indigo

Turquoise

Violet

Naples Yellow

Burnt Umber

Perylene Violet

Raw Umber

Permanent Brown

For details
White gouache

Gold gouache

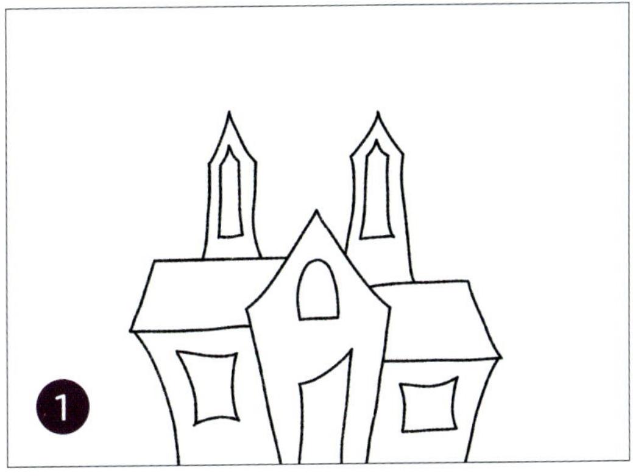

Step 1

Place your paper horizontally. Lightly sketch an asymmetrical house with uneven rooftops in the center of the page. Draw a mysterious structure that sparks curiosity.

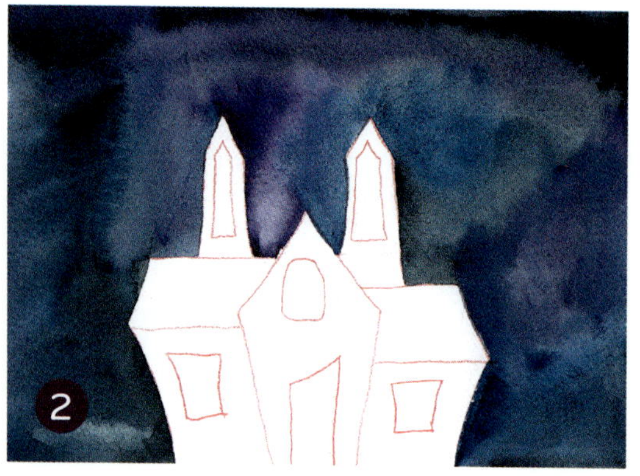

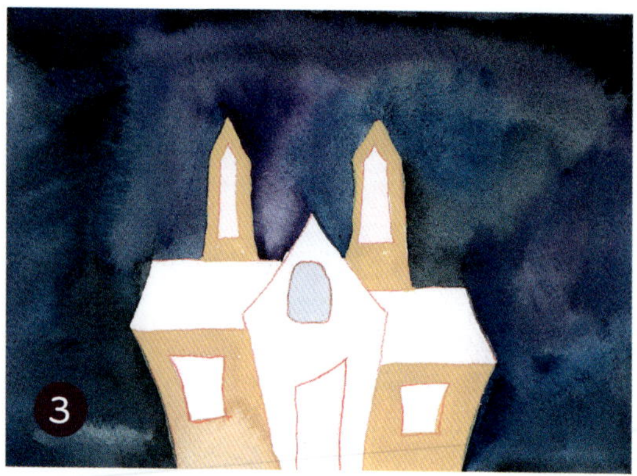

Step 2

Activate your paints with a bit of water. Then, using the size 4 brush and a blend of Indigo, Turquoise, and Violet, paint the night sky that wraps around the scene. Begin by adding deep strokes of Indigo along the edges. Then, while the paper is still wet, blend in touches of Turquoise and Violet toward the center, allowing the colors to merge softly. Leave a few lighter spots to add depth and variation that look like subtle clouds drifting across the sky. The key to this step is to work quickly to keep the wash even and avoid harsh lines. Let the sky dry thoroughly before moving to the next step.

Step 3

Using Naples Yellow and the size 2 brush, paint the front of the house, giving it a gentle glow amid the darkness of the forest. Then, create a soft wash by mixing 10-percent Indigo with 90-percent water, and use it to paint the main window of the house, like a quiet reflection of the moonlit night.

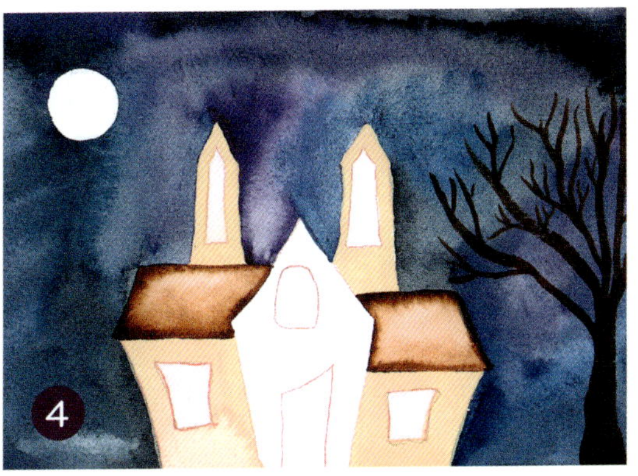

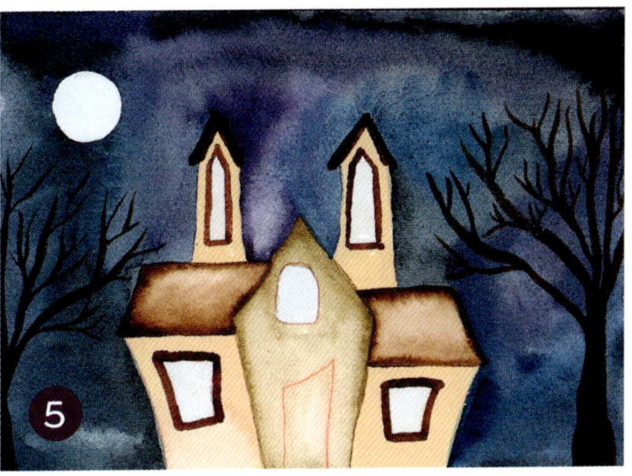

Step 4

Using Burnt Umber, paint the roofs of the house to give it a warm, weathered feel. Focus the concentrated pigment along the edges of the roofs, then rinse your brush and use clean water to gently pull the color toward the center. This gradual wash technique (page 21) creates a soft lighting effect and adds dimension to the roofs. Next, prepare this mix:

- 50-percent Perylene Violet +
  50-percent Burnt Umber

Paint a leafless tree on the right side of the scene with this mix. Starting from the ground, with the tip of the size 2 brush, let the trunk rise into the sky, extending delicate branches along the way. To add a hint of magic to this step, paint a glowing full moon in the upper left corner of the sky using white gouache.

Step 5

Using the tip of your size 2 brush and Burnt Umber, paint the window frames, adding depth and character to the house's details. Then, with Raw Umber, paint the main facade of the house, giving it a warm, earthy tone that beautifully contrasts with the night sky. Using the same Perylene Violet and Burnt Umber mix from Step 4, bring another bare tree to life, this time on the left side of the painting, adding a touch of eerie balance. With this same rich and moody blend, paint the rooftops of the small towers, giving the structure a sense of unity and shadowy charm. Once the frames are completely dry, finish painting all the windows of the house with the diluted Indigo from Step 3, giving them a soft touch of midnight blue.

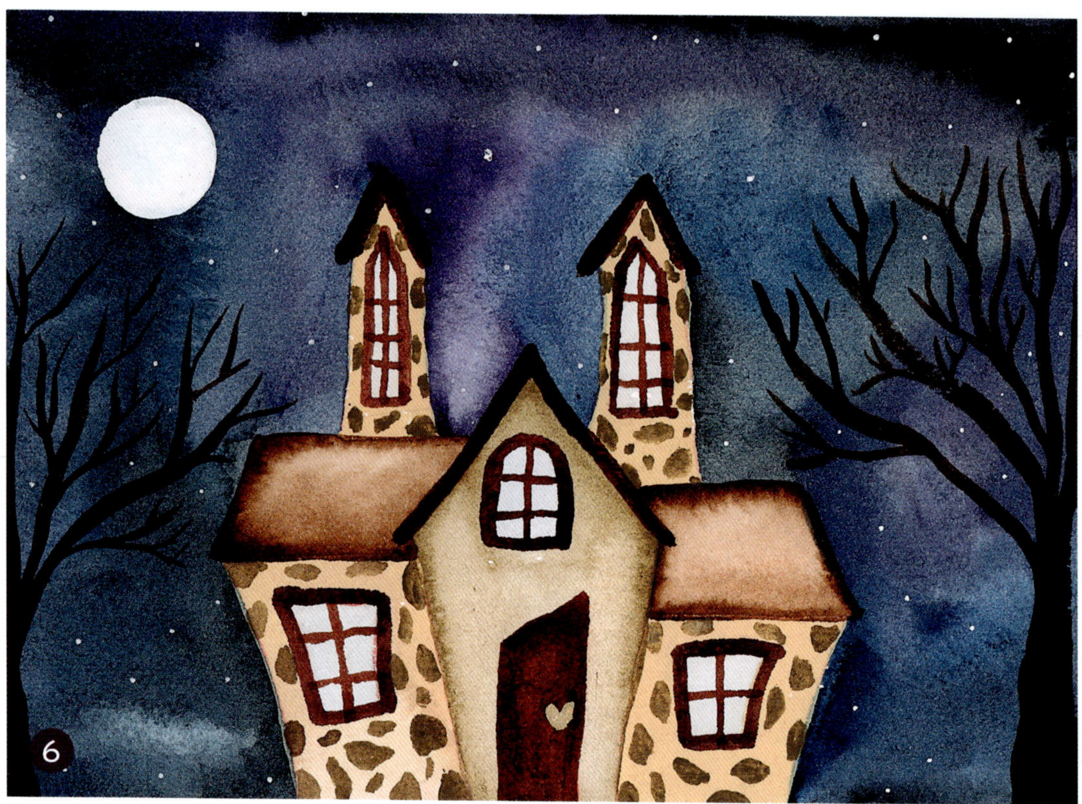

Step 6

Finish painting the window frames and panes using Burnt Umber and the tip of your size 2 brush, carefully enhancing each shape so they stand out against the night. With Raw Umber, add small, uniform shapes across the facade of the house to simulate stones, as if the walls were built from old forest rocks.

Next, use the tip of your size 2 brush and white gouache to add little stars scattered across the night sky. Then, paint the door Permanent Brown, concentrating the pigment along the edges and softening toward the center to add depth and character. To complete this richly textured step, add a final touch: Use gold gouache to paint a doorknob in the shape of a heart . . . a subtle spark of warmth within this mysterious scene.

Magic Jungle

Step into an imaginary jungle where leaves don't follow perfect patterns but dance freely in irregular, organic shapes full of character. In this exercise, we'll create a warm forest of overlapping and intertwining plants, evoking the richness and energy of a tropical jungle. We'll use a vibrant palette of greens, yellows, earthy browns, and deep touches of Perylene Violet, adding contrast and texture to every corner of this wild, mysterious world.

Materials

Paper size
5 x 7" (13 x 18 cm)

Brush
Size 2

Watercolors
Naples Yellow
Raw Umber
Permanent Brown
Perylene Violet

Green Apatite
Nickel Azo Yellow
Shadow Green
Quinacridone Lilac
Bohemian Green
Olive Green

For details
Size 12 fineliner
Gold gouache
White gouache

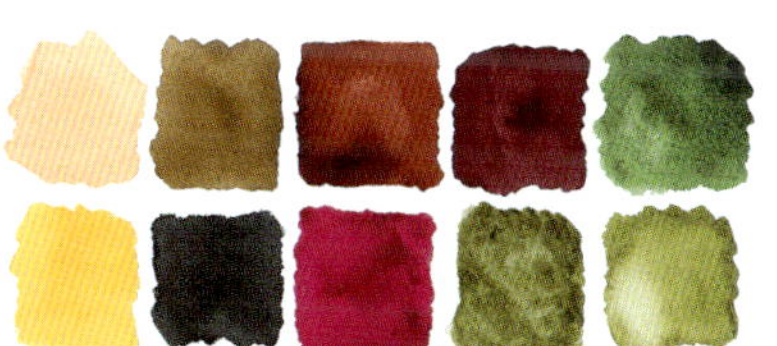

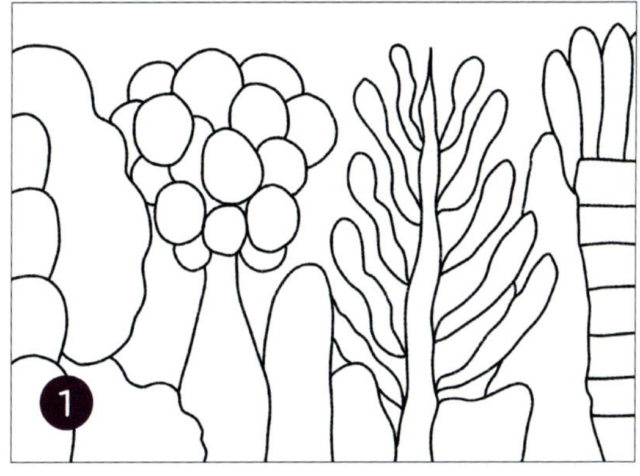

Step 1

Place your paper horizontally. Lightly sketch four trees with shapes that feel both uniform and irregular. Let them follow a rhythm or pattern, but keep the lines free-flowing and organic. You can overlap shapes on the trunks, use circles to suggest foliage, or draw long, uneven leaves reminiscent of palms—just more abstract. Between the trees, add a few bushes to complete the layout of your imaginary jungle.

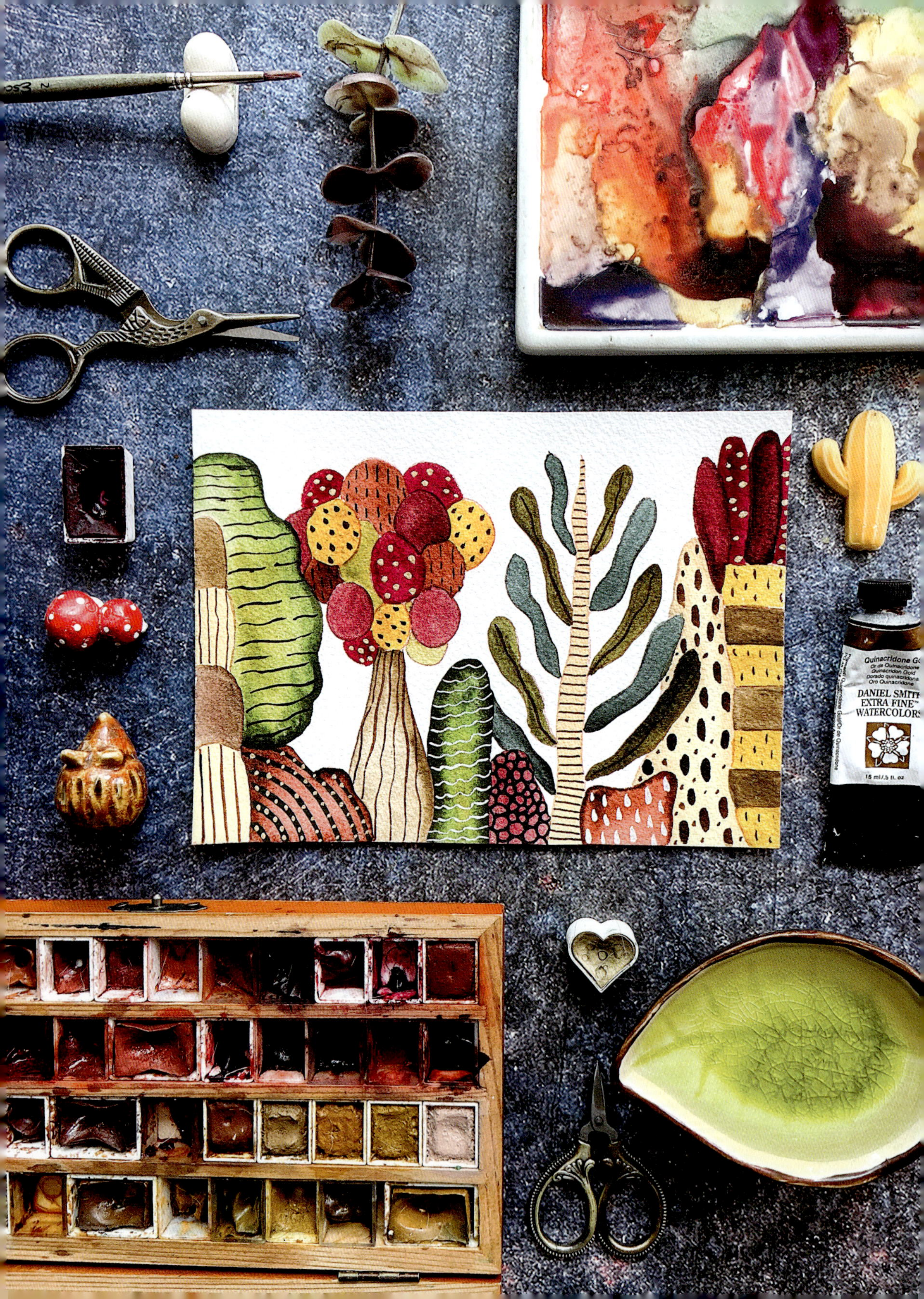

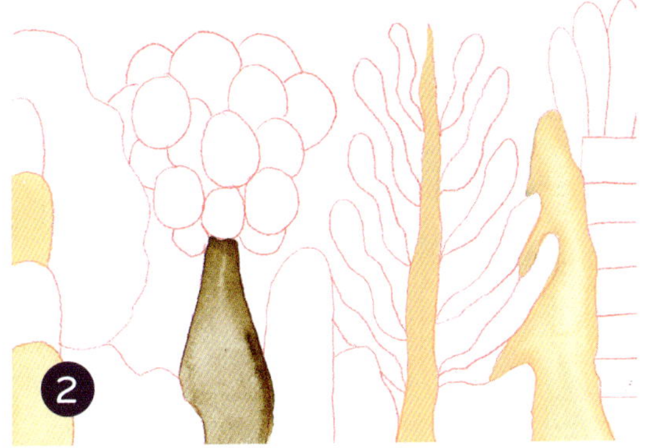

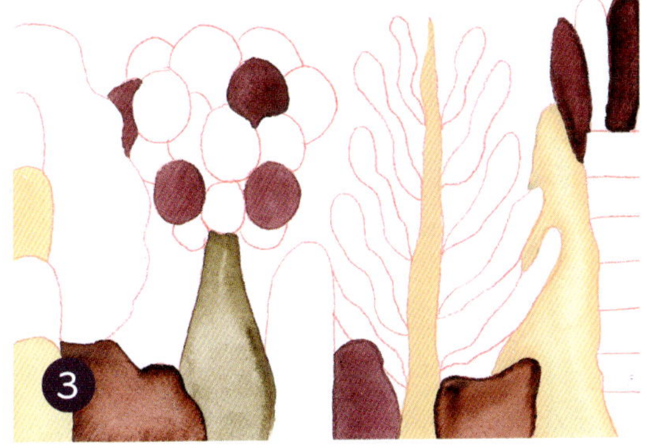

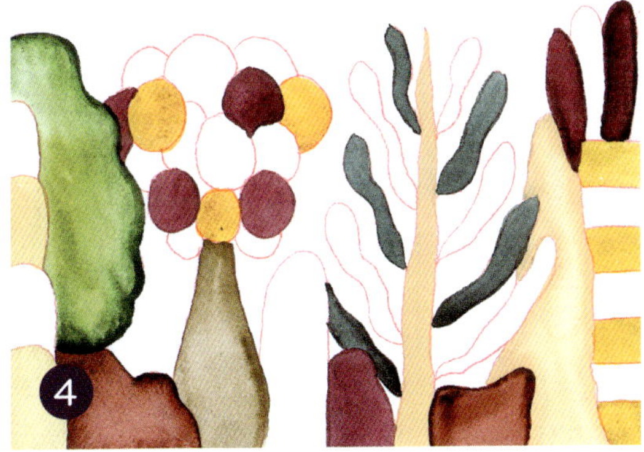

Step 2

Activate your paints with a bit of water. Using Naples Yellow and the size 2 brush, paint two of the overlapping shapes on the first tree trunk (from left to right), alternating one painted, one left blank to create contrast. Then, use the same color to paint the entire trunk of the third tree. Also, paint the bush located just to the left of the fourth tree with Naples Yellow. To finish this step, paint the trunk of the second tree with Raw Umber. Let everything dry completely before moving to the next step.

Step 3

Paint the first bush (from left to right) using Permanent Brown. Then, with Perylene Violet, paint some of the circles in the canopy of the second tree and the bush located before the third tree. Use Permanent Brown to paint the bush after the third tree. For the leaves of the last tree, alternate Perylene Violet (one leaf yes, one leaf no) to create contrast and visual rhythm in the composition.

Step 4

Paint the first tree canopy Green Apatite. Then, color some of the circles on the second tree with Nickel Azo Yellow. On the third tree, use Shadow Green to paint every other leaf. For the trunk of the fourth tree, alternate sections using Nickel Azo Yellow to create an engaging pattern of light and texture.

Step 5

Using Raw Umber, finish painting the remaining blank areas on the first tree. Then, on the second tree, paint some of the circles with Quinacridone Lilac, making sure that no two colors are directly next to each other. Next, paint the bush located after the second tree with Green Apatite. Fill in the remaining white leaves on the third tree with Bohemian Green. For the last tree, paint the remaining leaves with Quinacridone Lilac, and use Raw Umber to complete the trunk.

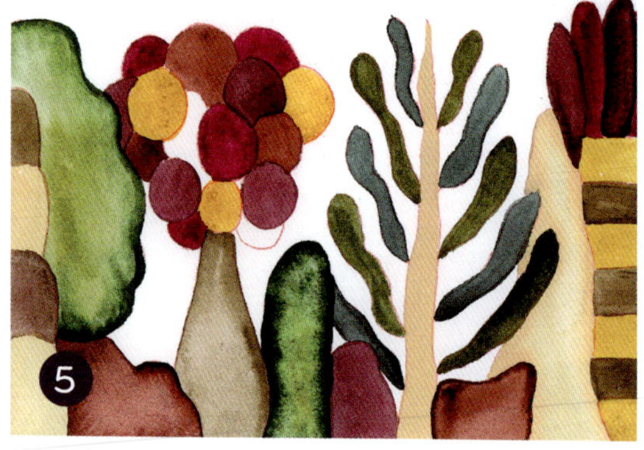

Step 6

Use Olive Green to paint the remaining circles on the second tree. Now begins the magical process of bringing this jungle to life through texture. With the fineliner, gold and white gouache, and richly pigmented watercolors such as Perylene Violet and one of your greens, draw lines, dots, and waves across trunks, leaves, and bushes. Use very concentrated pigment and the tip of your brush to add expressive patterns and details that echo the wild rhythm of nature. Let each mark tell its own story in this vibrant jungle corner.

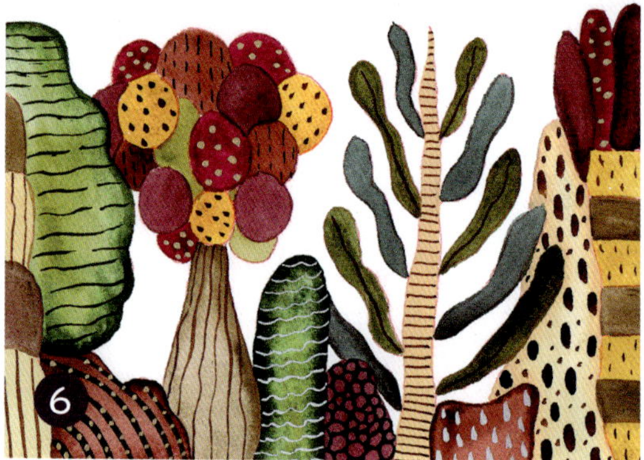

Forest in the Galaxy

In this exercise, we'll paint a magical forest that seems to float among the stars. The horizontal format is designed to become a beautiful bookmark, perfect to add a touch of wonder to your readings. We'll create a galactic sky in shades of indigo, violet, and turquoise, scattered with stars and a line of trees in various greens, standing like silhouettes in a stellar dream.

Materials

Paper size
2½ x 8" (6 x 20 cm)

Brush
Size 2

Watercolors
Indigo
Turquoise
Violet

Shadow Green
Green Apatite
Olive Green
Bohemian Green
Burnt Umber

For details
White gouache
Gold gouache
Size 12 fineliner

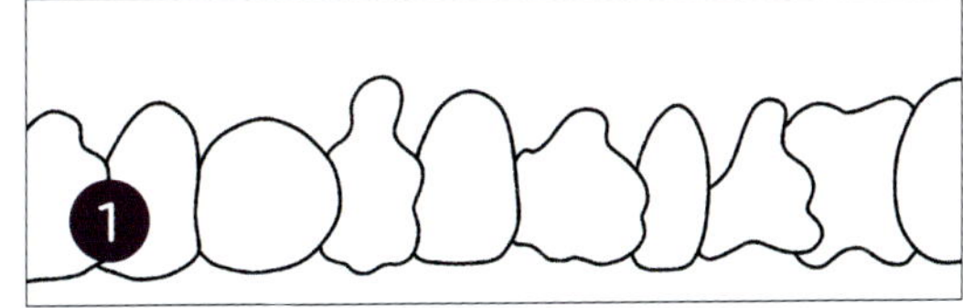

Step 1

Place your paper horizontally. Lightly sketch a series of oval shapes across the center of the page. Keep the ovals even but slightly irregular, letting them overlap as they move from left to right across the sheet. These shapes will serve as the treetops of your galactic forest.

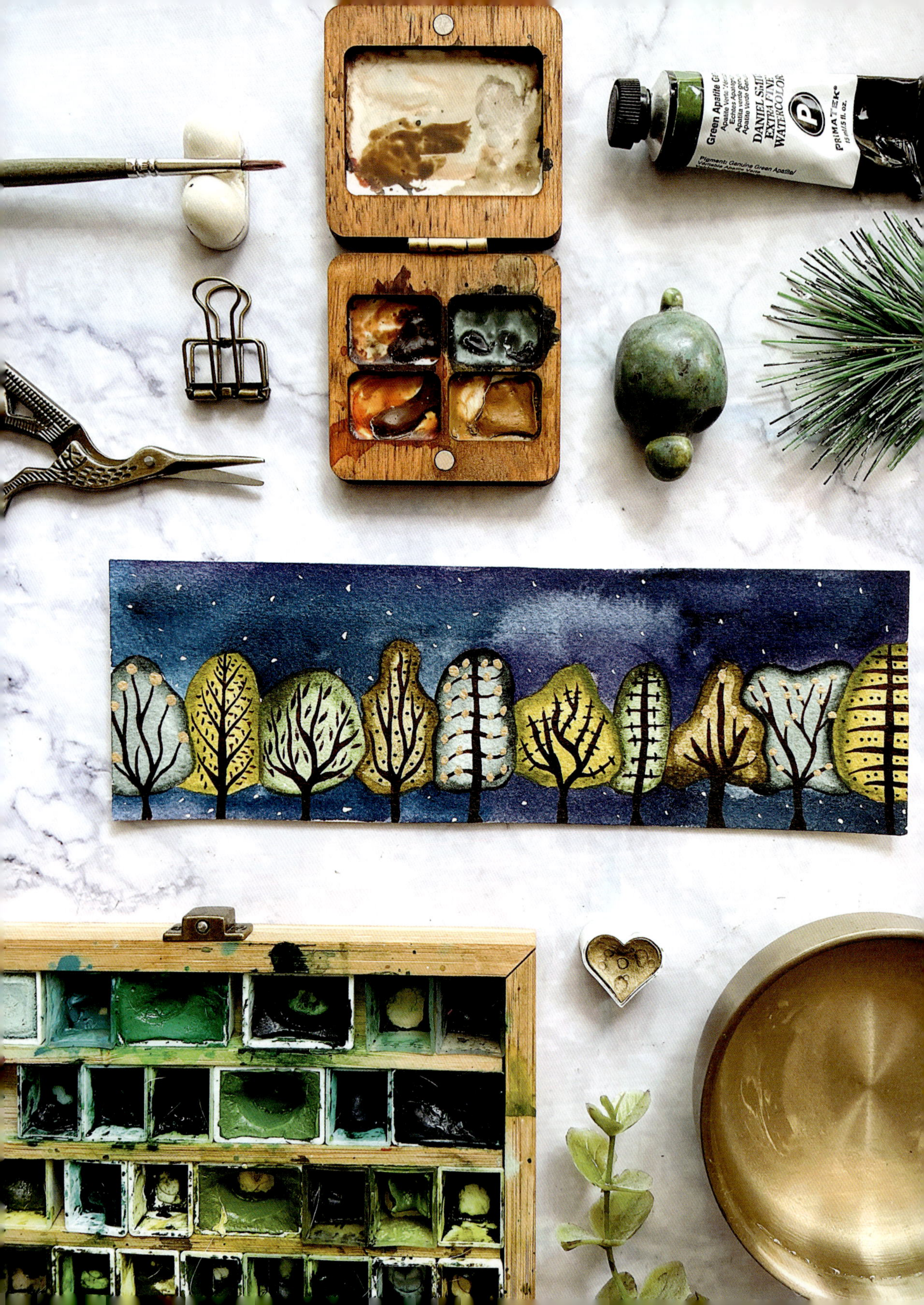

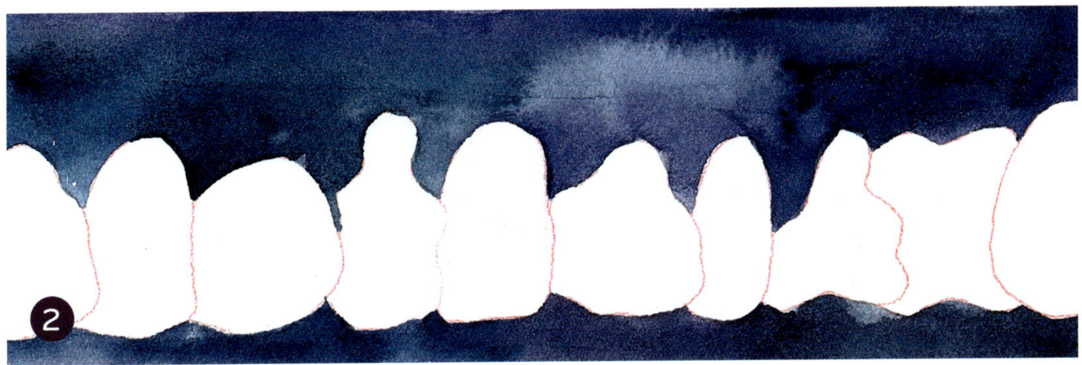

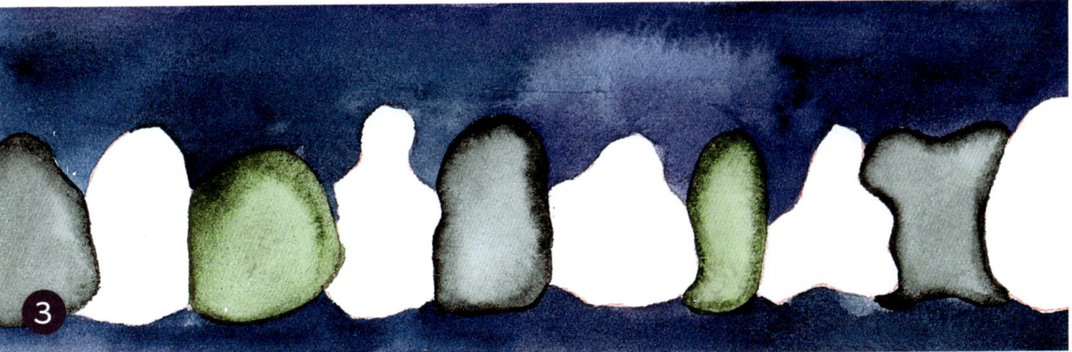

Step 2

Activate your paints with a bit of water. Now let's paint the background of your galaxy. Start by applying Indigo around the edges of the sky and blend it gently with water. Then add strokes of Turquoise in the center, followed by Violet to create depth and mystery. This step should be done quickly and smoothly to prevent the watercolor from drying before the soft transitions between colors are achieved—just like in a dreamy galaxy sky.

Step 3

Let's start bringing your forest to life. Paint the first, fifth, and ninth trees Shadow Green, making sure to leave space between them so the pigments don't bleed into each other. Then, using Green Apatite, paint the third and seventh trees.

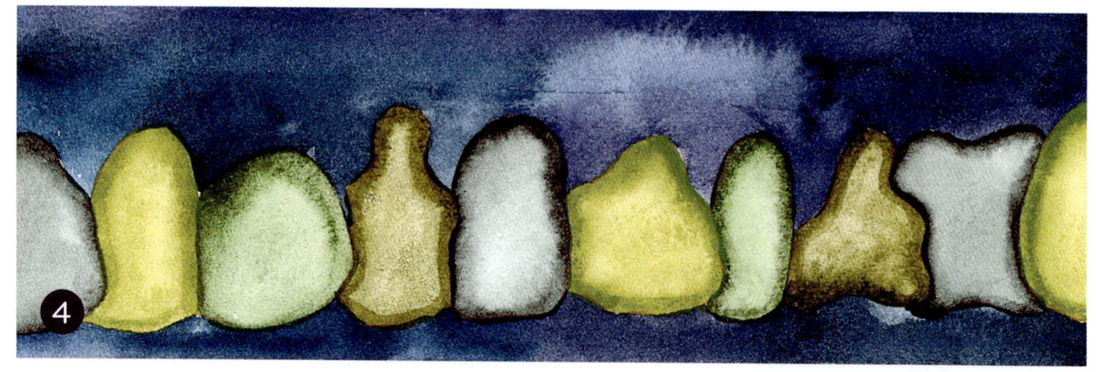

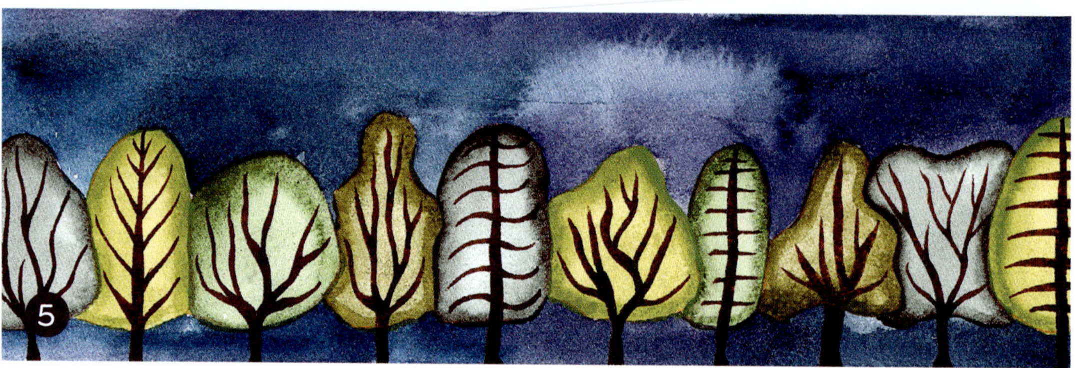

Step 4

Our galactic forest begins to come alive with rich, soulful hues. Paint the second, sixth, and tenth trees Olive Green, bringing soft, earthy tones to the scene. Then, with Bohemian Green, add a whisper of mystery to the fourth and eighth, as if they were swaying to a cosmic breeze. Let the trees dry completely so each color can settle and breathe beneath the starlit sky above.

Step 5

With the tip of your brush and Burnt Umber, bring your galaxy forest to life by painting delicate branches. Starting at the base of each tree, let the brush flow gently, allowing branches to grow in organic and expressive forms. Each tree becomes unique, telling its own quiet story through its graceful lines.

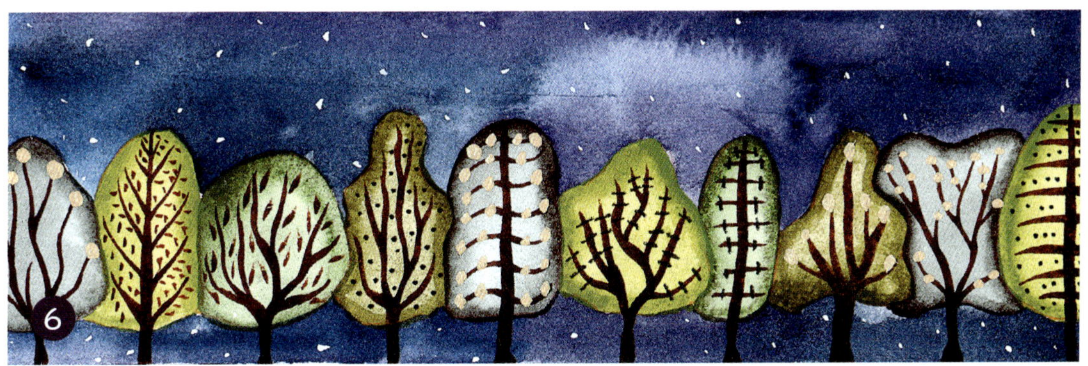

Step 6

Now, using white gouache and the tip of your brush, fill the sky with tiny stars—delicate dots that light up your galaxy. On the tree branches, paint small dots and lines to mimic shimmering leaves, using gold gouache and the fine-liner pen. These golden and inky details create the feeling of an enchanted forest under an endless night sky.

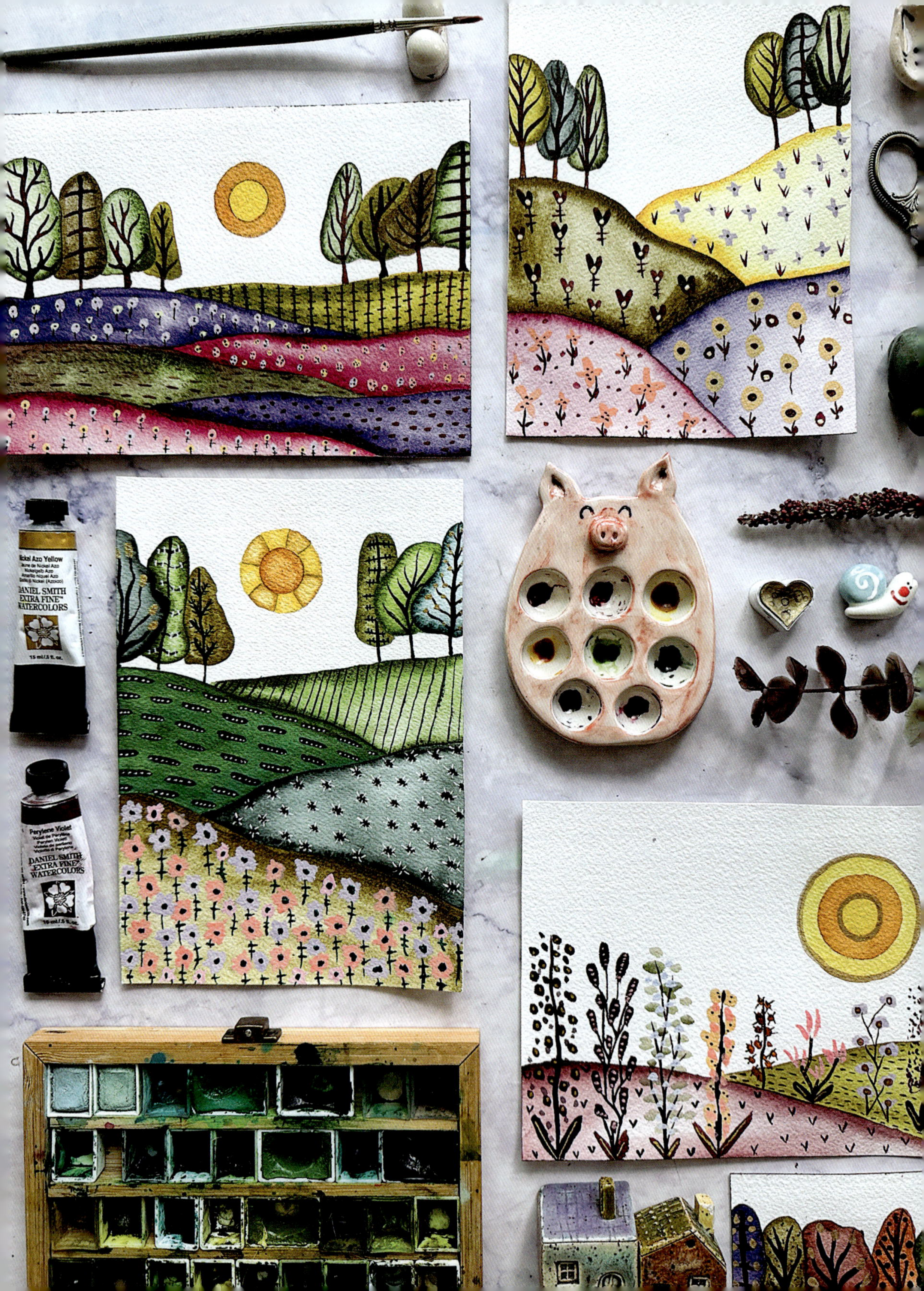

The Secret Garden

Behind every wildflower lies a story blooming in silence. In this chapter, we unlock the gate to a hidden garden where spring never fades, with gentle hills draped in blossoms, colorful peaks that breathe with life, and starry skies sheltering dreamy villages tucked among the trees. Here, landscapes are bathed in warm tones, sunlight brushes the leaves like golden strokes, and each painted petal becomes a whisper of beauty and renewal. This is a journey into a secret corner of the soul, where nature hums softly and watercolor turns into visual poetry.

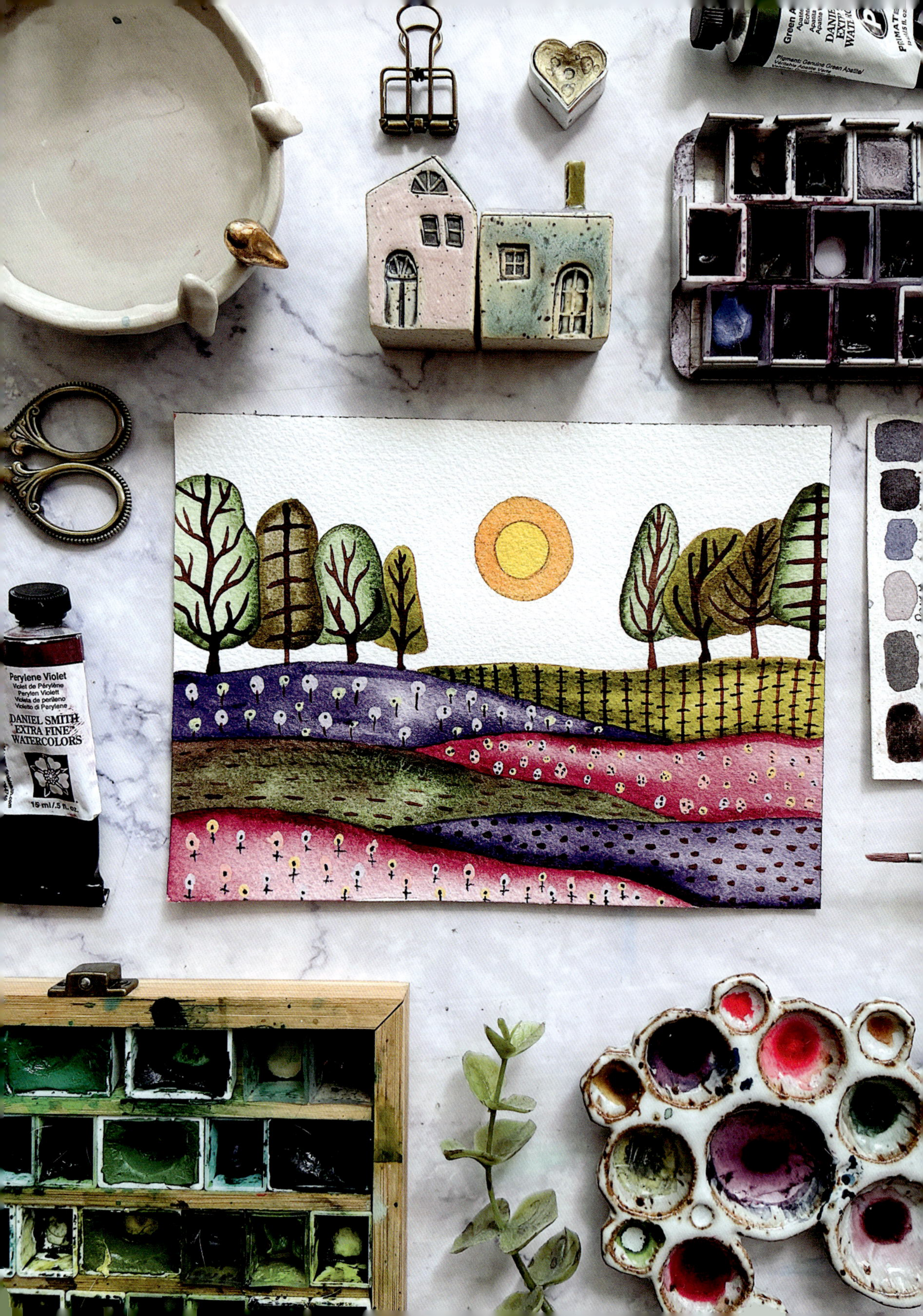

Taste of Spring

This painting is a tribute to the warm days when everything blooms. Here, flower-covered mountains and joyful colors merge into a vibrant, hopeful landscape. At the top, tall trees rise to welcome spring, while a radiant sun glows at the heart of the sky. It's a lively composition that invites you to paint with a light heart and the brightest colors on your palette.

Materials

Paper size
5 x 7" (13 x 18 cm)

Brush
Size 2

Watercolors
Green Apatite
Nickel Azo Yellow
Quinacridone Lilac
Bohemian Green
Quinacridone Gold
Violet
Olive Green
Burnt Umber

For details
White gouache
Size 12 fineliner

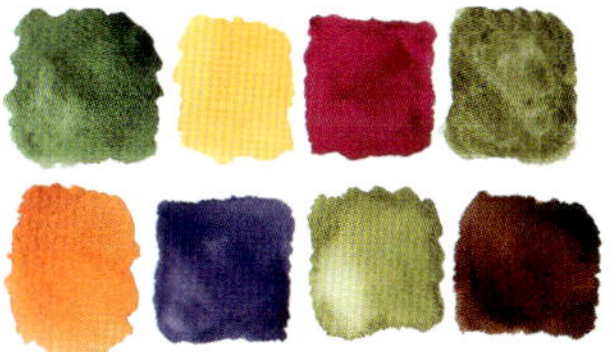

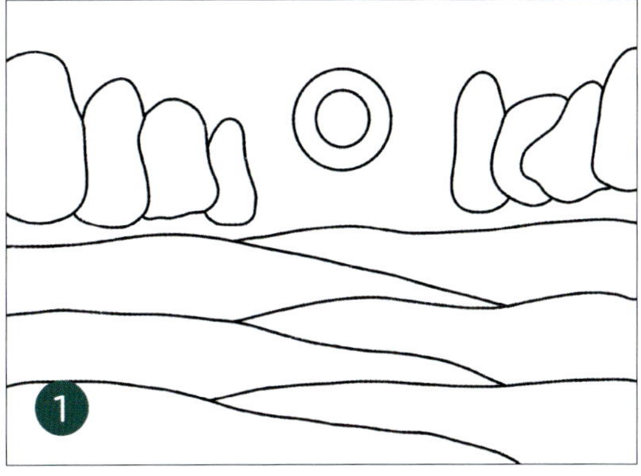

Step 1

Place your paper horizontally. Lightly sketch six overlapping wavy lines from left to right and back again. These flowing lines will become your six cheerful spring hills. At the top of the last two, draw four little trees on each—guardians of the blooming horizon. Between them, sketch a medium-sized circle with a smaller circle inside. This will be our warm, glowing sun—the heart of the scene.

Step 2

Activate your paints with a bit of water. Then, using Green Apatite, paint the first, third, fifth, and eighth trees (starting from the left). This fresh and vibrant green will capture the spirit of spring. Next, fill the inner circle of the sun with Nickel Azo Yellow to create a warm, golden glow at the heart of the scene. Now, move to the mountains. Paint the first mountain (the one at the bottom left) and the fourth with Quinacridone Lilac—a gentle and charming hue that adds sweetness to the landscape. Let all painted areas dry completely before continuing.

Step 3

From left to right, paint the second and seventh trees with Bohemian Green—a deep, rich green that brings harmony to the scenery. Next, with Quinacridone Gold, brighten the large outer circle of the sun, infusing the whole landscape with vibrant warmth and glowing energy. Now, to the mountains. From bottom to top, paint the second and fifth with Violet, adding a touch of magic and mystery that deepens the charm of this blooming springtime world.

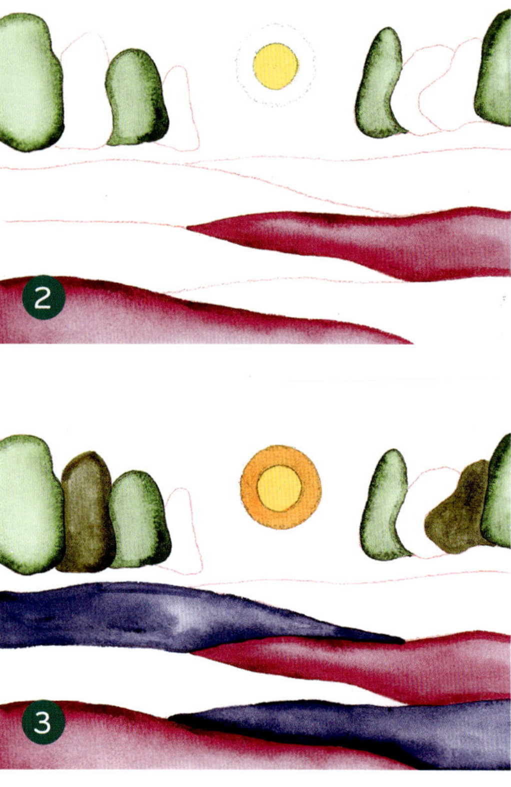

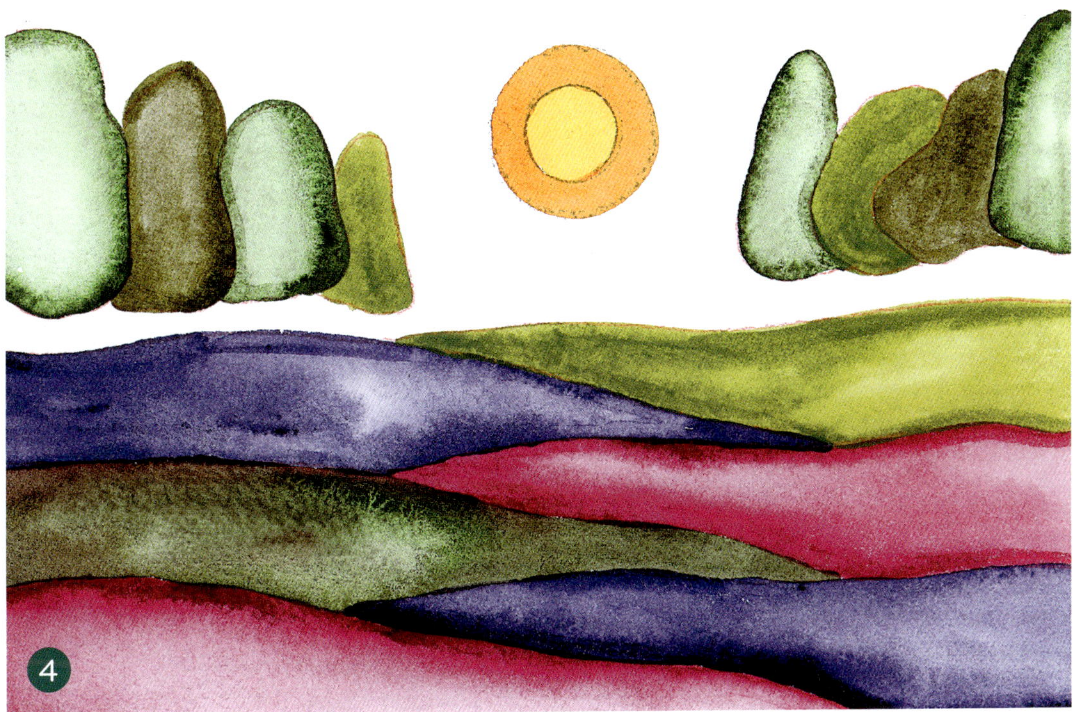

Step 4

Paint the fourth and sixth trees from left to right with Olive Green, a soft, tender shade that evokes the freshness of young leaves in the sunlight. Next, paint the third mountain from the bottom with Green Apatite and the sixth with Olive Green. Let all painted areas dry completely before moving to the next step.

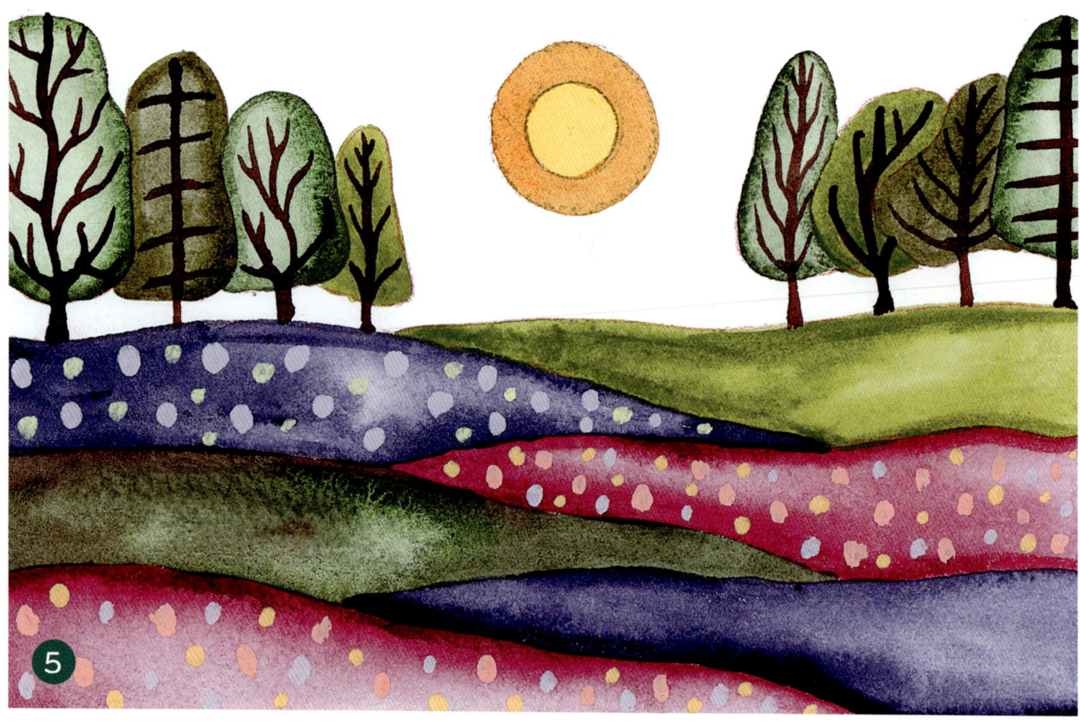

Step 5

With the tip of your brush and Burnt Umber, paint branches gently growing from the trunks of the trees. Some branches can reach upward, while others can extend horizontally to add natural variation and a more organic look. Next, prepare these three delicate mixes that will bring the spring scene to life:

- 90-percent white gouache + 10-percent Violet
- 90-percent white gouache + 10-percent Nickel Azo Yellow
- 90-percent white gouache + 10-percent Quinacridone Lilac

Use these soft tones to add small circles and dots of different sizes across the mountains. These shapes will become the base of the spring flowers, as if a gentle shower of petals had just fallen from the sky.

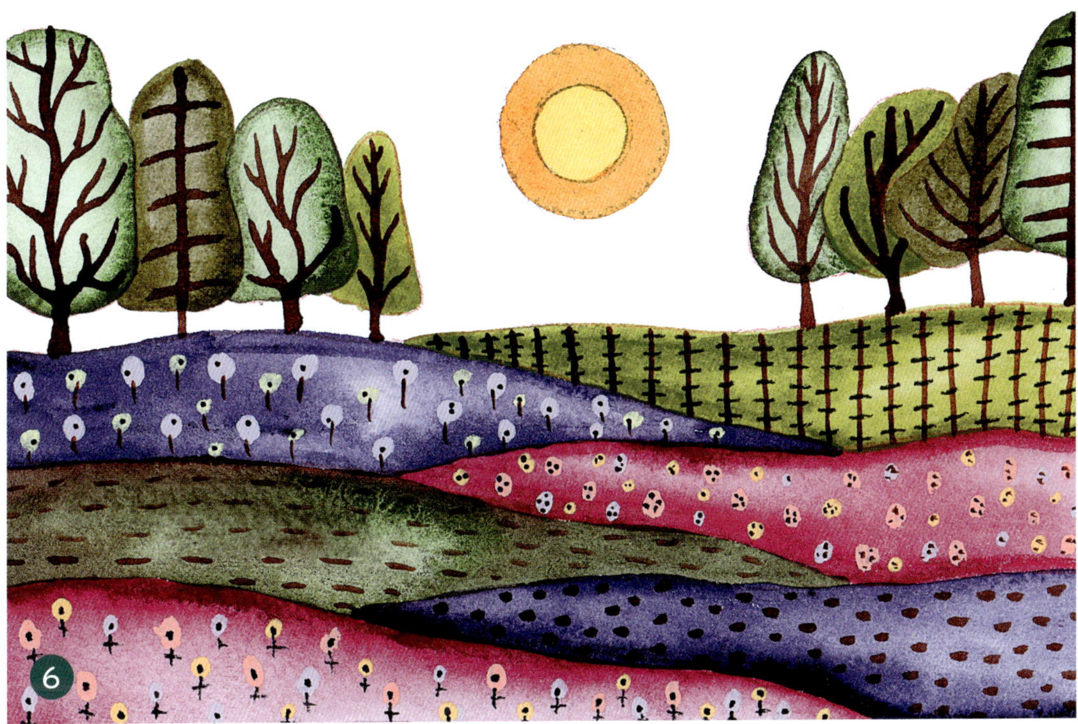

Step 6

With Burnt Umber, paint small dots on the second mountain. On the third and sixth mountains, add lines in different directions to suggest stems and branches peeking through the blossoms. Once these textures are dry, use the fineliner to bring each flower to life by adding delicate details such as stems, centers, and tiny accents that give them charm and character with every stroke. With these finishing touches, your spring landscape is complete: a scene filled with light, color, and the joyful sense of blooming hope.

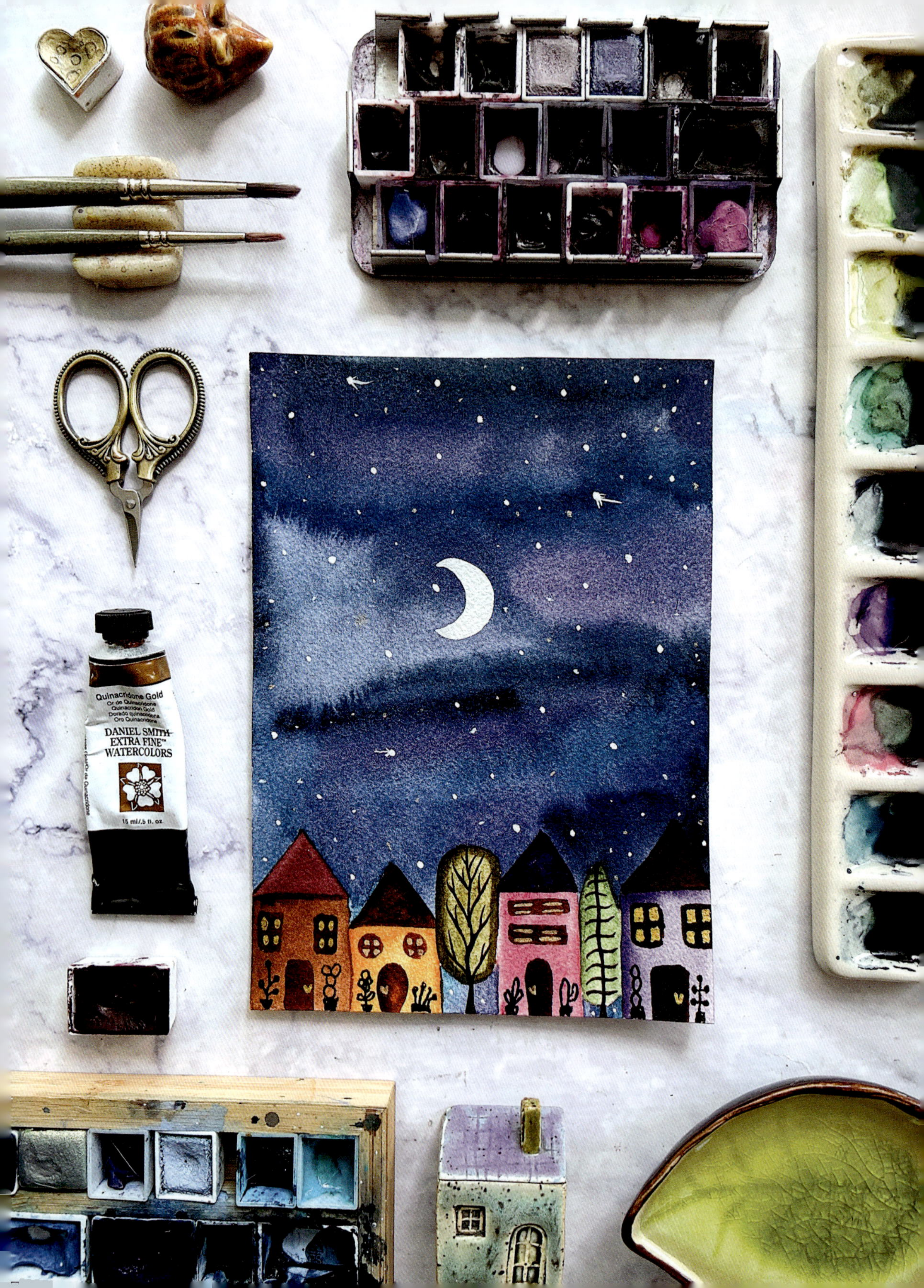

Quinacridone Gold
Or de Quinacridone
Quinacridon Gold
Dorado Quinacridona
Oro Quinacridona
DANIEL SMITH
EXTRA FINE™
WATERCOLORS
15 ml/.5 fl. oz.

Starlit Village

In this exercise, we'll be chasing starlight over a tiny village resting beneath the magic of the night. The sky takes center stage, scattered with stars that shimmer like distant promises and a gentle crescent moon that softly lights the rooftops below. With soft brushstrokes and moody tones, we'll paint a peaceful scene that feels like a dream you never want to wake up from.

Materials

Paper size
5 x 7" (13 x 18 cm)

Brushes
Size 4 and size 2

Watercolors
Indigo
Violet
Turquoise
Burnt Umber
Quinacridone Lilac
Perylene Violet
Quinacridone Gold
Green Apatite
Bohemian Green

For details
White gouache
Gold gouache
Size 12 fineliner

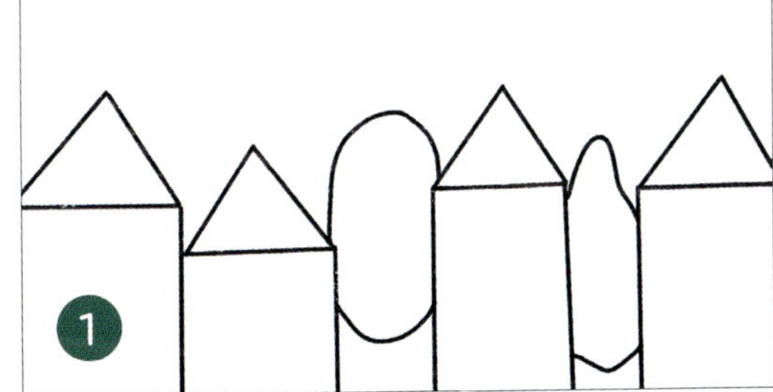

Step 1

Place your paper vertically. Lightly sketch four small houses at the bottom of the page, using simple shapes like squares and triangles. Between them, draw two tree canopies to bring life to this quiet little village. Keep the houses small so they take up only a portion of the page. The focus of this painting will be the starry sky stretching above them.

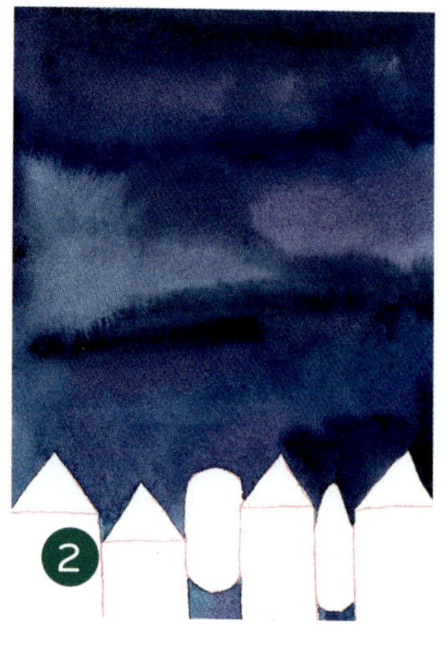 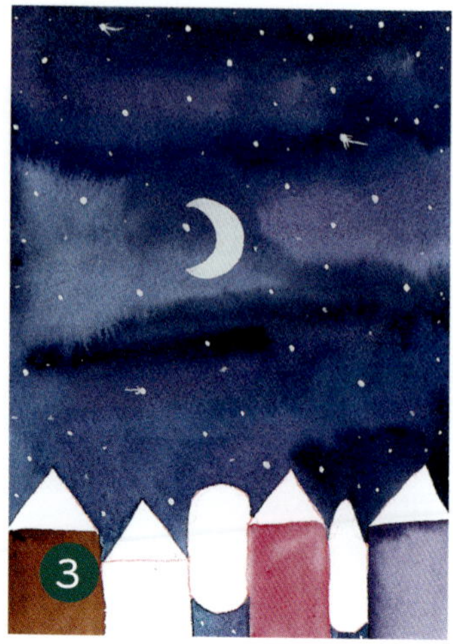 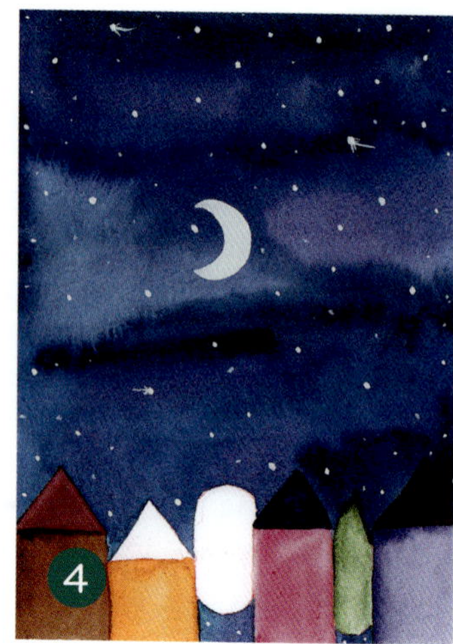

Step 2

Activate your paints with a bit of water. Now let's paint the background of our starry sky. Using the size 4 brush, begin by applying Indigo, then add touches of Violet and Turquoise in different areas of the sky. Gently blend the colors on your paper with a damp brush, allowing them to flow naturally to create a soft, magical texture. Work quickly so the watercolor stays wet—this will help you achieve a smooth, even sky full of dreamy depth.

Step 3

Once the sky is completely dry, use the tip of your size 2 brush and white gouache to paint small dots across the sky for stars. In the middle, add a crescent moon. Next, with the same brush and Burnt Umber, paint the first house on the left. Then, paint the third house Quinacridone Lilac. Finish by painting the fourth house Violet.

Step 4

Paint the roofs of the first, third, and fourth houses with Perylene Violet, Violet, and Burnt Umber, respectively. Then, use Quinacridone Gold to paint the second house, adding a warm glow to the village. Finally, paint the second tree from the left with Green Apatite to bring a touch of life to the scene. Be sure to let everything dry completely before moving to the next step.

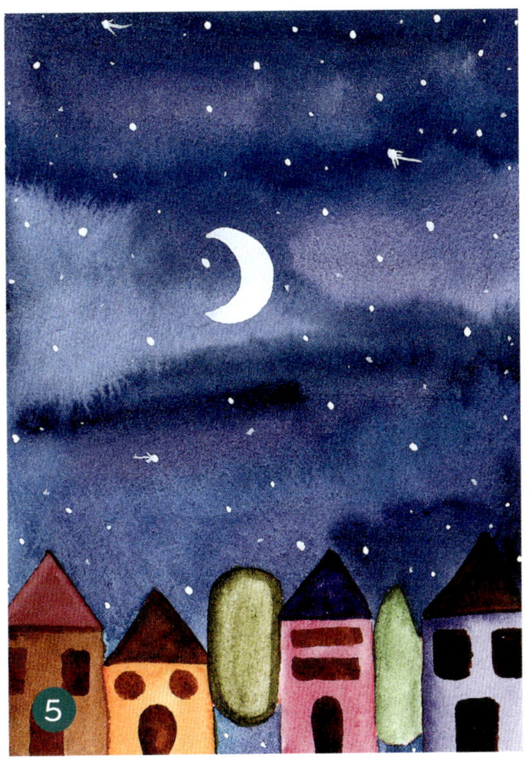

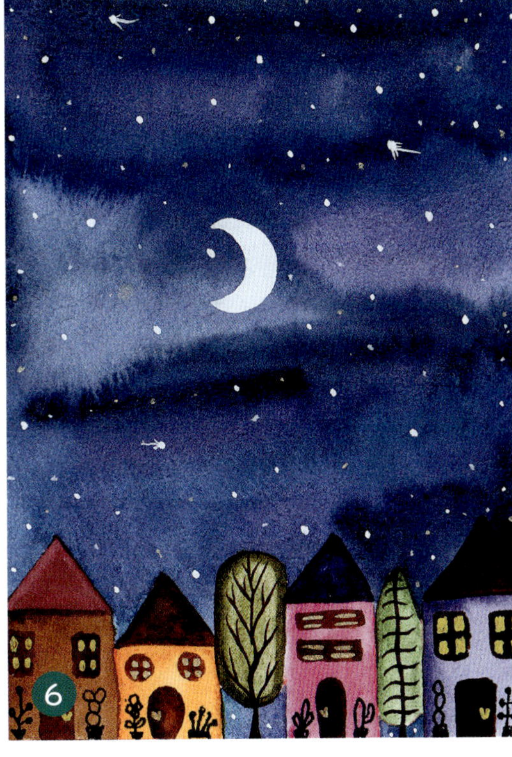

Step 5

With Burnt Umber, paint the roof of the second house. Then, paint windows and doors on all the little houses, using different geometric shapes such as arches, rectangles, and triangles to give each one its own character. Finally, paint the first tree with Bohemian Green, bringing balance and a touch of nature to this starlit village.

Step 6

Using gold gouache, paint the warm lights glowing inside the windows and the door handles, bringing this starlit village to life. Then, with a fineliner, add potted plants on the facades. These can be little cacti, flowers, or whimsical leaves to add charm and detail. Next, paint the tree branches Burnt Umber, starting from the trunk and letting them branch out naturally in soft, organic shapes. Finally, with the tip of your brush, add a few tiny dots of gold gouache in the sky to suggest glowing stars, completing the magical nighttime atmosphere.

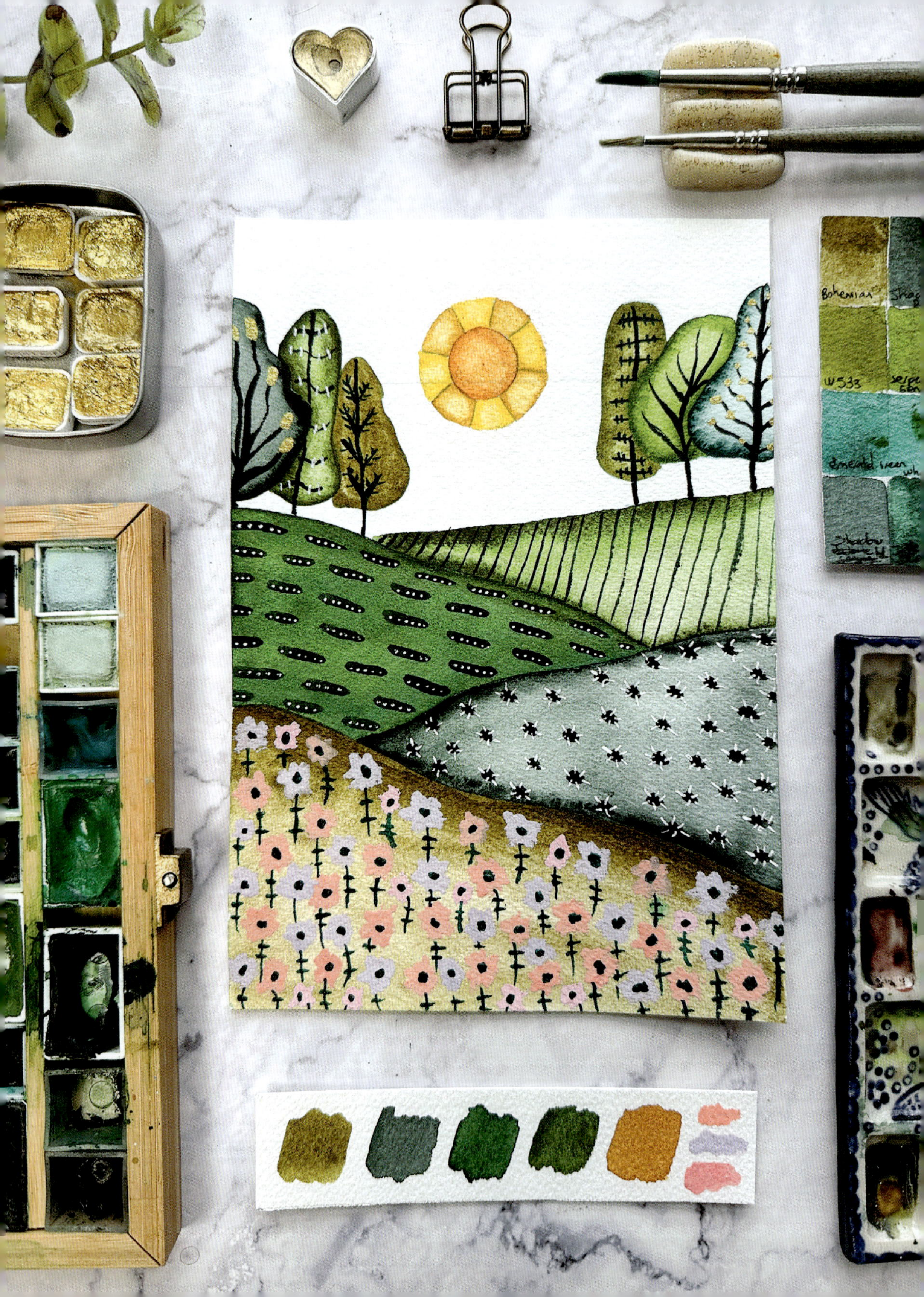

Blooming Peaks

The vibrant colors of wildflowers blossoming from the earth symbolize hope and renewal, reminding me that even after the coldest months, nature will flourish once again. Each stroke of my brush reflects the aliveness of spring, as the mountains come to life with a tapestry of colors that uplifts my spirit.

Materials

Paper size
5 x 7" (13 x 18 cm)

Brushes
Size 4 and size 2

Watercolors
Bohemian Green
Green Apatite
Shadow Green
Olive Green
Quinacridone Gold
Nickel Azo Yellow
Perylene Violet
Violet

For details
White gouache
Gold gouache

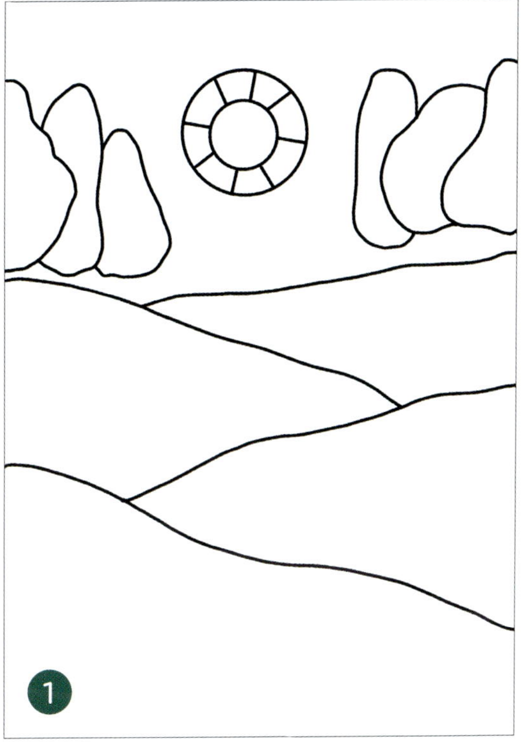

Step 1

Place your watercolor paper vertically to create a composition that emphasizes the majesty of the mountains and the serenity of the landscape. Lightly sketch crossed lines to form the bases of the mountains. At the top of the top two mountains, add distant trees—these can have rounded canopies or a more angular profile, depending on the effect you want. Finally, in the sky, draw a small circle for the sun. Around it, sketch a larger circle and divide it with short lines to suggest rays.

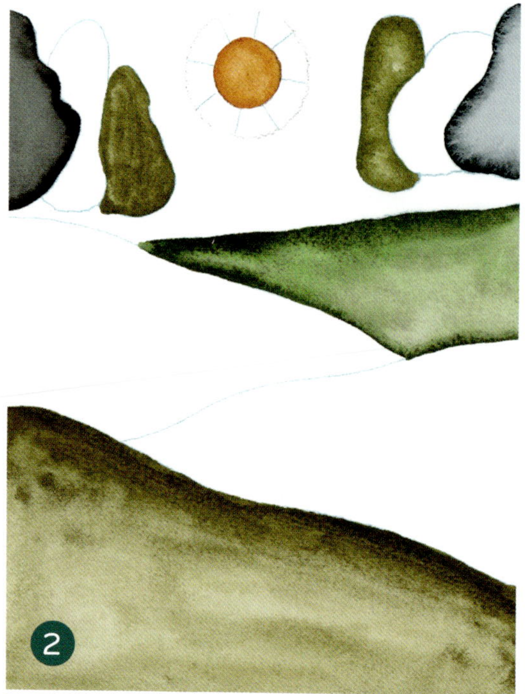

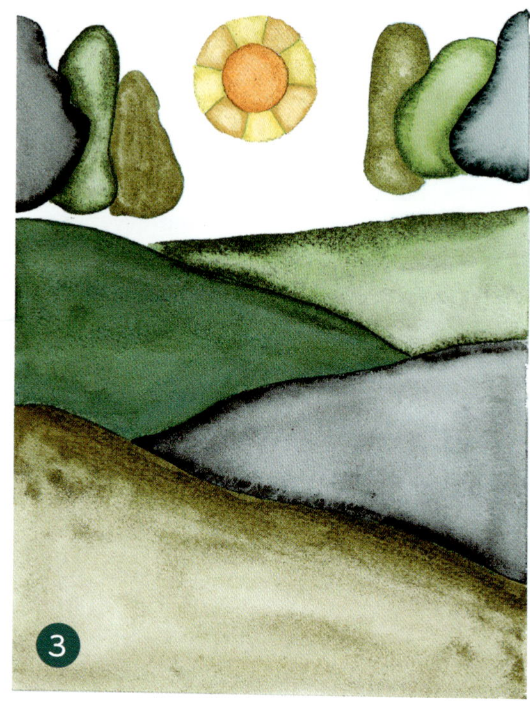

Step 2

Activate your paints with a bit of water. With a size 4 brush, load Bohemian Green and lay a generous band of color along the lower mountain's edge where you want the hue to be most intense. Rinse the brush, reload with clean water only, and pull the pigment in from the edges toward the center to create a soft, gradual gradient wash (page 21) that shapes the form and adds subtle shadows. Clean your brush and repeat on the top-right mountain with Green Apatite, varying the pigment strength to bring the landscape to life.

For the trees, repeat this same process. Paint the first tree on the left with Shadow Green, the third tree with Olive Green, the fourth with Bohemian Green, and the sixth with Shadow Green. Use Quinacridone Gold to paint the circle in the middle of our sun.

Step 3

Paint the second mountain from the bottom with Shadow Green. Once the watercolor dries, paint the third mountain with Olive Green. Then switch to your size 2 brush to paint the second tree from the left with Green Apatite and the fifth tree with Olive Green. To finish the sun, paint each of the sun's rays with a different shade of yellow, varying between Quinacridone Gold and Nickel Azo Yellow. It's important to remember to let each area dry completely before moving to paint adjacent areas.

Step 4

Now we are ready to begin the second layer—an exciting moment where we will bring our landscape to life through patterns and textures. Here is where your creativity can shine, allowing you to experiment with different shapes and designs.

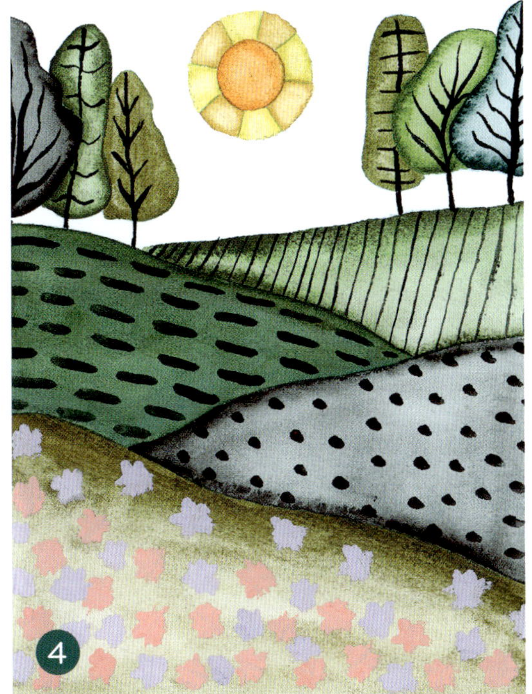

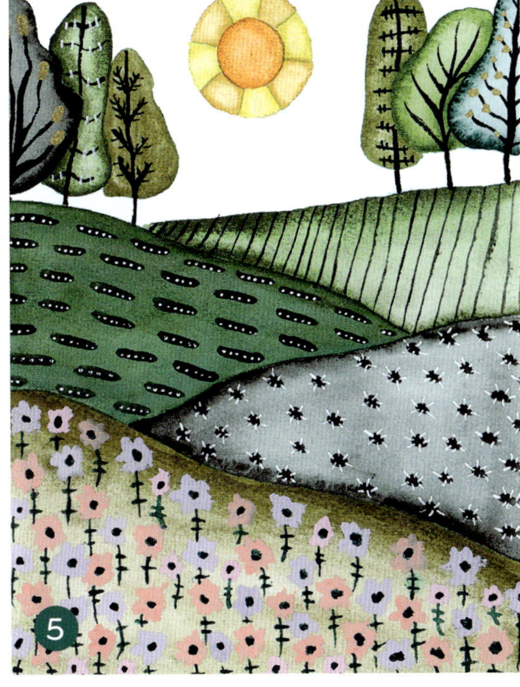

We will paint our flowers using two light pastel color mixes:

- 90-percent white gouache + 10-percent Perylene Violet
- 90-percent white gouache + 10-percent Violet

On the first mountain, paint small asterisks with the two pastel gouache mixes. Pick up a good amount of these mixtures with the tip of your size 2 brush without any water. These asterisks will represent our wildflowers. Using Shadow Green, we will create all the remaining textures. Paint spots on the second mountain, some thick lines on the third mountain, and thin lines crossing completely over the third mountain. Paint the branches of the trees with Shadow Green.

Step 5

Using white gouache, add details over the patterns we created earlier with Shadow Green on the mountains. To me, details are never excessive; they are what bring magic to our painting, so don't be afraid to be generous with your final touches and watch as your landscape comes alive with each one.

Move to adding details on the flowers. Using the tip of your brush, pick up a little amount of Shadow Green and paint the stems and centers of the flowers you previously painted. Also, add small leaves that complement the composition. Finally, with gold gouache, add golden touches to the trees. Apply these details in areas you want to highlight, as if they were fruits or glimmers of light. These touches not only add a charming appearance but also bring a feeling of warmth and joy to your composition.

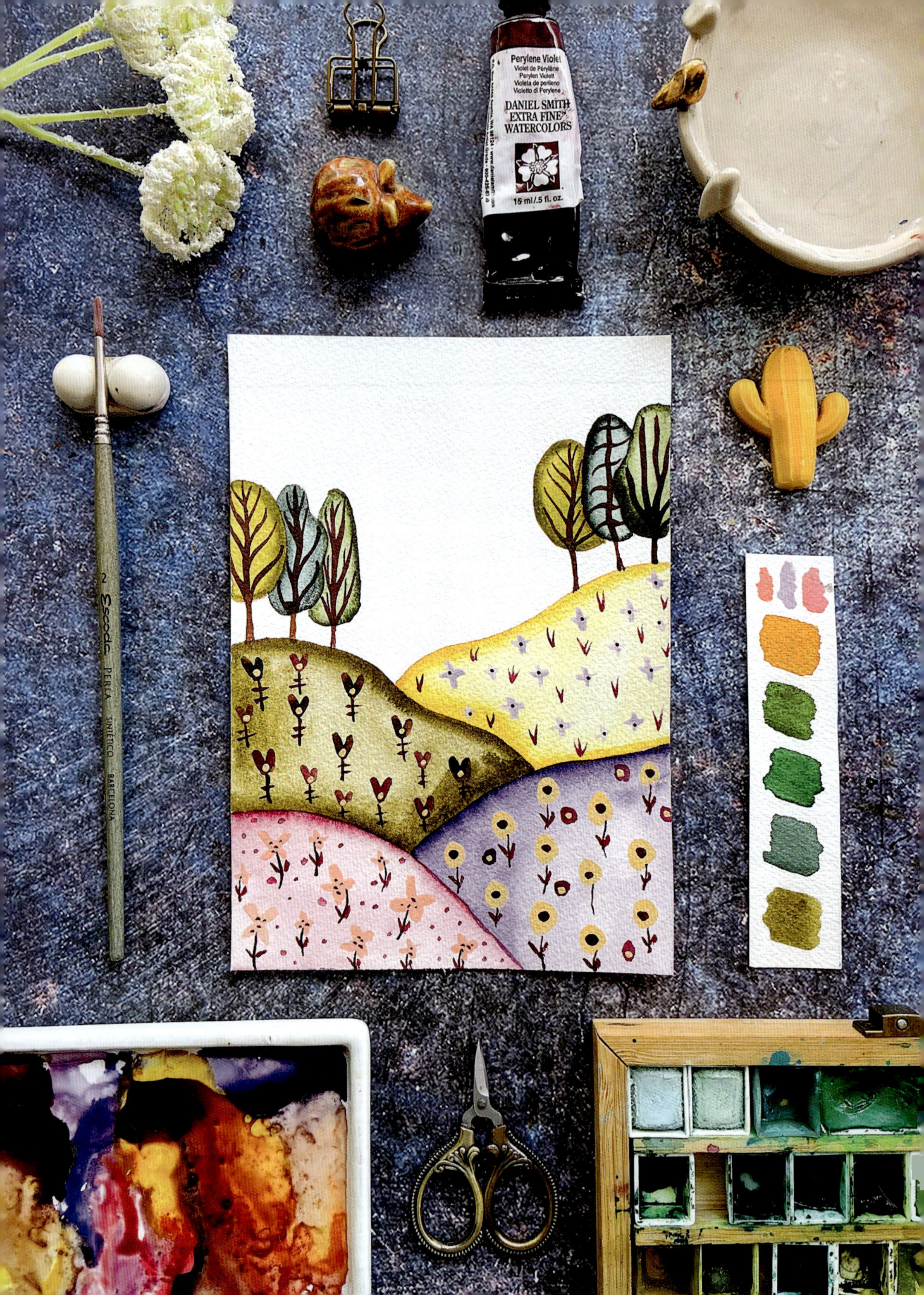
Perylene Violet
Violet de Perylène
Perylen Violett
Violeta de perileno
Violetto di Perylene
DANIEL SMITH
EXTRA FINE
WATERCOLORS
15 ml/.5 fl. oz.

Floral Whispers

In this vertical landscape, the mountains weave together like whispers carried on the spring breeze. Each soft, rolling hill is painted in cheerful pastel tones and comes alive with tiny blossoms, as if responding to the sun's gentle song. At the peaks, little trees stand tall, silent witnesses to this charming scene where nature unfolds in perfect harmony. This exercise invites you to let your brush tell quiet stories, as flowers bloom like warm thoughts across a canvas full of hope.

Materials

Paper size
5 x 7" (13 x 18 cm)

Brushes
Size 4 and size 2

Watercolors
Olive Green
Green Apatite
Nickel Azo Yellow
Quinacridone Lilac

Shadow Green
Violet
Permanent Brown
Naples Yellow
Bohemian Green
Burnt Umber
Perylene Violet

For details
White gouache
Gold gouache

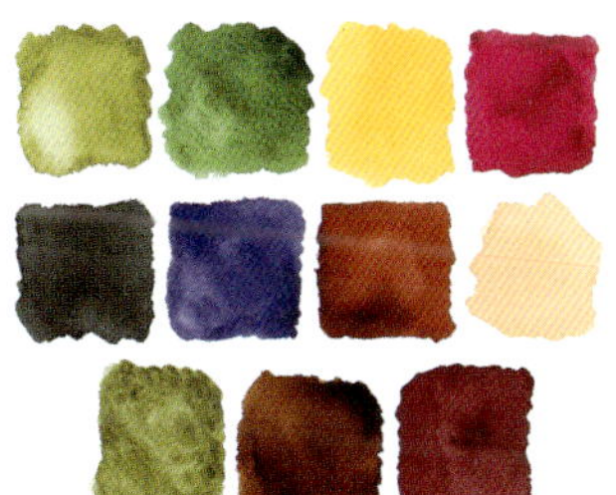

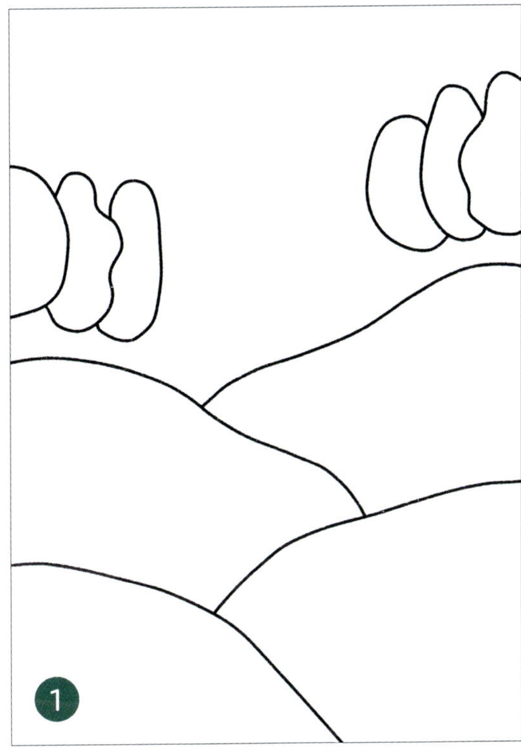

Step 1

Place your paper vertically. Lightly sketch four overlapping mountains, starting from the bottom of the page and building upward. At the top of the third and fourth mountains (counting from the bottom), draw three small trees on the left side and three more on the right. These trees will crown the scene, adding balance and a delicate touch to the composition.

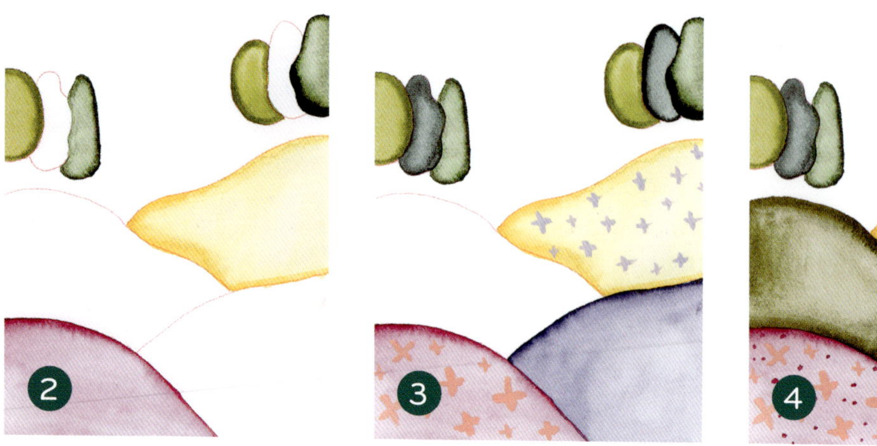

Step 2

Activate your paints with a bit of water. Using Olive Green and the size 4 brush, paint the first and fourth trees from left to right. Then, with Green Apatite, paint the third and sixth trees. Moving a bit lower, paint the fourth mountain (counting from the bottom) with Nickel Azo Yellow and the first mountain with Quinacridone Lilac.

Note: This top-to-bottom painting app-roach helps prevent unwanted smudges that can happen as your hand moves across the paper.

Step 3

Use Shadow Green to paint the second and fifth trees, bringing a deep freshness that balances the harmony of the scene. Next, paint the second mountain with Violet, letting its vibrant hue breathe life into the landscape.

Then, prepare two delicate mixtures:

- 90-percent white gouache + 10-percent Permanent Brown
- 90-percent white gouache + 10-percent Violet

With these soft blends and the size 2 brush, paint small crosses on the first and fourth mountains. These will become the base for our blooming flowers—gentle whispers of spring emerging through color.

Step 4

Use Naples Yellow and Quinacridone Lilac to paint circles of different sizes on the second mountain. These little shapes suggest flow-ers gently blooming across the landscape. Then switch to your size 4 brush to paint the third mountain with Bohemian Green, adding a fresh and calm contrast that brings balance to the whole composition.

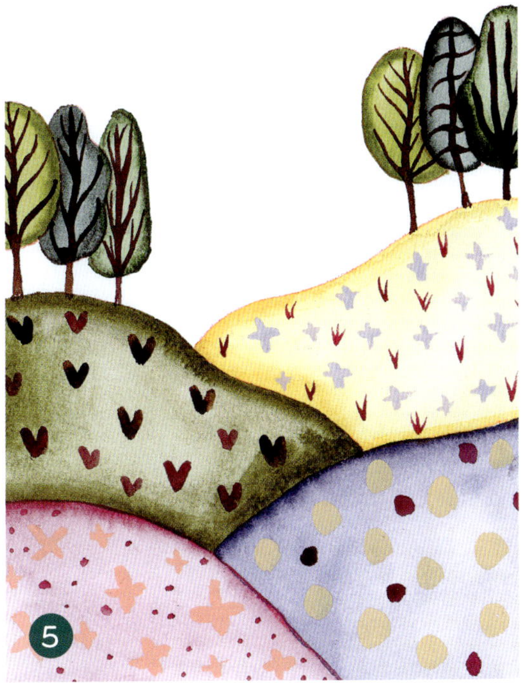

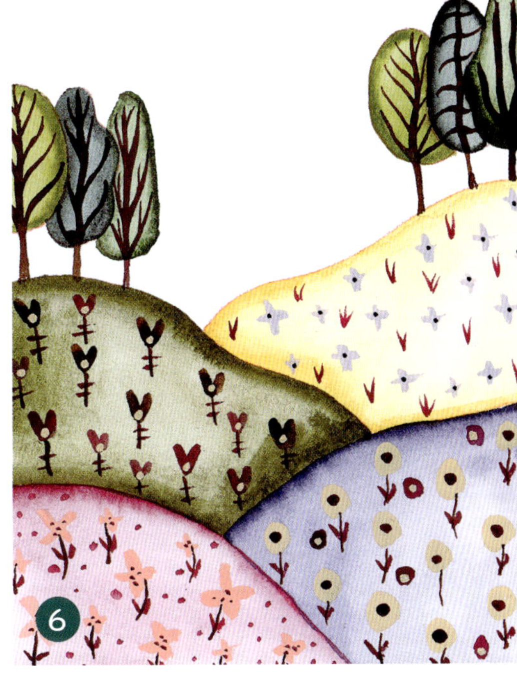

Step 5

Use Burnt Umber and the tip of your size 2 brush to paint the tree branches, starting at the trunk and letting some branches grow upward, while others reach sideways toward their neighbors (for example, the second tree from the right). This variation creates a more natural and organic look. On the third mountain, paint small hearts using both Burnt Umber and Perylene Violet. Once they are completely dry, add delicate golden touches with gold gouache to make these details glow and enhance the warmth of the landscape.

Step 6

With Perylene Violet, paint the stems and centers of the flowers scattered across the scene. Vary the shapes so each bloom feels unique and expressive. Finally, add subtle highlights with gold gouache on the flowers to give them sparkle and charm, making your spring landscape full of life and light.

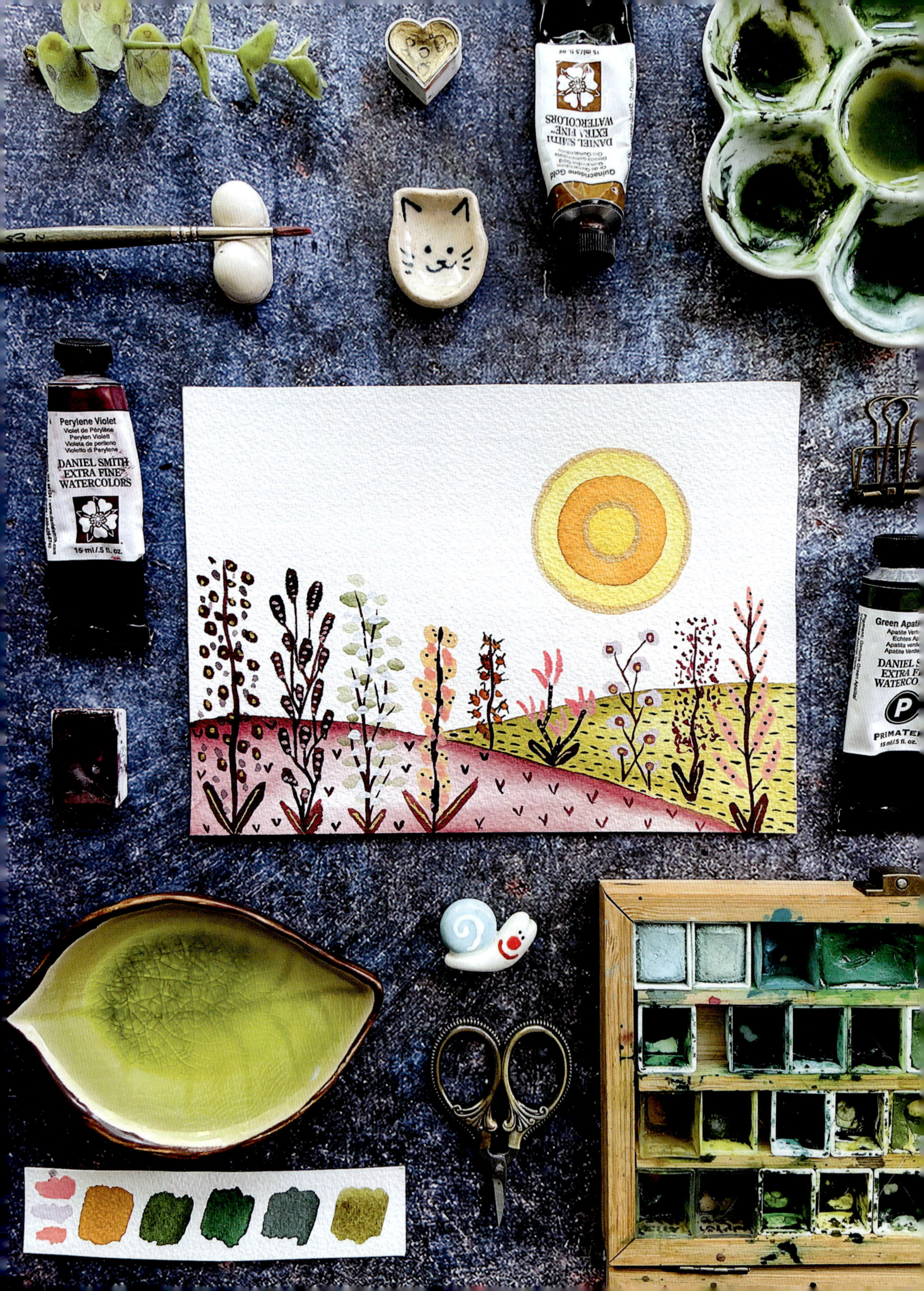

Whimsical Wildflowers

This painting explores a place where the earth awakens in a thousand colors, and the wind whispers secrets through brave petals. Flowers bloom freely with no rules or direction, as if each one carries a longing for the sky. Warm tones burst into gentle harmonies, and the golden sunlight caresses them tenderly, making them glow like small, everyday miracles. It is a celebration of wild growth—spontaneous, untamed, yet full of meaning.

Materials

Paper size
5 x 7" (13 x 18 cm)

Brushes
Size 4 and size 2

Watercolors
Perylene Violet
Nickel Azo Yellow
Olive Green
Quinacridone Gold
Quinacridone Lilac
Green Apatite
Naples Yellow
Violet
Permanent Brown

For details
White gouache
Gold gouache
Size 12 fineliner

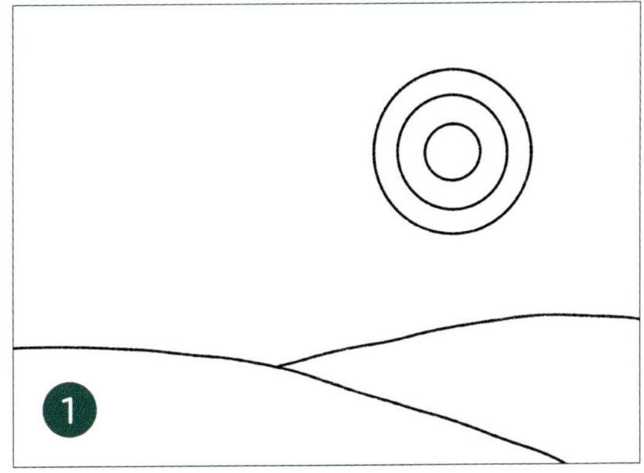

Step 1

Place your paper horizontally. Lightly sketch two gently overlapping mountains just below the middle of the page. In the upper right area of the sky, draw a large circle. Inside it, add a medium circle, and within that, a smaller one. These will form the glowing layers of our radiant sun.

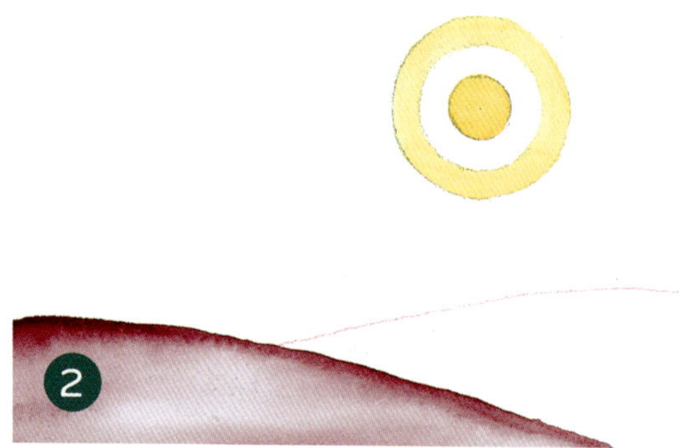

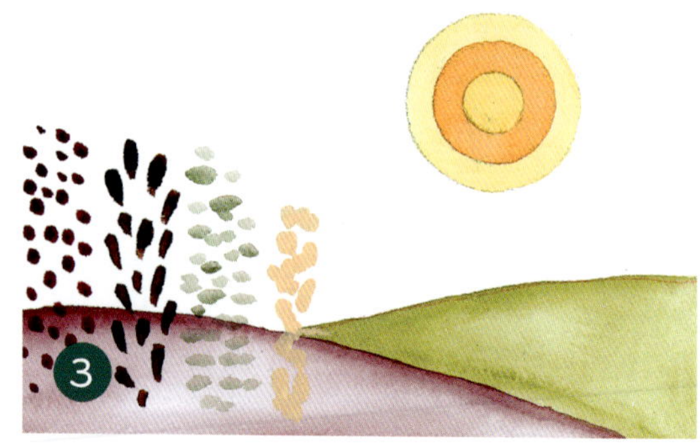

Step 2

Once you've activated your watercolors with a bit of water, begin to bring your landscape to life with the size 4 brush. Paint the first mountain on the left with Perylene Violet, concentrating the pigment along the edges and gently blending it toward the center to create a soft, gradual wash (page 21). Then, using Nickel Azo Yellow, paint the largest and smallest circles of the sun, leaving the middle circle blank. Let these areas dry completely before moving on.

Step 3

Using Olive Green, paint the second mountain with a smooth, flat wash, creating a soft and natural foundation for the scene. Then, with Quinacridone Gold, fill in the middle circle of the sun to complete its warm and glowing radiance. Be sure to let these areas dry completely before moving to the next step. Now it's time to let wildflowers bloom on our first mountain, which is already dry. Using your size 2 brush, begin with dots of Quinacridone Lilac for the petals of the first plant on the left. For the second, paint delicate leaves with Perylene Violet. For the third, add horizontal leaves with Green Apatite, and for the fourth plant, use Naples Yellow to bring light and cheer to the foliage.

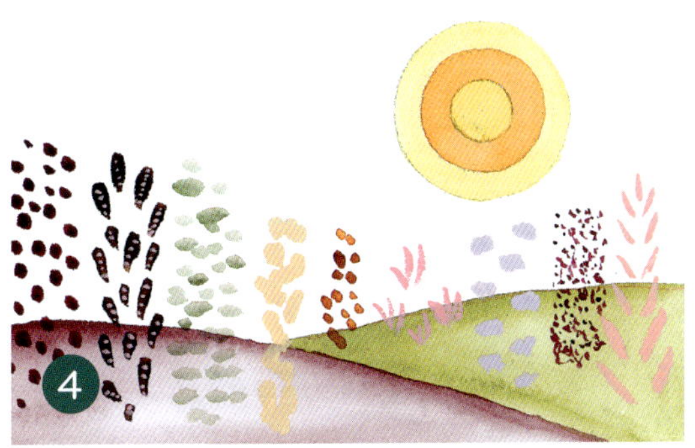

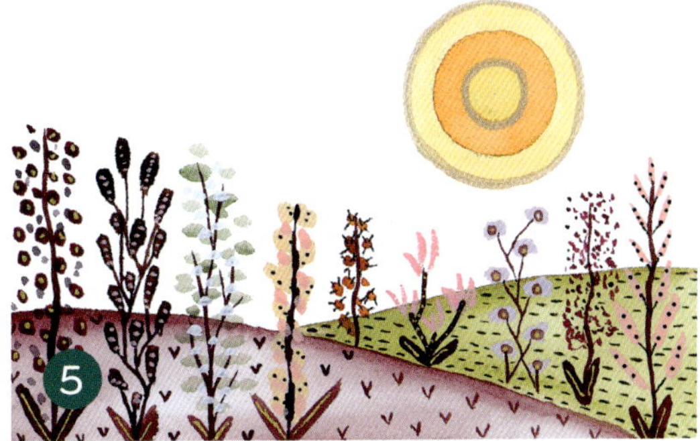

Step 4

Prepare three gentle mixes to paint softer wildflowers in the background:

- 90-percent white gouache + 10-percent Violet
- 90-percent white gouache + 10-percent Quinacridone Lilac
- 90-percent white gouache + 10-percent Permanent Brown
- 90-percent white gouache + 10-percent Perylene Violet

Once ready, use these mixtures to paint four or five wildflower leaves and shapes on the second mountain. These should be smaller and with different shapes and directions than the ones on the left mountain, as they're meant to appear farther away in the composition, adding a lovely sense of depth to our scene.

Step 5

Now, using highly pigmented Perylene Violet and the tip of your brush, draw the wildflower stems. Connect each petal and leaf with gentle strokes, or simply paint a small stem in the center of each group of leaves. Vary the design from plant to plant, and add two larger leaves at the base of each flower to ground them with personality. With the same color, create textures on the mountains with lines and tiny heart shapes that add movement and depth.

Once everything is completely dry, outline both the large and small circles of the sun with gold gouache to create a radiant glow. Then use it to add lines and dots on a few of the flowers, giving them a luminous touch that enhances the scene with light and magic. Then, with the fineliner, draw additional textures on the leaves and stems—tiny lines or patterns that bring more definition. If you wish, return to the pastel mixes from Step 4 to add extra petals or foliage. This combination of ink, pastel tones, and shimmering gold will make your scene bloom with depth and magic.

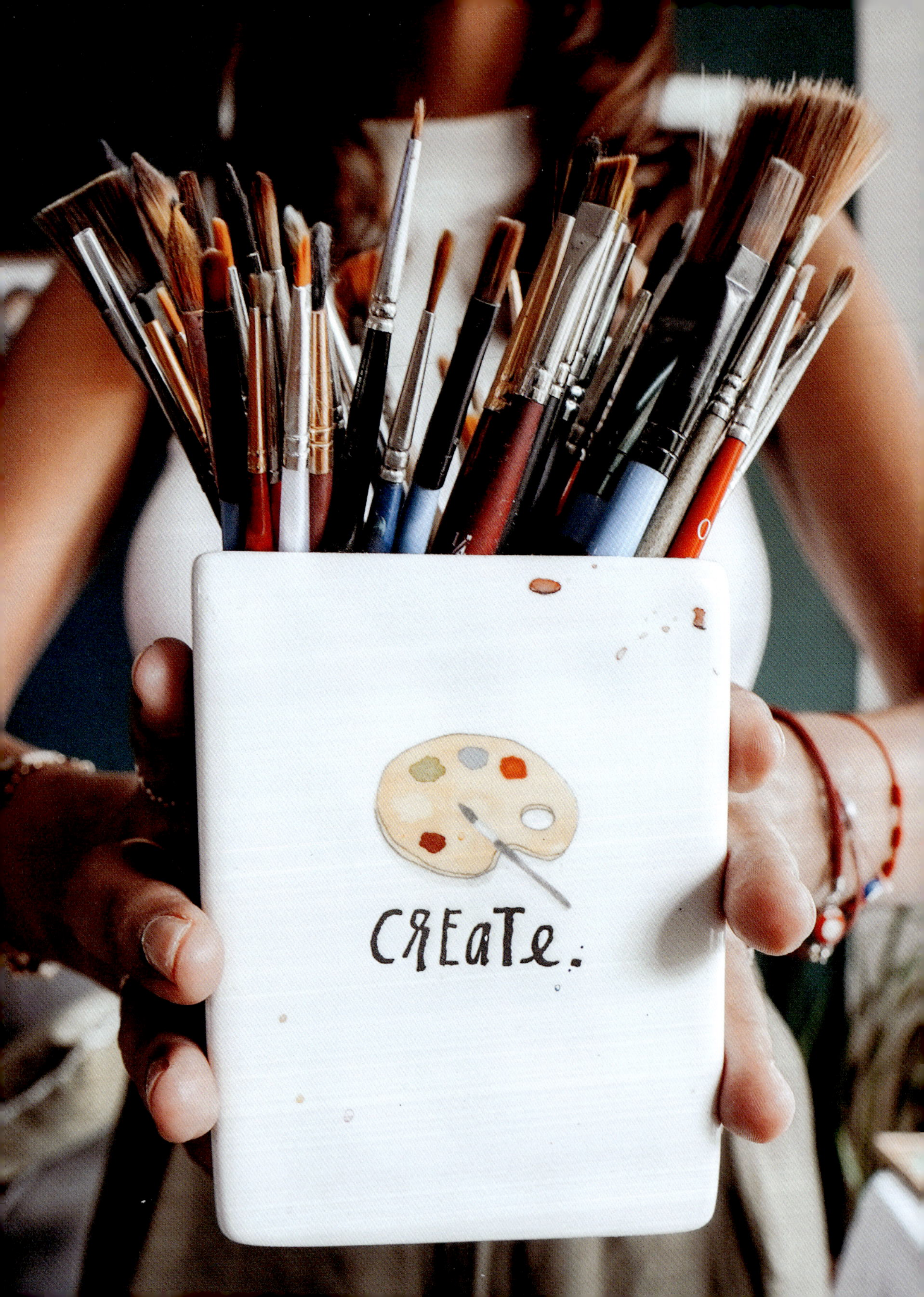

CREATE.

Acknowledgments

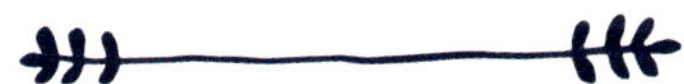

I feel deeply grateful to all my students and followers who have encouraged me every single day to keep walking this magical watercolor journey. Your kind messages, curiosity, and constant support have been beautiful sources of inspiration that fill my heart and fuel my art.

I also want to thank my editor, Sadie, for being such a wonderful guide throughout this entire process, and to Page Street Publishing, for believing in my voice and motivating me to create my very first book. I truly hope it's just the beginning of many more to come.

To my little son Ben, thank you for being my greatest source of joy and motivation. Every time I see how proud you are of your mom, it gives me strength to keep working hard for this dream. And thank you, Eddy, for helping me create the time and space I needed to focus and finally do what I've always dreamed of.

To my dear friend Laura, thank you for being my confidant, my support, and my source of laughter and light in both the hardest and happiest moments. This book carries traces of your friendship on every page.

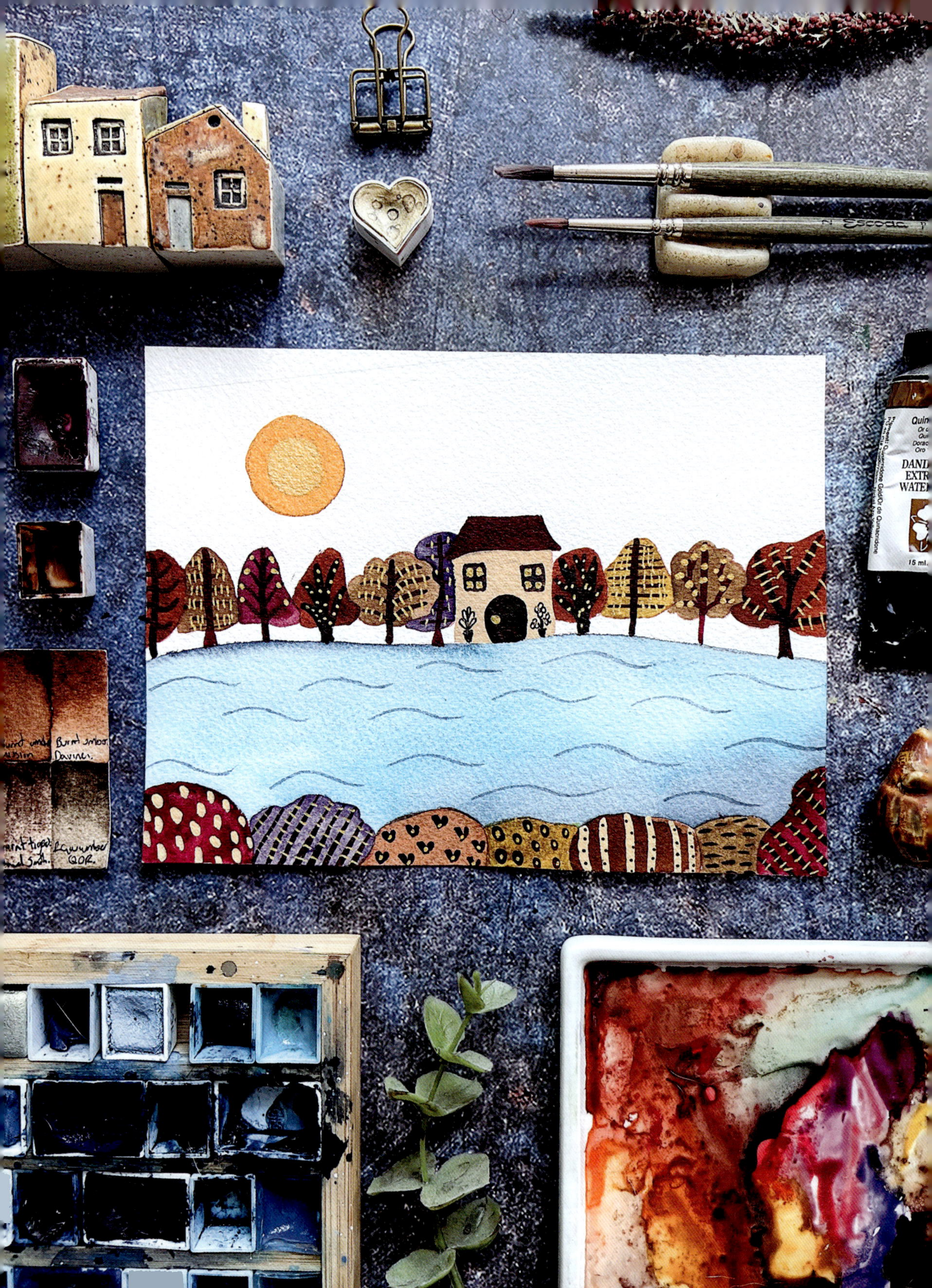

About the Author

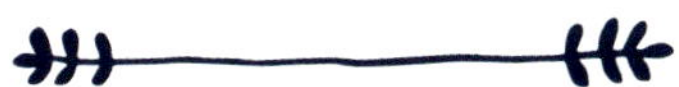

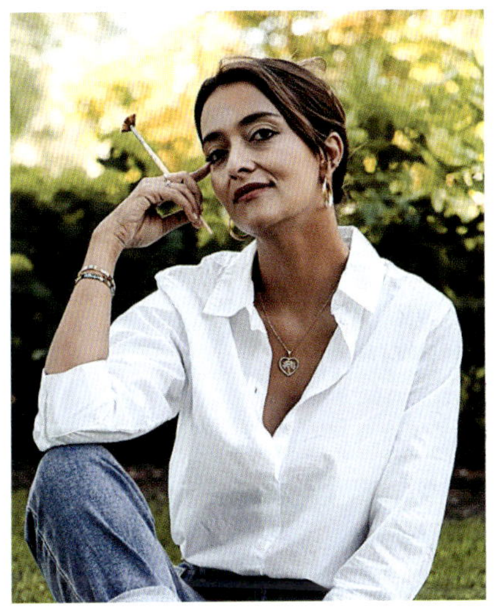

Mayo Moreno is a Colombian watercolor artist based in vibrant Chicago, Illinois, and is the creator of Safari of Ideas, her art brand and online shop where she shares her whimsical, nature-rich artwork with the world. She studied design in Argentina, where she developed her creative vision and love for storytelling through art.

Deeply inspired by the lush magic of her Colombian homeland—its jungles, mountains, music, color, and folklore—her work celebrates the way place shapes imagination. In her paintings, forests glow, desert light shimmers, animals wander through dreamlike landscapes, and botanical forms bloom in joyful harmony. Every brushstroke is an invitation to slow down, notice beauty, and feel wonder again.

Mayo also teaches watercolor classes, where she shares her creative process and love for color with students around the world. If you'd like to explore more of her work or join one of her classes, visit safariofideas.com or find her on Instagram @safariofideas.

Index